AF361293

The Trinity in History

A Theology of the Divine Missions

ROBERT M. DORAN

The Trinity in History

A Theology of the Divine Missions

VOLUME 2: MISSIONS, RELATIONS, AND PERSONS

UNIVERSITY OF TORONTO PRESS
Toronto Buffalo London

© University of Toronto Press 2019
Toronto Buffalo London
utorontopress.com
Printed in the U.S.A.

ISBN 978-1-4875-0483-0

∞ Printed on acid-free paper with vegetable-based inks.

Lonergan Studies

Library and Archives Canada Cataloguing in Publication

Doran, Robert M., 1939-, author
The Trinity in history : a theology of the divine missions / Robert M. Doran.

(Lonergan studies)
Includes bibliographical references and indexes.
Contents: v. 2. Missions, relations and persons.
ISBN 978-1-4875-0483-0 (v. 2 : hardcover)

1. Theology, Doctrinal.   2. Trinity.   3. Catholic Church – Doctrines.
4. Lonergan, Bernard J. F. I. Title. II. Series: Lonergan studies

BT75.3.D668 2012   230   C2012-903073-2

This book has been published with the help of a grant from the Federation for the Humanities and Social Sciences, through the Awards to Scholarly Publications Program, using funds provided by the Social Sciences and Humanities Research Council of Canada.

University of Toronto Press acknowledges the financial assistance to its publishing program of the Canada Council for the Arts and the Ontario Arts Council, an agency of the Government of Ontario.

Funded by the   Financé par le
Government   gouvernement
of Canada   du Canada

Canadä

Contents

Preface

I originally intended this book to be not only the second but also the last volume in *The Trinity in History: A Theology of the Divine Missions.* In the summer of 2017, I realized that I had enough material for a volume, that the remaining work I intended to do would be enough for a third volume, and that attempting to put the two projects together in one book would unnecessarily delay the publication of the present chapters and would make the single book uncomfortably long. I have thus decided to divide what was to be one book into two. The third volume will be subtitled *Redeeming History* and will come full circle on the proposals I first offered in *Theology and the Dialectics of History.*

I have decided to continue the format whereby summary statements are offered in thesis form. I have added an appendix to the present volume that provides the theses offered thus far.

My sincere thanks are offered especially to the graduate students I have taught over the years when this book was being written and to the members of the newly founded International Institute for Method in Theology, a collaborative venture of the Marquette University Lonergan Project, the Lonergan Research Institute of Regis College in the University of Toronto, and the Faculty of Theology at the Gregorian University, Rome. My hope is that this work will contribute to their important efforts to implement the work begun by Bernard Lonergan in some of the most crucial areas of research and praxis in our time.

Many thanks also to two anonymous readers of the manuscript for their many helpful suggestions, and to Stephen Shapiro of University of Toronto Press for his encouragement and careful stewardship of this work and of other Lonergan-related manuscripts published by the Press.

The abbreviations DB and DS refer to two editions of H. Denzinger, *Enchiridion Symbolorum,* a compilation of official ecclesiastical pronouncements.

The Trinity in History

A Theology of the Divine Missions

1

Imitating the Divine Relations

1   Overall Introduction to the Present Volume

This opening chapter offers a brief summary of some of the principal points of the first volume in this work[1] and a detailed response to one set of comments about that volume.

The first volume begins to mine the riches of a theological hypothesis found in the chapter on the divine missions in Bernard Lonergan's systematics of the Trinity.[2] The hypothesis links the four divine relations – paternity, filiation, active spiration, and passive spiration – to four preeminent self-gifts of the triune God. Three of these self-gifts occur in history, and the fourth in the life to come, both in life after death and in life after life after death, that is, in the life of the resurrection.[3]

In the refined and purified Scholastic framework that Lonergan was forced to employ and that in some cases he managed, against great odds, to develop further, these gifts were called, respectively, the *secondary act of existence of the Incarnation, sanctifying grace, the habit of charity,* and *the light of glory.* In Lonergan's hypothesis, where the meaning of these categories is developed and enriched, the secondary act of existence of the Incarnation is a created participatory imitation and communication of divine paternity, sanctifying grace a created participatory imitation and communication of active spiration, the habit of charity a created participatory imitation and communication of passive spiration, and the light of glory a created participatory imitation and communication of filiation. The first three of these are self-gifts of God in history. They are not simply participations in divine life but also communications of that life, or, in the Scholastic language of Lonergan's first systematic work, created communications of the divine nature.[4] The fourth is the consequent created condition of beatific vision in the new creation that we anticipate in hope.

In his expression of the four points themselves, Lonergan does not mention "imitation" or "communication," but only "participation," but prior to listing the four points he writes, "… there are four real divine relations, really identical with the divine substance, and therefore there are four very special modes that ground the external *imitation* of the divine substance."[5] And he writes later in the same chapter, "although the other goods of order externally imitate that supreme good of order that we observe in the Holy Trinity, nevertheless it was appropriate that the economy of salvation, which is ordered to participation in divine beatitude itself, should not only *imitate* the order of the Holy Trinity but also in some manner participate in that order."[6] As for "created communication," it is clear from "The Supernatural Order" that this is the preferred term to refer to the principal instances of divine grace: the grace of union in the incarnate Word, sanctifying grace and charity in this life, and the light of glory in eternal life. I am emphasizing the theme of imitation because of points I wish to make vis-à-vis Girardian mimetic theory. And clearly the imitation of "the order of the Holy Trinity" suggested in *Missions and Processions* is not simply what Lonergan refers to as an "external" imitation. It is a likeness based in the communication of divine life itself. Moreover, the participation to which Lonergan draws attention and the imitation to which I wish to draw attention and with which I want to identify that participation are *conscious*. In our case, of course, though not in the case of Jesus, participation and imitation, while conscious, most often are not known as what they are, though spiritual development and theological reflection can raise what is conscious to the status of what is in some manner understood and affirmed, and so known.

Because these self-gifts on the part of the triune God are, according to the hypothesis, created participations in and imitations of the divine relations, we may speak of three of them – the secondary act of existence, sanctifying grace, and charity – as "the Trinity in history."[7] And, of course, the Trinity in history is what Trinitarian theology calls the divine missions; hence the subtitle of this entire work: "A Theology of the Divine Missions."

Moreover, in the theologies of both Thomas Aquinas and Bernard Lonergan (and, for that matter, in the thought of Hans Urs von Balthasar), the divine missions are the divine processions linked to a created external term. Lonergan is more emphatic than either Aquinas or Balthasar in emphasizing that the term is a created consequent condition of a procession immanent to the triune God being also a mission of the proceeding divine person in history.[8]

The first volume of this effort at a systematic theology of the divine missions set forth the links between the divine processions and the missions.

Efforts were made in the book to establish foundational statements in the theology of grace and in Christology as well as in Trinitarian theology. The mediation to history of the divine self-gifts was understood through the integral scale of values,[9] where these self-gifts constitute "religious values." While the principal effort in that volume was to relate religious values to personal value, the scale of values in its entirety provides the central set of categories in a theological theory of history.

As the subtitle of the present volume indicates, we are moving here to further considerations, under the rubric of "Missions, Relations, and Persons." As in the first volume, so here an effort will be made both (a) to present and interpret the relevant portions of Lonergan's systematics of the Trinity, and (b) to transpose the metaphysical terms and relations of that work into the general and special terms and relations of interiority analysis and religiously differentiated consciousness in all their dimensions: intentional and psychic, natural and supernatural. It is hoped that these efforts will move to a new level the development of a theological theory of history as the context for the further systematic task of understanding other mysteries of Christian faith.

The first volume, while not in any way neglecting the mission, visible and invisible, of the Word, concentrated more on the mission of the Holy Spirit, and so on created participations in active and passive spiration. The present volume, while not in any way neglecting the mission of the Holy Spirit, will concentrate more on the mission of the Word. The first volume's emphasis on the mission of the Holy Spirit is linked to that volume's preoccupation with the relation between religious and personal values in the scale of values and with the consequent universality of the offer of divine grace. Shifting our emphasis now to the mission of the Word will entail extending the relation of grace beyond personal value to the realms of cultural and social values and to the crucial issue of the equitable distribution of vital goods to the entire human family. The Incarnation of the divine Word is the palpable entrance into history of the expression of God's meaning, Logos, Word, and so it has multiple implications for the realm of cultural values. The principal role of culture within the functioning of the scale of values is to provide the meanings and values that inform integral dialectics of community at the level of social values, where spontaneous intersubjectivity and the practical intelligence that establishes systems of capital formation, economy, and polity function in dialectical tension with each other as principles of social existence.[10] The Incarnation of the Word makes explicit meanings and values that can transform both social structures and human intersubjective responses.

The almost exclusive attention paid in the first volume to the connection of missions with processions here gives way first to the connection of divine missions with divine relations, and then to the connection of divine missions with the divine persons, and especially the connection of the Incarnation with the person of the Word. I will propose in this volume and the next that the participations in the divine relations to which the hypothesis refers are a matter of positive mimesis. They are conscious imitations of divine life, prompted by the grace of God that communicates divine life. Thus, whether known as such or not, they are grounded in the communication of the Trinitarian relations to human interior process and human relationality.

2   A General Note on Lonergan and Girard

If a major concern in *Missions and Processions* was with the relation of religious values to personal values in the scale of values that constitutes the immanent intelligibility of history, among the aspects of that relation that have drawn the most attention from commentators on the work are the connections that I posited between Lonergan's philosophical and theological contributions and the mimetic theory of René Girard. This chapter addresses these connections once again, partly in an effort to respond to the comments, both positive and critical, and partly to anticipate further developments that I intend to make in the rest of the work. Our treatment of the relation of the divine missions to the divine relations and of our participation in the relations and imitation of them will bring us more deeply into the connections that can and should be drawn between Lonergan's work and Girard's.

Lonergan and Girard are both students of human desire, and the divine self-gifts that we will be studying are simultaneously fulfilments and transformations of that desire. A synthesis of the respective positions of Lonergan and Girard would provide at least some of the elements in a broad outline of a heuristic structure for the study of desire. I propose that the basic categories of such a heuristic structure would be "natural desires," "elicited desires," "sensitive-psychic desires," and "spiritual desires."

Natural desires emerge from the very structure of human reality, as is the case, for instance, with what Lonergan calls the desire to know and with what both Thomas Aquinas and Lonergan recognize as the natural desire to see God.

Elicited desires are prompted by the cognitive recognition of some object.

Sensitive-psychic desires are affective responses to objects, often mediated through others.

Spiritual desires reflect the capacity of human intentional consciousness for self-transcendence in knowing and choosing. In the authentic pursuit of knowledge, we want to know what is really and not merely apparently so, and in authentic deliberative process we want to choose what is really and not merely apparently worthwhile.

Lonergan has elucidated desires that may be termed natural and spiritual, and Girard has elucidated desires that are elicited and sensitive-psychic. But Lonergan has also alerted his readers to interferences that may arise from elicited, sensitive-psychic desires in the pursuit of the natural desire for intelligibility, being and truth, and the good, and from related biases that affect both psyche and spirit. And Girard not only has provided a set of core insights for understanding elicited, sensitive-psychic desires but also offers a compelling theory of these desires, a theory that complements and indeed fills out aspects of Lonergan's work on bias.[11]

In volume 1, I drew on the following statement from Lonergan's systematic work on the Trinity to elucidate the distinction between spiritual and sensitive-psychic dimensions of consciousness, and so of desire:

> … we are conscious in two ways: in one way, through our sensibility, we undergo rather passively what we sense and imagine, our desires and fears, our delights and sorrows, our joys and sadness; in another way, through our intellectuality, we are more active when we consciously inquire in order to understand, understand in order to utter a word, weigh evidence in order to judge, deliberate in order to choose, and will in order to act.[12]

Lonergan has provided a thorough explanatory account of the second of these "ways of being conscious," a careful analysis of the unfolding of the eros of the human spirit as we move by inquiry from data of sense and of consciousness to insight into the data, from insight to conceptualization and formulation of our understanding, from formulation to critical reflection, from critical reflection to a grasp of evidence, from grasp of evidence to judgment of fact, from judgment of fact to deliberation, from deliberation to deliberative insight and judgment of value, and from judgment of value to decision.[13] This eros is driven by the native desire to know, which is Lonergan's transposition of the Aristotelian-Thomist "agent intellect," a desire that he extends beyond knowledge to an orientation to the good[14] and that he also identifies with Aquinas's natural desire to see God.[15]

All of this is "nature." "Nature" is a category that Girardian theory urgently needs to incorporate. Obviously, in the concrete and real order of things there is no such thing as pure human nature. The concrete existential situation of human beings is infected by sin and stands under the offer of divine elevating and healing grace, which we may either accept or reject. But sin distorts nature while grace elevates and perfects it and indeed divinizes it by the gift of participation in the divine relations of active and passive spiration because of the consequent created conditions that have been known as sanctifying grace and charity. Both the distortions and the elevation are reflected in the realm of desire. A complete theory of human desire is impossible without the heuristic of human nature, and for the latter I turn to the proposals provided by Lonergan, where natural law is reflected in the transcendental precepts: Be attentive, Be intelligent, Be reasonable, Be responsible.

Among the effects of "basic sin," which is a failure to reject a morally reprehensible course of action or a failure to choose a morally obligatory course of action, and especially among the effects of the first basic sin known as "original sin," are the myriad combinations of bias that distort the regular and consistent unfolding of the eros of the human spirit for being and the real, for the good, and for God, and thus increase the probability of further basic sin, which in turn accentuates the hold of bias, etc., etc., etc., in a vicious spiral of decline. Lonergan distinguishes individual, group, and dramatic bias, as well as a general bias of common sense against the ulterior exigencies of attentive, intelligent, reasonable, and responsible intentional operation as these exigencies call for a move to theory, the long-range point of view, and reflection on ultimate issues.[16]

Girard's mimetic theory provides a powerful analysis of the distortions that arise from what Lonergan calls bias. In particular, Girard has contributed an elucidation of the mimetic and so elicited sensitive-psychic desire involved in bias of all varieties.

Lonergan has called for and promoted through his writings the self-appropriation of one's rational and existential intentional operations. But even before becoming familiar with Girard, I insisted that there is also required a self-appropriation of the vagaries of sensitive-psychic desire.[17] I now find that Girardian mimetic theory is a powerful means of fulfilling this second requirement. From a Lonergan-based position, we may regard Girard's basic contribution as the elucidation of the vagaries of the sensitive-psychic dimensions of elicited desire as these interfere with or even prevent the efforts of the subject to be attentive, intelligent, reasonable, responsible, and loving – in a word, self-transcendent.

But Lonergan also makes a contribution to Girard. Part of that contribution lies in the distinction I have already summarized between spiritual desire and sensitive-psychic desire, and part of it lies also in the distinction between natural desire and elicited desire.

A primary instance of a natural spiritual desire is what Lonergan calls the pure, unrestricted desire to know. It is native to human beings in any culture to raise and want answers to questions for intelligibility (what is it?), for truth (is that so?), and for morally responsible action (is this truly good or only apparently good?). Contrasted with such a natural desire would be what is known as elicited desire: desire for something that arises out of perception of what is desired. Girard has shown, conclusively I believe, that such elicited desires are usually mediated by models, that their structure is triangular, that the relation of subject to object in such desires is not immediate, that the desire passes through the mediator or model from whom our desires are elicited through the dynamics of mimesis, that mediation through the model can become obsession with the model, that such obsession is contagious, and that the result is some form of violence.

Girardian mimetic theory, then, is a theory of elicited sensitive-psychic desire. It can be related to Lonergan's project insofar as such desire is responsible for the distortion and deviation of the operations of the human spirit in search of intelligibility, truth and being, the good, and God. The distortion and deviation of these operations subverts the operations of intelligence and reason so that they become instruments for the satisfaction of elicited, sensitive-psychic, mimetic desire, thus frustrating their natural function in human unfolding. Intelligence can be conscripted as an instrument of ultimately irrational and irresponsible behavior.

We saw in *Missions and Processions* a further clarification that Lonergan provides to Girardian theory. He offers a refinement of the notions of autonomy and spontaneity, specifying a legitimate meaning to these two terms, a meaning that, if it is mimetic in any way, is so in a manner quite different from the acquisitive mimesis whose dynamics Girard has elucidated.[18] I wish to suggest a fruitful mutual self-mediation[19] between Lonergan and Girard, where Girard offers Lonergan a more precise maieutic of a major source of interference with the unfolding of the natural desire for intelligibility, the true and the real, the good, and God, and where Lonergan offers Girard a more precise understanding of the meaning of "nature," a more differentiated understanding of spontaneity and autonomy, a distinction between them where Girard tends to conflate them, and, most basic of all, a theology of the graced imitation of divine goodness.

This relation will at least begin to play out in the present volume in ways that take us into culture and social structures, that is, into cultural and social values, and will be expanded in the next volume.

3   The Divine Relations and Their Imitations

The four-point hypothesis points to a very different kind of imitation from the mimesis studied by Girard, a graced imitation of the divine relations rendered possible by the gift of God's love, that is, by divine self-communication. That imitation is most often conscious but not known as the kind of imitation it really is. It is *vécu* but not *thématique*, implicit and not explicit, or in Scholastic terms *exercitus* (exercised in practice) but not also *signatus* (reflectively objectified).

These distinctions reflect Lonergan's grounding distinction between consciousness and knowledge. Consciousness is simply awareness, the self-presence of the subject, while knowledge is a complex function of three kinds of conscious acts: empirical, intelligent, and rational. Immanently generated human knowledge is the correct understanding of experienced data, while consciousness is simply interior experience, the self-presence of the subject to herself not only in these operations but in all the operations and states that qualify for the adjective "conscious." Lonergan specifies the acts that constitute immanently generated knowledge in a shorthand manner as experience, understanding, and judgment. These operations can be applied to conscious acts themselves, and then one undergoes what Lonergan calls self-appropriation: experiencing, understanding, and affirming one's own operations of experiencing, understanding, and affirming. Then what was conscious, *vécu, exercitus,* becomes known, *thématique, signatus.*[20] But consciousness itself is simply awareness, the experience of these and other operations and states.

The distinction enables us, I believe, to acknowledge the quotidian, indeed secular, nature of grace itself as it is lived in the daily life of believers and nonbelievers alike.[21] It also makes possible a Christian theology of the world's religions that would identify de facto conscious participation in Trinitarian life in those whose religious traditions do not explicitly recognize the triune nature of God.[22]

The Trinitarian theology of both Aquinas and Lonergan speaks of four divine relations: paternity, filiation, active spiration, and passive spiration. Lonergan's Trinitarian systematics of the divine missions adds mention of created imitations of each of these divine relations. Lonergan's statement, which has come to be called the "four-point hypothesis," was proposed in a systematic work on Trinitarian theology published in 1957. As I already mentioned, the hypothesis begins, "... there are four real divine relations, really identical with the divine substance, and therefore there are four very special modes that ground the external imitation of the divine substance."[23] The three divine persons *are* relations: the Father *is* paternity, the Son *is* filiation, and the Holy Spirit *is* passive spiration; and in Trinitarian theologies based, as Lonergan's is, on Thomas Aquinas's spiritual or psychological analogy, the Father and the Son together *are* the active spiration from which the Holy Spirit, passive spiration, proceeds precisely as the proceeding Love of Father and Son. Thus, active spiration is only conceptually distinct and not really distinct from the Father and the Son together.

The four created imitations of divine being participating in the four divine relations are the following.

First, Lonergan adopts from late material in Aquinas the notion of the "secondary act of existence" of the incarnate Word, in an effort to delineate an understanding of how it can be true that the eternal divine Word subsists in both a divine and a human nature. The proper act of existence of the incarnate Word is the divine act of existence. The person, the one who says "I," is the eternal Son of the Father, the eternal divine Word. But that eternal Son become incarnate is present to himself not only with the divine consciousness that is his as Son but also with the human consciousness of a complete and developing human being, like us in all things but sin. Aquinas attempted to arrive at some remote and hypothetical understanding of this mystery of faith, and in doing so eventually, in one late document (*Quaestiones disputatae de unione Verbi incarnati*), hit upon the notion of a "secondary act of existence" as the basis of the relation of his assumed human nature to the divine person of the Word. The secondary act of existence is the "is" in the statement, "The eternal Word of God *is* this man Jesus of Nazareth." *Esse*, to be, is a verb, not a noun; the proper *is* of the incarnate Word is the divine *Is*, but the consequent condition of the truth of the statement, "The eternal Word of God *is* this man Jesus of Nazareth," is the created "is" in that statement, a secondary "is," a contingent "is" consequent upon the assumption of the human nature, an "is" that enables the foregoing statement to be true.

Lonergan adds to Aquinas's Christology the hypothesis that this secondary "is" may be regarded as a created participation in and imitation of divine paternity, of the Father, of the one whom Jesus called "Abba." The reasoning behind this hypothesis is that (1) the secondary act of existence, this "is," is the created base of a created *relation* of the assumed humanity to the eternal and uncreated Son, and (2) any such created relation to the Son, precisely as consequent condition of the procession of the Son being also the mission of the Son, must share in the divine relation to the Son. But the divine relation to the Son is the Father. The relation of the assumed human nature, as a created relation precisely *to the eternal Son of the Father*, thus imitates the eternal relation to the Son that is the Father. It participates in and imitates divine paternity. Thus, Jesus says, "Whoever has seen me has seen the Father" (John 14.9). Again, the divine Word as such does not speak but is spoken. Its notional act is not *dicere*, to speak, but *dici*, to be spoken. However, the incarnate Word speaks in time, as the divine Father speaks eternally. But the incarnate Word speaks only what he has heard from the Father (John 8.28, etc.). The secondary act of existence of the Incarnation, the created base of a created relation of the assumed human nature to the eternal divine Word, enables the incarnate Word to do the works, and speak the words, of the Father.

For Christian theology, the grace of hypostatic union that Aquinas and Lonergan partly explain through the hypothesis of a secondary act of existence is truly affirmed to be, from the standpoint of divine eternity, the basic created grace on which all others depend, and so in some sense the foundation of supernatural life wherever it is found.[24] Still, this is not the created imitation of divine life that most concerned me in *Missions and Processions.* The two divine relations that have been most relevant to my concerns up to now are active spiration and passive spiration, and so the communications of the divine nature that have occupied me most are sanctifying grace and charity. But I have always presented Lonergan's statement in full and have spoken briefly about the created imitations also of paternity and filiation. In the previous volume, I wanted to find something that is available not only to the human being Jesus of Nazareth, but to all of us. The secondary act of existence is a communication of divine paternity unique to the incarnate Son of God. What I was looking for in *Missions and Processions* was expressed in the participations in divine life that a theoretical and metaphysical theology calls sanctifying grace and the habit of charity.

In Lonergan's hypothesis, the elevation to participation in divine life that in a second-stage-of-meaning or theoretical-metaphysical theology was called sanctifying grace was understood as a created participation in and imitation of the active spiration that *is* the Father and the Son together "breathing" the Holy Spirit. The created gift of participation in God's active loving (*notionaliter diligere*) is a created base of a created relation to the uncreated Holy Spirit. The Holy Spirit, Trinitarian Proceeding Love, says Lonergan, dwells in us not as some kind of formal cause, as Karl Rahner maintains, but as an uncreated term of a created relation.[25] We are divinized not by a quasi-formal cause but by elevation to conscious *relations* to each of the divine persons, relations that participate in the divine relations because of the communication of divine life conditioned in a consequent manner by the created graces that Scholastic theology calls sanctifying grace and the habit of charity. Because the relation is a relation to the Holy Spirit, it both imitates and consciously participates in the uncreated relation to the Holy Spirit that is the Father and the Son together actively "breathing" love in their acknowledgment of each other as infinitely lovable. The Word that the Father speaks from eternity is "God is love." The Son *is* that Word. The Spirit "hears" that Word and "does" the truth of that Word in love.[26] The reception of the divine favor, of the grace that makes us pleasing to God (*gratia gratum faciens,* in the medieval expression), is the reception of our own lovableness in the sight of God, a lovableness that when received enables us to love with the very love of the Father and the Son, and so to "breathe" charity in a manner that is analogous to, and participates in, the way in which the Father and the Son "breathe" the Holy Spirit.

The charity that is "breathed" from the reception of actively spirating love, that is, from what a metaphysical theology calls "sanctifying grace," is love of the God who gave the gift of love. It is love issuing forth in grateful remembrance of and return for the gift. It is a created participation in and imitation of the passive spiration, the divine Proceeding Love, that is the Holy Spirit. Charity is an infused habit, or perhaps in Lonergan's more modern terms an infused circle or scheme of operations consequent upon our "hearing" the Word of divine love. As such it is the created base of a created relation to the uncreated Father and Son, who thus also dwell in us as uncreated terms of created relations.[27] Charity is a dimension of what Lonergan calls the dynamic state of being in love with God. Because it is a relation to the Father and the Son, it imitates the Holy Spirit, who *is* an uncreated relation of passive spiration, uncreated Proceeding Love, with respect to the eternal Father and Son who together "spirate" the Spirit of their mutual love. In Christians, this love of God in return is companionship with the incarnate Word, who relates us in transcendent hope to the Father. In those to whom the same gift has been given but without the objectification that comes from Trinitarian and Christological belief, we may speak of its manifestations in such dispositions as the love of wisdom and the transcendence that relates us to the ultimate, a transcendence manifest in diverse ways in the various religions of the world and often in secular relations as well. In either case, faith and hope may be said to accompany the charity that responds to the gift: faith as the knowledge born of the love, and so as a participation in the Word invisibly sent and breathing love in return, and hope as a relation to the transcendent origin of all, the Father.[28]

Finally, what Thomas and Lonergan call the light of glory is the created condition of the "vision," that is, the immediate knowledge of God that we already hope for in this life as we yearn to "see" the Father. When the light of glory is bestowed upon us, it will be a created participation in and imitation of divine filiation, as the incarnate Son leads the children of adoption perfectly back to the eternal Father. In this way, it is the created base of a created relation to the uncreated Father to whom we are related in hope in this life, whether that hope be explicitly related to Christian belief or not: it is found wherever the transcendental aspirations of the human spirit for intelligibility, truth, and goodness are kept alive in a sustained and consistent fashion, at times against all odds.

The first and the fourth of these created imitations of the divine relations, namely, the secondary act of existence and the light of glory, are not available to our human consciousness in this life. The first is peculiar to the incarnate Son of God, Jesus of Nazareth, and is determinative of his human consciousness in its conscious relation to the divine Word and so to his divine consciousness: a relation consciously participating in divine paternity. Chapter 5 of the present volume will be consumed with an attempt to develop an understanding of this relation.

The light of glory will be available to human consciousness in the beatific knowing that is our destiny. It is available to us now by anticipation in the supernatural virtue of hope.

What *are* available to human consciousness in this life are the second and the third of these created imitations of divine life, and it is on these that I have focused to date in speaking of imitations of the divine relations.

Lonergan's four-point systematic-theological hypothesis thus proposes that sanctifying grace is to charity as active spiration is to passive spiration, and so that created habitual grace in its totality has a Trinitarian structure, that it participates in and imitates the Trinitarian relations of active and passive spiration. In my elaborations on this hypothesis, I have suggested that God's offer of this gift of participation in divine life through created relations to the three divine persons is universal, that it is offered to all men and women at every time and place, but also that it is differentiated, revealed, made known, *thématique, signatus,* explicit, through the divine revelation recorded in the Jewish and Christian scriptures, and especially in the human beatific knowing of Jesus, the primary site of revelation.[29]

The universal mission of the Holy Spirit, the gift of divine love, is not only intensified but also revealed, made thematic, in the visible mission of the Son, where it plays a constitutive role. A visible mission of the Holy Spirit at Pentecost fulfils the twofold mission of the Son and the Spirit, invisible and visible, and enables a public acknowledgment that what happened in Jesus was indeed the revelation of the triune God in history. The mutual interplay of divine and human freedom can now be carried on in explicit recognition of what, prior to the revelation that comes to its fulfilment in the mission of the incarnate Word, necessarily remained *vécu* (lived) but not *thématique* (reflectively objectified), implicit but not recognized, conscious but not known, present *in actu exercito* (in practice) but not *in actu signato* (as signified).[30]

The interpersonal state of grace establishes imitations of divine life that run directly counter to the relations of mimetic rivalry elucidated by Girard. I regard Girard's thought as a substantial contribution to the theology of the Christian word, and so to the theology of revelation. The visible mission of the incarnate Word is among other things the explicit revelation, through linguistic and incarnate meaning, of what God has always been doing and continues to do in the invisible missions of the Word and the Holy Spirit. Entailed in that revelation, intrinsic to it, is the solution to the evils consequent on mimetic infection and contagion, namely, the command to "be perfect as your heavenly Father is perfect," where perfection means "love your enemies and pray for those who persecute you, so that you may be children of your Father who is in heaven; for he makes his sun rise on the evil and on the good, and sends rain on the just and on the unjust" (Matthew 5.44–45). That is a command whose implications reach far beyond the strictly spiritual dimensions of human understanding, judgment, and moral choice, and into the psyche and its neural base: nothing short of what I have called a psychic conversion, explicit or implicit, is often required if it is to be fulfilled.

One of the ways in which this gift of mutually reciprocal relations to the divine persons can be made available to consciousness is through recollection or memory providing evidence sufficient for the silent, indeed ineffable, judgment of value in which one assents to being on the receiving end of unqualified love. For Augustine, *memoria*, memory, is the state in which the mind (*mens*) finds itself, and there is a graced *memoria*, a transformed state in which the mind finds itself, a recollection that functions as the analogue for the divine Father. I am suggesting that it does so precisely as it provides evidence grasped as sufficient for the judgment of value that assents to the gift of divine love.

That assent, to the extent that it is made and clung to, changes everything in a person's life. The proceeding judgment of value Lonergan calls the faith born of religious love, and it establishes a new horizon for everything.[31] It functions in the same analogy as the analogue for the divine Word. From recollection and faith operating together, there proceeds charity, love in return of the givers of the gift. For Christians, as I said above, that love becomes more and more an explicit relation of companionship with the divine Word made flesh and an explicit relation of hope for the vision of the divine Father, while for those who do not know the revelation that makes this explicit, that love is a love of wisdom and a hope that keeps the quest for truth alive against all odds. The Trinitarian structure of active and passive spiration is present in the graced dimensions of all who have received the gift, whether or not it is articulated thematically as Trinitarian on the basis of God's revelation in the incarnate Word. A Christian theology of the world's religions in their positive moments will thus be Trinitarian at the core.[32]

4   Autonomous Spiritual Processions

I wish now to return to the notion of nature, which I believe is an important qualification to be added to Girardian anthropology. Theological understanding of the divine relations is grounded in an understanding of the divine processions, and for Lonergan as for Aquinas the key to reaching an obscure and analogical understanding of the divine processions lies in what Aquinas calls *emanatio intelligibilis*, intelligible emanation, precisely in the order of nature.

What do Aquinas and Lonergan mean by "intelligible emanation"?

If I grasp that there is sufficient evidence to posit a conception as true, the inner assent, the silent "yes" of the judgment of fact that I utter, emanates with rational exigency from the grasp of the evidence as sufficient.

Again, if I grasp that there is sufficient evidence to affirm something or someone as a genuine value, the silent "yes" of the judgment of value that I utter emanates with existential autonomy from the grasp of the evidence.

The judgment of value, moreover, is a word that breathes love (*verbum spirans amorem*), and so from the evidence grasped and the consequent judgment of value together there proceeds or emanates love, at least in the form of responsible decision.

Thus, the intelligible emanation of a judgment of value, "Yes," from a reflective grasp of evidence regarding what is good provides one variant of the so-called "psychological analogy" to enable us to have some very remote and imperfect understanding of what the procession of the Son from the Father might be. And the intelligible emanation of a loving decision from this grasp of evidence and judgment of value operating together as a unified principle provides one variant of the psychological analogy for the procession of the Holy Spirit from the Father and the Son.

This analogy, unlike the one I suggested above from the structure of grace, is taken from the natural unfolding of the eros of the human spirit for intelligibility, truth and being, and the good. It manifests what is meant by *emanatio intelligibilis*. It also manifests what is meant by the law of human nature, thus offering a clarification that Girard needs. It is a law whose observance is always precarious, in fact one whose consistent observance is statistically close to impossible without grace. But it is nature, and it allows theological anthropology to be based in the tripartite structure of nature, sin, and grace, rather than in the twofold structure of sin and grace characteristic of Girard's at least implicit anthropology.

I have chosen to render *emanatio intelligibilis* as "autonomous spiritual procession." It is precisely in the notion of *autonomy* that we will find, I suggest, the contribution to mimetic theory that comes from the clarifications of the notion of nature to be found in Lonergan's work.

Girard speaks of the illusion we entertain regarding the autonomy of our desires. More precisely, he conjoins the two terms "spontaneity" and "autonomy," so that they mean various aspects of the same thing, aspects that he claims are illusory.[33] I wish to distinguish them. *Processions of act from act in the spiritual realm* are autonomous. The legitimacy of the autonomy results from the fact that these processions in their integrity are not governed by the interdividual field.[34] That field constitutes what I called above the first way of being conscious. This first way of being conscious includes preeminently the sensitive-psychic passive reception of desire and fear within the realm of primordial intersubjectivity, and it can infect the second way of being conscious with all the vagaries of mimetic contagion that Girard elucidates. Autonomy is present in an authentic way only when the second way of being conscious has not been negatively infected by the first.

This autonomy is also not present in the spiritual emergence of insights from questions, for that is an emergence of act from potency, not of act from act. As such, however, it constitutes what Lonergan would regard as a legitimate *spontaneity* in the second way of being conscious. Thus, he distinguishes spontaneity from autonomy, whereas Girard tends to conflate them. Lonergan assigns to each a possible legitimate and authentic meaning that is not subject to Girard's hermeneutic of suspicion.

What, then, is this rare thing called authentic human autonomy? The eros of the human spirit, in its movement from experience through understanding and judgment to right decision, manifests along the way not only the spontaneous emergence of act from potency as answers suddenly emerge from questions but also careful, self-possessed, assured originations of new acts from previous acts. Included in these are the emergence of inner words of hypothetical conceptualization from insightful grasp of intelligibility, the emergence of judgments of fact from the reflective grasp of the sufficiency of evidence, the emergence of judgments of value from loving grasp of the evidence of goodness, and the emergence of loving acts or responsible decisions from the collaboration of loving grasp and the word of value that it has uttered.

In the emergence of act from potency, the principle is the object; in the emergence of act from act, the principle is the subject. What I am calling autonomous spiritual processions *are* indeed a function of human desire, but of the natural and spiritual desire that is to be distinguished from the elicited and sensitive-psychic desires whose mimetic structure Girard has elucidated. Especially when those processions entail authentic operations of value judgments and loving decisions, the desire that they express and indeed inchoately fulfil is quite different from the acquisitive mimetic desire that Girard illuminates. There are desires that are best understood as natural participations in divine light and love: the desire for intelligibility, the desire for the truth that is the medium of the knowledge of the real, the desire for the good. These participations always are conscious, but frequently they are not known for what they are. And even the consistent exercise of these natural desires is a function of grace.

We may provide more detail concerning what is meant by "spiritual" in contrast to "sensitive-psychic." In *Insight* Lonergan draws a distinction between the intelligible and the intelligent. Empirical objects are *potentially intelligible*: they can be understood. The unities and laws of things are *formally intelligible*: understanding has grasped unity and law, form. The existence of these unities and the occurrence of events in accord with the laws are *actually intelligible*: the formal intelligibilities are affirmed to *be*. But the disinterested, detached, unrestricted desire to know is *potentially intelligent*: when its promptings revealed in questions are followed upon, they will lead to understanding, to insight. Insights grasp unities and laws, and they ground conceptions of the unities and laws. As such, they are *formally intelligent*: understanding has occurred. The further reflective insights that grasp the sufficiency of evidence to pronounce judgment on our understanding, and the judgments that emanate from such reflective understanding and posit being as known, are *actually intelligent*. Thus, as known to ourselves, we are intelligible, as every other known is, but that intelligibility, unlike the intelligibility of other known realities, is also intelligence and knowing.

Now for Lonergan intelligibility that is also intelligent is precisely what is meant by "spiritual," and that is the sense in which I am using the word "spiritual" here. Thomas Aquinas's *emanatio intelligibilis* refers to what Lonergan calls spiritual intelligibility, the intelligibility that is also intelligent, the intelligibility of intelligence, reasonableness, and moral responsibility in act, where "act" is manifest in such operations as insight, conception, grasp of evidence, and judgment.

We proceed now to the meaning of "autonomous." When a judgment of value proceeds *because of* and *in proportion to* the evidence grasped, and when a loving decision proceeds *because of* and *in proportion to* both the evidence grasped and the judgment of value, the human subject has attained an authentic autonomy. A sound judgment is sound because it proceeds (a) from a grasp of sufficient evidence that I know is sufficient, and (b) in accord with or in proportion to the evidence that has been grasped. A good decision is good because it proceeds (a) from the grasp of evidence and the sound judgment, and (b) in accord with or in proportion to both sources together grounding the decision. The relation conveyed by the phrases "because of" and "in accord with" and "in proportion to," precisely as this relation is known to, and acted on by, the acting subject, constitutes genuine autonomy. This is what I mean by rendering Thomas's and Lonergan's "intelligible emanation" in the language of "autonomous spiritual processions." In the expression "autonomous spiritual procession," the word "autonomous" refers precisely to the "because of" and "in accord with" or "in proportion to" aspect of the procession of word from understanding and of loving decision from understanding and word together, precisely as that aspect is known by the subject to constitute the relation between what grounds the procession and what proceeds from that ground. This is part of the very notion of human *nature* that, I suggest, Girardian theory needs for its completion.

I distinguish, then, in a manner that Girard does not, between "autonomous" and "spontaneous." I find a genuine meaning for both terms, even while acknowledging that Girard has exposed illusions regarding them. There are in human consciousness processions, even spiritual processions, that are not autonomous but spontaneous. One example of a spontaneous as contrasted with an autonomous spiritual procession is the emergence of an act of understanding from data organized by imagination under the dynamism of inquiry. This procession is distinct from the subsequent autonomous spiritual procession that is the emergence of an objectification or conceptualization from the act of understanding or of a judgment from the reflective grasp of evidence. What is the difference? From reflecting on our own experience, we can, I believe, verify that the emergence of insight from data organized by imagination under the dynamism of inquiry is an instance of what anyone influenced by Aristotle would call the emergence of *act from potency*, whereas the emergence of hypothetical conceptualizations from the insight itself is an emergence of *one act from another act*. Since there is no movement from potency to act in God, who is pure act, what I am calling spontaneous processions will not provide a fitting or suitable analogy for understanding divine processions. The processions in human consciousness that will provide such an analogy must be processions of act from act. Even then, of course, the analogy is deficient. God is one act, consciously participated in in distinct ways by three divine persons, whereas insight and subsequent conceptualizations or objectifications in human consciousness are distinct acts, as are reflective grasp of the sufficiency of evidence and consequent judgments of fact or of value.

The dimension of spiritual autonomy that provides Lonergan with the appropriate realm in which to locate an analogy for Trinitarian processions lies in what he calls existential self-constitution, that is, in the emergence of good decision from an authentic judgment of value based on a reflective grasp of evidence, *precisely with regard to the question, What am I to make of myself?* The evidence grasped by an authentic person is, first and foremost, evidence regarding existential self-constitution: What would it be good for me to be? The consequent judgment of value is an assent to that grasped ideal. The proceeding love that leads to self-transcendent decision flows from the grasped evidence and consequent judgment. In an analogous manner, the divine Word is a judgment of value resting on *agapē*, Loving Intelligence in act, originatively constituting divine being. Divine Proceeding Love, the Holy Spirit, is spirated from such a dual origin: from Loving Grasp and the divine "Yes, this is very good!" as the two acknowledge each other's lovableness and breathe the Spirit of Love that both proceeds from and unites them.

In this section, we have been presenting a version of the Thomist-Lonerganian psychological analogy from human nature for understanding what Christians profess in faith regarding divine procession: "God from God, Light from Light, true God from true God." But as we saw in the previous section, Lonergan's four-point theological hypothesis adds the possibility of constructing an analogy in the supernatural order, one that posits graced imitations of, participations in, created communications of, the divine relations themselves. The secondary act of existence of the incarnate Word participates in and consciously imitates divine paternity. The reception of the gift of divine love participates in and consciously imitates divine active spiration. The habit of charity – loving God in return – participates in and consciously imitates divine passive spiration. The light of glory participates in and consciously imitates divine filiation. All four of these created supernatural realities are analogues for divine relations. But they are also more than that. They are imitations-by-conscious-participation because of divine self-communication conditioned in a consequent manner by the created realities.

The full analogy in the order of grace for understanding the divine processions would be based on the imitations-by-conscious-participation in active and passive spiration. The structure of this analogy is the same as that of the analogy from nature. There is the procession of assent from intelligent grasp of evidence, providing the analogy for the procession of the Son, and there is the procession of acts of love from grasp-and-assent considered as the one principle of love, providing the analogy for the procession of the Holy Spirit. But in the analogy within the supernatural order, the grasp of evidence is explicitly a grasp on the part of a lover who has been loved with an unqualified love that has now become one's own love, and the assent is that loving assent to that gift that we know as faith. The dynamic state of loving with God's love, not our own, and so the gift of loving in an unqualified fashion, governs the entire movement from beginning to end. This is the meaning of "created communication of the divine nature."

5   The Duality of Consciousness and the Dialectic of Desire

The integrity of spiritual process, whether natural or supernatural and whether spontaneous or autonomous, entails fidelity to a natural, transcendental orientation of human spiritual desire to the intelligible, the true and the real, and the good. This transcendental orientation is a natural participation in uncreated light. Within our present context, we should emphasize as well that it is a natural, not elicited, desire in the spiritual order for being, for the true, for the good, for God.

Lonergan consistently emphasizes that there are other desires that would interfere with the unfolding of the transcendental, spiritual, sometimes autonomous, active desire for being and value – with the pure, unrestricted, detached, disinterested desire to know what is and to do what is good, a desire ultimately for union with God. We can approach an understanding of this problem from what Lonergan says about the two ways of being conscious, and we can enlist the invaluable assistance of Girard in doing so.

Discriminating these two dimensions of human self-presence is an extraordinarily sensitive and delicate enterprise. Christian ascetical tradition, and, for that matter, even some supposedly Lonergan-based anthropologies, have often neglected the positive importance of the sensitive-psychic dimension, while much psychological theory tends to overlook the spiritual dimension. The first way of being conscious permeates the second, either in support of the transcendental orientation to the intelligible, the true, the real, and the good, or in conflict with it. Again, and more precisely, the first way of being conscious precedes, accompanies, and overarches the intentional operations that constitute the second way of being conscious. It precedes the operations in the transition from the neural to the psychic, with all the ambiguities of dreaming consciousness and myth, but also with the release of the images that are needed for insight and the symbols that manifest our higher aspirations and beckon us to follow them. It accompanies the operations in the feelings that are the mass and momentum of intentional consciousness. And it overarches the operations in establishing us as lovers and beloved, as members of community, as subjects whose consciousness or self-presence is itself interpersonal, not with the interdividuality of the purely psychic but with the communion characteristic of those who are principles of benevolence and beneficence.

Thus, distinguishing the two ways of being conscious and negotiating their relations calls for what Christian spiritual tradition has called discernment. What we undergo rather passively in what we sense and imagine, in our desires and fears, our delights and sorrows, our joys and sadness, affects the entire range of our spiritual orientation as it actually unfolds. Under optimal circumstances, this first way of being conscious bolsters and supports the second, where we consciously inquire in order to understand, understand in order to utter a word, weigh evidence in order to judge, deliberate in order to choose, and will in order to act. But those optimal circumstances are relatively rare. In fact, they are never reached without help from others and ultimately from the grace of God. To the extent that they are not achieved, there is a statistical near-inevitability of distortion precisely in the spiritual dimensions of human operation. Integrity in those dimensions, and especially in autonomous processions of act from act in human spirituality, is ever precarious, and is always reached by withdrawing from inauthenticity.

Girard has called attention to the extremely precarious nature of human claims to autonomous subjectivity. These precautions are salutary for anyone hoping to resurrect the psychological analogy in Trinitarian theology. Lonergan has called attention to authenticity and inauthenticity in the very realms of understanding, truth, moral development, and religion, the realms that are also appealed to for the analogy. These areas are positively treated when he speaks of intellectual, moral, and religious conversion, but these conversions are required for the consistent integrity of spiritual performance. And in my own writings I have called attention to a distinct dimension of authenticity and conversion that affects primarily the first "way of being conscious." I have spoken of psychic conversion. Girard gives us a better purchase on this psychic dimension of desire than do other current or recent explorations, and being very clear with him about the character of false mimesis and deviated transcendence precisely as they affect and distort intellectual, moral, and religious operations will help students of Lonergan and of theology in general to isolate much more clearly just where in consciousness the genuine *imago Dei* really lies.

Thus, I propose (1) that what Girard has written about desire concerns directly the first "way of being conscious," that is, the sensitive, psychic dimension of consciousness, but also (2) that this dimension penetrates our spiritual orientation to the intelligible, the true and the real, and good, and that it does so for better or for worse.

I presume that we are all aware of Girard's explication of mimetic or triangular desire, and of his distinction between acquisitive or appropriative mimetic desire and a possible desire, even a form of mimetic desire, that functions in positive ways. I would suggest

- that what Lonergan calls the first way of being conscious is precisely interdividual, in Girard's sense,
- that psychic development entails the negotiation of this interdividual field, a negotiation that (1) would take the subject through something like what C.G. Jung calls individuation, but without the vagaries and confusions of Jungian explications,[35] and (2) would lead beyond individuation to genuine interpersonal relations as one moves consistently into the dynamic state of being in love,
- that this negotiation calls upon the operations of the second way of being conscious, that is, upon inquiry, insight, conceptualization, weighing evidence, judging, deliberating, and deciding,
- that inadequate negotiations of the interdividual field can and will distort the second way of being conscious, and
- that authentic negotiation of the same field will allow the second way to flourish in the development of the person.

It seems important to stress that Girard's complex conceptions of mimetic desire presuppose a radical insufficiency in the very being of the desiring individual. There is a radical ontological sickness at the core of internal appropriative mimetic desire. The individual is at some level painfully aware of his or her own emptiness, and it is this awareness that leads one to crave so desperately the fullness of being that supposedly lies in others. The figures onto whom such desire is projected mediate being itself for us. It is via them that we seek to become real, and it is through wanting the very being of these models or mediators that we come to imitate them. The wish to absorb the other or to be absorbed by or into the substance of the other implies an insuperable revulsion for one's own being. Such metaphysical desire is masochism or pseudo-masochism, a will to self-destruction that manifests itself in attempts to become something or someone other than what one is. The self-sufficiency attributed to the model is, of course, illusory, and so the project to attain it is doomed from the outset. But even if one vaguely perceives the fruitlessness of the quest, one does not give it up, because to do so would mean admitting that the salvation one craves is impossible to achieve. One may even become the tormentor, torturing others as one was oneself tortured, and thus transforming masochism into sadism.

I find a threefold benefit to be gained from a serious study of Girard's exposure of these dynamics. First, Girard's position shows that there is a much greater complexity than might be obvious to the two ways of being conscious to which Lonergan refers; in particular, much more enters into the first way of being conscious than might be obvious from Lonergan's description of it. The passive reception of what we sense and imagine, of our desires and our fears, our delights and sorrows, our joys and sadness, is not some simple, one-dimensional reality. It is extraordinarily complex, and the mimetic model of desire throws more light on that complexity than any other position of which I am aware.

Second, Girard also shows the interrelations of the two ways of being conscious. For one thing, it is ultimately a spiritual emptiness that leads to the derailments of mimetic desire, an emptiness that recalls Augustine's "You have made us for yourself, and our heart is restless until it rests in you."[36] But also, the only resolution of mimetic violence is the complete renunciation of the rivalry to which triangular acquisitive desire leads us, and that renunciation is an intensely spiritual act flowing from a decision that itself proceeds from acknowledging the facts in true judgment. In other words, the resolution of the problems to which acquisitive mimetic desire gives rise takes place through a series of autonomous spiritual processions that are precisely the sort of emanations that Lonergan regards as appropriate for the psychological Trinitarian analogy.

Finally, I regard the vagaries of mimetic desire to which Girard gives us entrance as principal instances of what Lonergan calls dramatic bias and also as frequent psychological components of the other forms of bias that Lonergan exposes, components that introduce the blind spot that Lonergan describes so powerfully in his description of dramatic bias.[37]

My questions to Girard would be the following. First, his work raises for me the question of the significance precisely for mimetic theory of the natural spiritual desire for intelligibility, truth and being, and the good, and ultimately for God, that Lonergan has clarified. There is a radical ontological desire that itself is not mimetic but that is involved in various ways in all mimetic desire. And so I ask: Is imitative desire brought on by a sense of spiritual inadequacy that is endemic to the human condition? Is the story of imitative desire a story of the successes and failures of mutual self-mediation in the attempt, itself completely legitimate, to find the completion of one's being in relation? Is mimetic violence, which springs from imitative desire, the fate of mutual self-mediation gone wrong? Is there healthy mutual self-mediation? Do we all suffer from such a radical ontological insufficiency that these double binds are inevitable for all of us? Or is there a mediation that can quiet the sense of spiritual inadequacy and enable human relations to be something other than the violent mimesis that Girard depicts? What is it that enables one to renounce mimetic rivalry completely without using this renunciation as a feigned indifference that is just another way to get what one wants? Is the tendency to compare oneself to others not rooted in an ontological emptiness that only God can fill? Is there a way of negotiating this emptiness that transcends victimization by the triangular situation that necessarily will be involved in the negotiation? What is the source of our fascination with the saints? Think of Ignatius Loyola asking, What would it mean if I were to do in my situation what Francis and Dominic did in theirs? Or again, think of Bernard Lonergan asking, as he must have, What would it mean if I were to do in my situation what Thomas Aquinas did in his? The mimetic quality of the questions is obvious. But in either case it led to something quite other than the tortured quality of internally mediated relations. It led to autonomous spiritual processions of word and love that were, at times at least, in fact created participations in triune life.

These questions can be answered, I believe, by appealing to the transcendental desires of the human spirit, to Lonergan's second way of being conscious. "All people by nature *desire* to know," Aristotle says at the very beginning of the *Metaphysics*. This becomes Lonergan's leitmotif throughout *Insight*, where he unpacks the dynamics of the desire to know in mathematics, science, common sense, and philosophy, as well as the devices that we employ to flee understanding when we do not want to face the truth. In his later work, he extends this transcendental desire to the notion of the good. Girard insists correctly that almost all learning is based on imitation, and so satisfying the desire to know involves mimetic behavior. But the present question is, Are the desire to know and the transcendental intention of value themselves a function of acquisitive mimesis? Are they acquisitive desires? Or is acquisitiveness a perversion of these desires? *Is* there such a thing as a detached, disinterested desire to know? Girard himself speaks of a true vocation of thought that lies in integrating isolated discoveries into a rational framework and transforming them into real knowledge.[38] Is not that an indication of what Lonergan calls the desire to know? Is it not an instance of Lonergan's second way of being conscious, where we inquire in order to understand, understand in order to utter a word, weigh evidence in order to judge? How does fidelity to this vocation differ from acquisitive mimesis? How can it be infected and derailed by acquisitive mimesis? These questions are worth pursuing. And in a further extension of the same set of questions, can Lonergan students ignore how Girard has clarified in an astounding fashion the influence that distorted mimesis has on the realm of the sacred, which in its authenticity pertains primarily to the second way of being conscious, an influence that Girard calls deviated transcendence? Will not these clarifications help us get straight just where the genuine *imago Dei*, and so the genuine *imitatio Dei*, resides?

6   *Imago Dei*

Where is the *imago* that is also an *imitatio*? We have seen two instances, one in human nature itself and the other in that nature as elevated to participation in the divine relations. Foundationally, the image of God lies in the created participation in active and passive spiration, the share in divine life given to us by God. That participation is, first, the gift of being on the receiving end of unqualified love. This gift prompts an existential judgment of value, a knowledge born of the gift of love, a word that breathes love in return, the word of faith. That love in return is the charity born of the reception of love and the acknowledgment of that reception, a charity that is inspired by gratitude for the gift given. This process may serve as an analogy for the divine relations of active and passive spiration, relations which encompass the entirety of immanent Trinitarian life.

But this supernatural *imitatio* may itself be understood by analogy with an imitation of God in the very order of nature, an imitation that lies within actively intelligent, actively reasonable, actively deliberative consciousness, that is, in the second way of being conscious that Lonergan specifies. In fact, it has been in the context of the autonomy of the operations performed in this natural unfolding of the transcendental orientation that we have found a fruitful encounter with Girard's mimetic theory. Girard has introduced a necessary hermeneutic of suspicion into the project of self-appropriation initiated by Lonergan, a hermeneutic that is probably the best categorical articulation to date of what my own work anticipated heuristically by speaking of a need for a psychic conversion. He has captured the interference of acquisitively mimetic desire with the unfolding of the transcendental orientation. But there *is* an *imago Dei*, and an *imitatio Dei* – *imago* and *imitatio* are from the same root – that is natural, that resides in our spiritual nature, where "nature" is understood in the Aristotelian sense of an immanent principle of movement and of rest. The *imago Dei* or *imitatio Dei* is not the whole of that spiritual nature, for that nature is "the human spirit as raising and answering questions" and so is potency in the realm of spiritual matters. But there are moments in which that nature precisely as nature imitates the pure act that is God, however remotely: when from understanding as act there proceeds an inner word of conceptualization in act, when from the grasp of evidence as sufficient there proceeds a judgment whether of fact or of value, and when from a judgment of value there proceeds a good decision or an act of love. That natural image can be used as an analogy from which we may understand the more radical image or imitation that lies in a created participation in the divine relations of active and passive spiration.

Lonergan writes, "The psychological analogy ... has its starting point in that higher synthesis of intellectual, rational, and moral consciousness that is the dynamic state of being in love. Such love manifests itself in its judgments of value. And the judgments are carried out in decisions that are acts of loving. Such is the analogy found in the creature."[39] The quotation is applicable equally, of course, to natural and graced states of being. But the dynamic state of being on the receiving end of a love that is without any reservations or qualifications, a love that makes us lovable because it elevates us to participation in divine life, is precisely the gift that the four-point hypothesis construes as a created participation in divine active spiration. From that love received there flows a knowledge born of love that is a silent judgment of value proceeding as act from act. These two together imitate divine active spiration, and what proceeds from this created participation in active spiration is the love in return that relates us to the Father and the Son who gave the love in the first place. The supernatural analogy imitates by participation the entire life of the triune God. It is in fact only by the grace of this created imitation, whether it is known as such or not – and most often it is not – that the natural transcendental unfolding of our spiritual aspirations remains authentic.

2

The Program

We have reviewed in chapter 1 some of the principal themes of *Missions and Processions*. All of these themes were introduced in an effort to develop the connection between the divine processions and the visible and invisible missions of the Son and especially of the Holy Spirit, and to do so in the framework of the theology of history whose basic general categories were developed in *Theology and the Dialectics of History* and *What Is Systematic Theology?* The present volume presents five further developments in the theology of the divine missions. Some of these developments will be elucidated in the present volume and others in the next.

1   Actual Grace

Within the overall framework of the theology of history that provides the unified field structure[1] of a contemporary systematics, the missions of the Son and the Holy Spirit, both their invisible-universal missions and their visible-public missions, provide the basic realities embraced by the category "religious values" in the integral scale of values, with all of the relations of those realities to the other levels of value in the scale. Authentic religion is reception of and collaboration with the missions of the Word and the Holy Spirit, whether that reception and collaboration be *vécu* or also *thématique,* conscious or also known, a function of the universal missions of Word and Spirit or also of their revealed missions, where the operative directive of collaboration is found in the words of Jesus, "As the Father has sent me, so I send you" (John 20.21).

This notion of authentic religion calls for one step beyond what I was able to provide in *Missions and Processions.* That step lies in a development in the theology of what has been known as actual grace. The new material in the present volume begins with this development, which is provided in the next chapter.

The missions of Word and Spirit are always conjoined, and our effort now must be to try to understand how they work together. It will be in the cultural and social formal effects of grace that their collaborative endeavor in mission from the Father is clearest. In this endeavor the theology of actual grace is needed to complement the transposition of sanctifying grace and charity offered in *Missions and Processions*.

2   Divine Relations and Persons

While the divine processions, relations, persons, and missions are really identical, the relevant Trinitarian concerns from the standpoint of theological *conceptuality* are not simply the divine processions, which were in the forefront in *Missions and Processions*, but also and especially the divine *relations*, as well as the divine persons not only in themselves but especially in their relations to one another, where perhaps we may speak of exemplary causality with respect to social grace. "… the three Persons are the perfect community, not two in one flesh, but three subjects of a single, dynamic, existential consciousness."[2] Social grace is about relations, and ultimately about the elevation of human relations and human communication and collaboration to the point of imitating and participating in divine circumincession. It is to this that we turn here. *What are elevated human relations, and how are they pertinent to the integrity of cultural and social values, that is, to the meanings and values that inform given ways of living and to the social structures that embody those meanings and values for better or for worse? And what connection do such relations have with the divine relations sent into history?*

We need to address, then, Lonergan's theology of the divine relations and the divine persons. A presentation of my understanding of Lonergan on divine relations constitutes the fourth chapter of this volume, and the divine persons begin to be treated in the fifth. I will draw from his theology of the divine relations and the divine persons implications relevant to my ulterior concerns.

The concluding chapters in volume 1 of this three-volume work, *Missions and Processions*, were devoted principally to interpreting and commenting on Lonergan's first few assertions in his work *The Triune God: Systematics*, that is, on chapter 2 of that work, which treated the theology of the divine processions. The same procedure will be followed here with regard to chapter 3 and parts of chapters 4 and 5 of that work. We will be focusing on Lonergan's assertions regarding the divine relations and on some of his work on the divine persons. I will intersperse the presentation and interpretation of Lonergan's theology of the divine relations and persons with the sublation of that material into the theology of history that is my overall project. Lonergan's theology of the divine relations is studied and developed a bit further in chapter 4, and his theology of the divine persons, including the incarnate person of the divine Word, is drawn on in chapter 5.

After his chapter on the divine processions, Lonergan moves closer to his specification of an analogical and obscure understanding of Trinitarian life by asking what *reality* is to be attributed to what were *conceived* as two specifically distinct divine processions. "Now that we have *conceived* the two specifically distinct divine processions, we must ask what *reality* is to be attributed to them."[3] The reality to be attributed to the divine processions is the reality proper to relations. The divine relations *are* the divine processions. "The processions are conceptually distinct from, but really identical with the relations."[4] But we have already seen that the missions are also the processions joined to created external terms. The missions must then also be understood as the divine relations *joined to the same created external terms.* This will be the first step, taken in chapter 4, beyond presenting a position on actual grace. It will be followed in chapter 5 by some treatment of the persons identical with the relations.

The presentation will be done again in the form of theses, as in the previous volume. There were sixty theses articulated in the first volume, and the numbering here will be consecutive with that alignment.

Thus, we begin with thesis 61.

> **Thesis 61:** *Since the reality of the two divine processions with which the divine missions are identical is the reality to be attributed to relations, the missions themselves will have a thoroughly relational structure. The missions of the Holy Spirit and the Son are themselves missions of relations, sendings of divine relations into the human world mediated and constituted by meaning and motivated by values, and so into the world of human relations. These missions are identical with the divine relations joined to created external terms. The Word and the Holy Spirit are sent or missioned to transform human relations, to lift or elevate them precisely as relations into conformity with the reign of God and so with the entire range of the scale of values.*

3   A Relational System among the Created Terms

One consequence of this logical stream of assertions is clear, and we may state it in a second new thesis.

> **Thesis 62:** *The created external terms that are the consequent conditions of the processions and relations also being missions – in Lonergan's*

> *hypothesis, the secondary act of existence of the incarnate Word, sancti-fying grace, charity, and the light of glory – must (1) be related to one another in a manner that shares in and imitates the order of the divine relations of which they are created external terms, and (2) have impli-cations for an elevation of human relations (not simply of individuals in their authenticity, that is, "personal values") to a participation in divine relations.*

Lonergan's "four-point hypothesis" already bears out the connection of the missions to the relations, for it correlates the preeminent created graces – hypostatic union understood in terms of the secondary act of exis-tence of the Incarnation, sanctifying grace, charity, and the light of glory – with the four divine relations. The secondary act of existence is a created participation in and imitation of paternity, sanctifying grace a created par-ticipation in and imitation of active spiration, charity a created participa-tion in and imitation of passive spiration, and the light of glory a created participation in and imitation of filiation.

But there remains the issue of specifying the *relations among the four cre-ated participations* in the divine relations. Correlating divine missions with the divine relations raises the question of how to specify relations among the four created external terms that correspond to, imitate, and participate in the di-vine relations, and that are the created consequent conditions of the commu-nication of the divine life, a communication constituted by those relations.

The relations among the created external terms are discovered in the transformation of human relations. Thus, we should be able to move to an attempt to understand how imitating the divine relations and participating in them affects the realms of cultural and social values and the equitable distribution of vital goods to the whole human family. Since interpersonal relations are at the heart of what Lonergan means by the human good,[5] conceiving the missions in terms of relations moves us directly into the re-lation between the missions and the levels of cultural and social values. To participate in the divine relations will be shown to have a connection with human relations, and so with the human good, with cultural and social val-ues, and with collective responsibility for the scale of values. That is the link or set of links that we must attempt to draw.

But just how will that show us something of the relations among the four created participations in the divine relations: among the secondary act of existence of the incarnate Word, sanctifying grace, charity, and the light of glory? The terms of the divine relations as immanent to Pure Act are the op-posed relations: paternity to filiation, filiation to paternity; active spiration to passive spiration, passive spiration to active spiration. The missions add a created external term to each relation: secondary act of existence to light of glory, light of glory to secondary act of existence; sanctifying grace to charity, charity to sanctifying grace. Not only must these created external terms be understood in relational terms, but the relational terms must follow the order of the divine relations. They will be shown to do so by analyzing their effect upon the entire realm of human relations.

We have already seen that the created external terms are the bases of created relations to uncreated divine persons. Thus, the secondary act of existence of the Incarnation, the "is" in the statement "The eternal Word of God *is* this man Jesus of Nazareth," is the created base of a created relation of the assumed human nature of Jesus to the uncreated divine Word. This relation, precisely as a relation to the divine Word, participates in and imitates paternity, the uncreated relation to the divine Word that is the Father. Thus, Jesus is able to say that anyone who sees him sees the Father (John 14.9). Again, the Word immanent to the Trinity does not speak but is spoken; the incarnate Word speaks, but he speaks only what he hears from the Father. Etc., etc., etc.[6] Next, sanctifying grace, an entitative habit elevating the core of personal identity to participation in divine life, is the created base of a created relation to the uncreated Holy Spirit. As the base of a relation to the Holy Spirit, it participates in and imitates the uncreated relation to the Holy Spirit that is active spiration, Father and Son together "breathing" Proceeding Love. Sanctifying grace is an actively spirating love that must "breathe" its own proceeding love. Third, a created participation in that same Holy Spirit, namely, charity, is the proceeding love breathed from the elevation into a share in divine life that is sanctifying grace, in a manner remotely analogous to the being-breathed of the Holy Spirit from the active breathing of the Father and the Son in their mutually opposed relations of paternity and filiation. That charity is the created base of a created relation to the Father and the Son. This relation, as a relation to the Father and the Son together, participates in and imitates the uncreated relation to the Father and the Son together that is passive spiration, the Holy Spirit. Fourth, the light of glory (of which we have yet to say very much) is the created base of a created relation to the Father. As such it participates in and imitates the uncreated relation to the Father that is the Son as he leads the children of adoption perfectly home in the reign of God. It is reflected in this life in the virtue of hope, and realized in one step in life after death and in a second step in the life after life after death that is the resurrection and the new creation.[7]

But that is not enough. This is but a first indication of the relationality constitutive of created grace.

A second set of relational terms must be established. For if the Father, the Son, and the Holy Spirit are themselves relations to one another, there must also be a set of created relations *among* the created terms of those uncreated relations, the terms that make of the relations *missioned* relations as God's entrance into the human world mediated and constituted by meaning and motivated by values. There is not simply a relation *between* each of the created terms and the uncreated reality to which that base, as the term of a mission, is related. Rather, since the reality of the two divine processions with which the divine missions are identical is the reality to be attributed to relations, the missions themselves and the external terms that allow the processions to be missions not only will have a thoroughly relational structure, but the structure of the relations of the terms must participate in the structure of the divine relations themselves. We must develop and complicate the four-point hypothesis by constructing a further relational system that unites the created terms in the foundational reality of the created supernatural order. Their relational unity must be a created participation in and imitation of the order of the divine relations.

We have already seen two of these *relations among the terms*: the relation of sanctifying grace to charity and the opposed relation of charity to sanctifying grace. But we must construct a relational system that unites all four created terms in the foundational reality of the created supernatural order, the order of grace in its fullest extent. We must consequently face the questions:

- What is the relation of the secondary act of existence of the Incarnation not only to the divine Word but also to sanctifying grace, to charity, and to the light of glory?
- What is the relation of sanctifying grace not only to the Holy Spirit, and not only to charity (which we have already established), but also to the secondary act of existence and to the light of glory?
- What is the relation of charity not only to the Father and the Son, and not only to sanctifying grace (which again we have already established), but also to the secondary act of existence and to the light of glory?
- And what is the relation of the light of glory not only to the Father but also to the secondary act of existence, to sanctifying grace, and to charity?

The answers to these questions must establish a relational unity that follows, imitates, and participates in the order of the divine processions and relations. The missions, again, are the processions and relations joined to created external terms. The terms must be related to one another in a manner that reflects the internal relations among the divine persons.

The basic structure of these relations has already been suggested. Paternity is to filiation as the secondary act of existence is to the light of glory; filiation is to paternity as the light of glory is to the secondary act of existence; active spiration is to passive spiration as sanctifying grace is to charity; passive spiration is to active spiration as charity is to sanctifying grace. But where are these realities to be located? In the communal experience of grace, in social grace, in grace as it reflects the transformation of human relations into participation in divine circumincession. That claim, however, remains to be substantiated, and most of this work will be left to the next volume, *Redeeming History*.

4   Social Grace and Imitation of and Participation in Divine Circumincession

The foundational thesis of what remains to come in this volume and the next states: *The Word and the Holy Spirit are sent or missioned to transform human relations, to lift or elevate them into conformity with the reign of God and so with the entire range of the scale of values.* Thesis 62 develops this a bit further. And we are now ready for a further development.

> **Thesis 63:** *The affirmation that the missions that are identical with the divine processions are real relations and the consequent affirmation that the created terms of these relational missions participate in the relationality that is divine life together constitute the firm theological ground of the theology of social grace already introduced in the first volume. It is in the realm of social grace that there will be found the relations among the created terms of the relational divine missions: the relations to one another of the secondary act of existence, sanctifying grace, charity, and the light of glory.*

I discovered in composing the index to *The Triune God: Systematics* that "relation" is the single most significant category in that work. My purpose now is not only to explicate why this is so in a pure theology of the immanent Trinity (chapter 4) but also to articulate the importance of this significance for the historical participation in divine life that is my major concern.

Grace is participation in the divine relations, a participation rendered possible by divine self-communication. Moreover, graced participation in the divine relations of active and passive spiration provides the "special basic relations" of systematic theology in its entirety.[8] These are immanent to and constitutive of the subject, of "personal value," as the subject is elevated to life in God, where the subject becomes what Lonergan calls the subject in Christ Jesus.[9] We have no direct conscious access to the created terms of the other two elements in the four-point hypothesis, namely, the secondary act of existence of the Incarnation and the light of glory. We must work from the experience of grace that we do have and extrapolate to these other supernatural realities as best we can. In the case of the *esse secundarium,* we may work as well from the intricate position expressed by Lonergan regarding the human consciousness and human knowledge of Jesus.[10] But whether our participation in divine life through created imitations of and participations in active and passive spiration be *vécu* (as it almost always is) or *thématique* (which perhaps is one of the great theological and ecclesial challenges of our age), it is constitutive, I suggest, of "religious values" in the normative scale of values. I have already studied in abundance the relation between religious values and personal development and integrity, both in the previous volume of this work and earlier in *Theology and the Dialectics of History* and *What Is Systematic Theology?* But as we move to the explicit connection between the divine relations and the divine missions, it is time to move as well to a consideration of *the relation of religious values to cultural and social values.* Charity is relational not only to God but also to neighbor, and from there the missions themselves, invisible and visible, take on their historical significance in establishing the realms of cultural and social values. Thus, as we move to the explicit connection between the divine relations and the divine missions, we move as well to a consideration of the relation of religious values to cultural and social values.

That relation is mediated through personal values, many of whose constitutive aspects we saw in considering Lonergan's chapter on the processions. Personal value can be understood largely in terms of the autonomous spiritual processions that form the natural analogue for the divine processions. No specifically theological theme is more appropriate for considering cultural and social values than that of the divine relations and our created participation in them through grace. For that participation will itself be relational, and personal relations are at the heart of the social mediation of the human good. In fact, the state of grace is an interpersonal situation, where the founding persons are the divine Three, and where we are all invited to allow ourselves to be caught up, in prayer and in life, individually and communally, in the circumincession of divine life. Our participation in the divine relations through grace is an elevation also of our relatedness to our fellow men and women, and in fact to all creation. That elevation will be mediated historically through cultural and social values. Social grace is a matter of *elevated human relationality.*

I have mentioned five distinct new issues to be introduced here and in the next volume, beyond the already established created relations of the created terms to divine persons, and have painted in broad strokes the outlines of four of them: the theology of actual grace as it enables us to understand the structure of the invisible missions; an understanding and development upon Lonergan's systematic theology of divine relations and persons; the establishment of a relational system *among the created terms,* a relational system that participates in and imitates the order of the divine relations; social grace as a participation in and imitation of divine circumincession as this participation and imitation becomes effective in the transformation of cultural and social values. The fifth new issue is social grace in its connection especially to the visible and invisible missions of the Word. Chapter 5 of *Missions and Processions* was devoted to this topic, but more can be said about it, for the topic opens upon a soteriology. The soteriology that completes our theology of the divine missions will be presented in the third volume in this project, but distinct anticipations of the shape that it will take will be offered in the present work.

5   Social Grace and the Mission of the Word

The scale of values, as I argued in *Theology and the Dialectics of History*, provides the immanent intelligibility of history.[11] Because the missions *are* the processions joined to a created external term, the missions, visible and invisible, are the "Trinity in history." They are the universal presence of grace in history precisely as constituting the fifth level in the scale of values, the level that ultimately is responsible for effective human functioning at all other levels.

But the scale of values also forces other considerations beyond the explicit developments found in volume 1. My principal though by no means sole concern to date in *The Trinity in History* has been with the relation of the missions, as constituting "religious values," to the realm of *personal values* in the same scale, where "personal value" means "the person in [one's] self-transcendence, as loving and being loved, as originator of values in [oneself] and in [one's] milieu, as an inspiration and invitation to others to do likewise."[12] The point of this is clear: the processions are understood on the basis of a psychological analogy, and that analogy names precisely what constitutes the realm of personal value, the person in his or her authenticity, the subject in whom what I call autonomous spiritual processions occur. That analogy can be constructed on several grounds, natural and supernatural, as is manifest by comparing the work of Augustine, Aquinas, the early and the later Lonergan, and the suggestion offered in *Missions and Processions*, where an analogy is drawn from the missions themselves. The structure of the analogy – speaker, word, love – remains the same in all these various renditions. What changes is the character of the created analogue for the Father speaking the Word. The analogue is *memoria* in Augustine, *intelligere* in Aquinas and the early Lonergan, *agapē* in the later Lonergan, and a graced *memoria* in my efforts.

But the reality of the Trinity in History is about much more than the relation of grace (understood as participation in and imitation of active and passive spiration) to the personal authenticity, integrity, indeed holiness, of individuated subjects. That consideration stresses the mission of the Holy Spirit. It does not ignore the mission of the Word, but it does not integrate it fully with the mission of the Holy Spirit. And even when we stress the mission of the Holy Spirit, we must consider the formal effects[13] of such grace in the realms of cultural and social values. These I have called "social grace." The category of social grace refers to the cultural transformation of the meanings and values that inform human living, as well as the transformation of social, economic, and political structures. It refers to the cumulative and transforming effect of the divine missions in the realms of cultural and social values, precisely through the agency of converted subjects working together on mission from the Word just as the incarnate Word was on mission from the Father. Ultimately "social grace" means the integrity of the whole scale of values. This integrity itself is measured against its bottom line, namely, the equitable distribution of vital goods to the entire family of God's children. This measure tells us how far we have to go before what we pray for when we say, "Thy kingdom come," actually occurs in our midst in any secure set of schemes of recurrence.

While these points are, I hope, constant throughout my work, the dynamics of operative and cooperative grace – whether habitual or actual – precisely as social, that is, in their formal effects at the cultural and social levels in the scale of values, remain to be specified in more detail. The present volume will make a contribution in this direction. As it does so it moves from a concentration in volume 1 on the mission of the Holy Spirit to an emphasis on the mission of the divine Word, visible and invisible. My principal hope is to link the formal effects of grace in cultural and social transformation to the mission, visible and invisible, of the Word, who enlightens everyone who comes into the world (John 1.9), and who became flesh and dwelt among us (John 1.14).[14] But a theology of the mission of the incarnate Word constitutes a soteriology, and so the final volume, *Redeeming History*, will represent my attempt to contribute to the development of a contemporary soteriology.

3

Actual Grace and the Elevation of the Secular

1   The Proposal

The first new development to be suggested in this second volume of *The Trinity in History* promotes a renewal of the theology of what traditionally has been called actual grace. This development occurs as I attempt to integrate several strands of thought represented in recent contributions I have tried to make first to the secularization-sacralization debate and also to the question of a Christian theology of religions.

The sacralization-secularization debate, which I already addressed in *Missions and Processions*, is both ecclesial and theological, or (perhaps better) both doctrinal and systematic, and the two contexts are related. The systematic-theological debate will not be resolved short of discovering in actual grace the key to discerning grace everywhere. Resolution of the doctrinal-ecclesial debate, I fear, may take much longer, if not in the *sensus fidelium* at least in some magisterial attitudes. I believe it will occur only to the extent that something along the lines of the theological advances on actual grace suggested here are accepted.

This chapter offers what I regard as the central element in the relevant discernment of ubiquitous grace. We begin with a bit of repetition of something we saw in *Missions and Processions*, namely, the linking of what Lonergan calls the law of the cross with genuine sacralization, true grace, in

Some of the material in this chapter appeared in an article, "Actual Grace and the Elevation of the Secular," *Australian eJournal of Theology* 22/3 (2015) 166–79. See also Doran, "Invisible Missions: The Grace That Heals Disjunctions," in *Seekers and Dwellers: Plurality and Wholeness in a Time of Secularity.*

history. In so beginning, we are also anticipating the soteriological themes that will be central in the next volume. My principal reason for stressing this theme will be clear in the references below to "Gaudium et Spes" and two of Pope John Paul II's encyclicals.

2   Sacralizations and Secularizations Welcomed and Resisted

As we saw in chapter 10 of *Missions and Processions*, in a lecture delivered at Trinity College, University of Toronto, in November 1973, "Sacralization and Secularization," Lonergan proposed the complex heuristic structure of (1) a sacralization to be dropped, (2) a sacralization to be fostered, (3) a secularization to be welcomed, and (4) a secularization to be resisted.[1] In *Missions and Processions* I provided "lower-blade" suggestions meant to give flesh to that heuristic structure. I wish now to review, reorder, and rework the proposals found there, though the reader should turn to that longer treatment for further details. I find this the best way to introduce the position I wish to suggest on actual grace, since it provides perhaps the paramount instance of what is meant by that theological category.

I propose to start here with "a sacralization to be fostered" and "a secularization to be welcomed." Fostering true sacralization will counteract various forms of deviated transcendence and so will facilitate the dropping of false sacralizations. And welcoming genuine secularization will entail resisting secularism; for genuine secularization is the fruit of attentiveness, intelligence, reasonableness, and responsibility, while secularism depends on neglecting or denying the finality, the upwardly but indeterminately directed dynamism, of authentic intentionality.

The key to discerning the genuine sacred in human history lies in what Lonergan calls "the just and mysterious law of the cross," particularly as the redemptive action of returning good for evil informs a praxis that works strenuously to implement the integral scale of values and so to extend the formal effects of grace to the realms of cultural and social values. The position I wish to suggest is that such discernment entails actual grace in one of its most obvious and dramatic instances, where actual grace consists, as Lonergan would argue, in divinely communicated insights and divinely effected transformations in the willing of the end, or in more contemporary language, in the establishment of one's fundamental option.[2]

Discerning the genuine sacred in history thus entails recognizing, implementing, and celebrating the transformation of evil into a greater good, indeed the supreme good of transformed human relations, precisely through the determination to absorb evil in love like a blotter[3] and to respond with both forgiveness and positive initiatives to work around the mischief occasioned by mimetic conflict and *ressentiment*[4] and continue to institute schemes of recurrence that will have a positive effect on the course of events. Such recognition and such determination are instances of actual grace.

The law of the cross was revealed progressively in its dynamics, though not in terms of the cross, in the Israelite scriptures, where it reached its highest expression in the servant songs of Deutero-Isaiah. It is embodied fully in the incarnate Word, Jesus of Nazareth, where it is revealed as the fulfilment of Israelite prophecy.[5] That revelation is, I believe, a specification or objectification of a genuine religious component that can be found to a greater or lesser extent in other religious traditions and in graced secular living. "What distinguishes the Christian … is not God's grace, which he shares with others, but the mediation of God's grace through Jesus Christ our Lord."[6] The revelation of the law of the cross is progressively insinuated in the Hebrew Bible, is presented with clarity in the Deutero-Isaian servant, and appears definitively in the New Testament. But fidelity to this law can be found everywhere, even if it often remains a coincidental departure from violent schemes of recurrence. What is specific to Christianity are the mysteries of the incarnate Word and the Trinity, and part of what is specific to the incarnate Word as embodying a Trinitarian mission is that in him there is *revealed and so made known* this law of utmost generality, a law that affects the very constitution of history, a law that has been operative whether the name of Jesus has been known and invoked or not. This reality, wherever it is found, is determinative of the genuine religious *word*, as that word affects historical action or praxis through the development and purification of cultural values. Any word that would purport to be religious but that runs counter to or neglects the precept that enjoins returning good for evil is fraudulent, a manifestation of deviated transcendence, no matter what "sacred" authority utters it. The revelation in the incarnate Word of God sets the standard for the genuine religious word everywhere.

The key to secularizations to be welcomed in the conduct and organization of human affairs lies in the precepts of Lonergan's generalized empirical method: Be attentive, Be intelligent, Be reasonable, Be responsible. The natural law consists in fidelity to those precepts. But there is also a dimension of mood or disposition or affect that precedes, accompanies, is transformed by, and goes beyond operations performed by attentive, intelligent, reasonable, and responsible subjects. This affective or psychic dimension is appealed to in what Christian tradition calls discernment. The natural orientation of the human spirit to intelligibility, the true and the real, and the good, and to beauty as the splendor and fulfilment of these other objectives, and the affective dispositions that match this orientation, will disclose over time and over the development of human culture those cultural and social arrangements that can and should be granted autonomy from the mantle of sacral authority. If sacral authority is itself determined as authentic only by fidelity to the law of the cross and not by the deviated transcendence of darkly sacrificial religiosity or by the false mantle of authoritarian preaching masking itself as proclamation of the gospel, there will be no conflict between genuine sacralization and authentic secularization. The secularization of cultural life and social institutions will continue to encourage the influence of genuine religious and personal values in the same cultural and social spheres, even while increasing its indictment of false sacralizations. Genuine secularization has no problem with returning good for evil, and returning good for evil is the determinant of what truly is sacred in historical relations. Moreover, as Lonergan makes abundantly clear, sustained fidelity to the precepts of generalized empirical method is possible only by the gift of God's love, whether recognized or not, and so only by some lived participation in the genuine sacred, and so ultimately in the love embodied in the law of the cross.

With this stress on positions to be advanced, we may turn to the antithetical considerations of sacralizations to be dropped and secularizations to be resisted. The reversal of these existential counterpositions will be relatively easy once fidelity to the existential positions of sacralizations to be fostered and secularizations to be welcomed is more or less securely in place.

Sacralizations to be dropped in the conduct of human affairs include all attempts to employ the name or word of God or any other sacral trappings to justify violence or otherwise to distort the scale of values, especially at the level of social values, where persecution, exclusion, and scapegoating not only of carriers of the genuine religious word but also of anybody else easily occurs. There is neither Jew nor Greek, male nor female, rich nor poor, straight nor gay, white nor person of color; if there is, and if the existence of such exclusions is based in some religious word, that word itself is inauthentic, and the sacralization of activities and groups based on such a word must be dropped.

Secularizations to be resisted are almost all based in efforts to locate human "coming of age" as a perfection to be attained exclusively in this life and exclusively on the basis of human resources. In other words, they head directly to secularism. Ironically, they often but not always are indistinguishable from sacralizations to be dropped, since the latter often originate in a neglect of the invitation of grace to acquiesce to the gift of God's love always offered. Pope Francis has indicated as much, for instance, in his denunciations of clericalism, which represents simultaneously a sacralization to be dropped and a secularization to be resisted. Much deviated transcendence is a cover-up for the rejection of genuine transcendence in humble, self-sacrificing love.

The four points that I am making are a theological elaboration of the implicit doctrine on grace in the historical and secular order already found in Matthew 25. "As often as you did it or did not do it to these, the least of my brothers and sisters, you did it or did not do it to me." No sacramental incorporation into the church is required to fulfil these demands, and if such incorporation is employed to skirt or replace these demands with others, it manages only to create a false sacralization, a case of deviated transcendence, precisely the sort of thing that Jesus railed against in a different religious context in his diatribes concerning the scribes and the Pharisees, the lawyers and the high priests, and in his parable of the good Samaritan. And Matthew 25 makes it very clear that such responses are what qualify as "pleasing" to the Son of Man, that is, as formal effects of *gratia gratum faciens*, the grace that makes us pleasing, sanctifying grace, or actual grace that, once accepted or acquiesced to, elevates to the supernatural order.

Lonergan's articulation of the law of the cross mentions a supreme good into which the "evils of the human race" are transformed. That supreme good is a new community in history and in the life to come: the whole Christ, head and members, in all its concrete determinations and relations.[7] In fact, the law of the cross enjoins, I believe, a three-stage developmental process: non-retaliation, forgiveness, and reconciliation. The last step, reconciliation, depends on the acknowledgment by all parties of the truth of what has happened. Moreover, the supreme good may be regarded (as it is by Lonergan) as the "form" of the economy of salvation introduced into the "matter" of a human race infected with original sin, burdened with actual sins, entangled in the penalties of sin, alienated from God, and divided both within individuals and between them or socially.[8] It is in effect an elevation of human relations to participation in the divine relations. But, like every form, its emergence is in accord with probabilities, and in this case the probabilities "regard the occurrence of [our] intelligent and rational apprehension of the solution and [our] free and responsible consent to it."[9] Such apprehension and consent are instances of actual grace. The probabilities of actual grace are greatly increased by God's revelation of the dynamics of the solution, a revelation that is progressive and cumulative over the history of Israel and fulfilled in the visible mission of the incarnate Word of God, in Jesus.

Thus the real key to increasing the probabilities of apprehending and consenting to the non-violent solution to the problem of evil lies in what the tradition has called actual grace. The universal missions of Word (apprehension, insight) and Holy Spirit (fundamental option, transformation of the end) may be understood partly in terms of a robust reconstruction of the theology of actual grace.

The "form" introduced into the "matter" of fragmented humanity, in its explicit Christian instantiations, takes shape on the basis of a fourfold communication of God to us (in the hypostatic union, in the uncreated gift of the Holy Spirit and the reciprocal movement of charity, and in hope for the fulfilment of human natural desire that in fact is given with the beatific vision). Consequent on these gifts is a developing order of personal relations brought about through apprehension of the divine self-communication (the apprehension we call faith) and the charity flowing from that apprehension. The form is really the communion of saints, a community of friendship with the three divine persons and among ourselves. Lonergan's emphasis on a new community, a new social reality, as the supreme good into which the evils of the human race are transformed corresponds to his position regarding the state of grace. The state of grace is a social, interpersonal situation grounded in the three divine subjects of the one consciousness of God.[10] The fourfold communication of God is an imitation of and participation in the divine relations, and so a mimesis that runs counter to the infected mimesis that constitutes or at least profoundly affects the evils of the human race from which we are freed by the law of the cross.

This much we have already seen. But the theology of actual grace that I intend to propose here will enable *the discernment of this state of grace even where the explicit appeal to Christian revelation does not occur.* The four-point hypothesis mentions sanctifying grace, that is, habitual grace, but not actual grace. Here I wish to affirm actual grace as *the usual, quotidian operative and cooperative grace – more usual and more quotidian, I dare say, than sacramental baptism – by which God elevates human beings into a share in Trinitarian life, whether they know this is happening or not.*

3   The Problem

We have spoken again of infected mimesis and of a mimesis that runs counter to it. This, of course, brings to mind the work of René Girard, who, as I indicated in chapter 1, has in my estimation discovered something very important about the "evils of the human race" that are transformed into this new community of human and divine subjects. These evils are often distortions of relations, distortions that hinder genuine community from ever being realized. Girard has pinpointed a basic dimension of that distortion.

Now Lonergan's well-known treatment of these evils speaks of "basic sin" and "moral evil," where "basic sin" is the *failure* to reject a morally reprehensible act or to perform a morally obligatory one, and "moral evils" are the consequences of basic sin, including deteriorating relations, systemic injustices, and bias of several kinds. It is in fact these moral evils that are transformed by the law of the cross into a new community.[11]

These evils are of course all traced ultimately to what the theological tradition has come to call original sin. And so with Girard I ask to what extent we may associate original sin with submission to a mimetic temptation. To what extent may we fruitfully regard *peccatum originale originans,* originating original sin, as an original and originating failure to reject the mimetic cycle represented in the temptation "You shall be like God" (Genesis 3.5), and *peccatum originale originatum,* originated original sin, as a violent cycle unleashed by that original failure, a cycle whose dynamics are manifested in the portrayal of the first murder in Genesis, which also entailed a similar failure to reject infected mimesis?

I ask as well to what extent what Lonergan calls basic sin in our own lives may fruitfully be understood as a matter of failing to reject infected mimesis. Is that failure one instance of basic sin, or is it more than that, perhaps the core of this basic root of irrationality in human rational consciousness? Cannot something like this be inferred from Lonergan's reference to *ressentiment* as understood by Max Scheler as perhaps the "most notable" aberration of human feeling?[12]

I ask, again, to what extent the moral evils that follow upon basic sin (the deterioration of human relations, the systematizing of injustice, and the elevation of various forms of bias so that they become the determining principles of human affairs) are consequences of failing to reject the mimetic cycle, and conversely to what extent the satanic sequence of events that follows from failing to reject the mimetic cycle is coincident with the consequences of basic sins that constitute moral evil.[13]

Furthermore, "to what extent do the biases that are structural elements in these consequences predispose us to further failures to reject the mimetic cycle?"[14] "Girard, by filling in a heuristic structure provided by Lonergan, helps us specify the evils of the human race that are transformed, and ... Lonergan is clearer on the reality into which these evils are transformed."[15] The heuristic structure to which I refer is the three-step dynamic of the law of the cross: (1) from basic sin to moral evil, (2) non-violent response that returns good for evil, (3) the transformation of the evil into a greater good.

The structure of the law of the cross, then, may be phrased in a way that complements Lonergan with Girard. Jesus (1) suffered and died because of the basic sin of others, their failure of will that brought him to this point, a failure that entailed massive mimesis. He (2) transformed the evil of suffering and death, accepted in love and obedience, into a supreme moral good, a new community emergent from these events, the whole Christ, head and members, in all their concrete relations and determinations, which were entirely different from the relations and determinations that preceded the event of the cross. And God the Father (3) raised him from the dead as the first-born into this new community of "the whole Christ, head and members."[16]

The way the law of the cross is observed in Christ is of course quite different from the way it is observed in the members. It appears in Christ as in the redeeming principle and exemplary cause, and in the members as in what is to be redeemed; we have to *learn and believe*, and come *freely to consent* to Christ, living in him, operating through him, being associated with him, so that we may be assimilated and conformed to him in his dying and rising. A fuller theology would regard these as formal effects of participating in and imitating active and passive spiration through sanctifying grace and charity, which, precisely because of this connection, may always be regarded as "the grace of Christ." Our imitation of divine active and passive spiration through sanctifying grace and charity is itself an imitation of the one whose ontological constitution is marked by a secondary act of existence that itself is an imitation of and participation of paternity, of the divine Father who is perfect in mercy. This, again, makes the remote proportionate principle of his operations, the created communication of the divine nature that is the secondary act of existence of the Incarnation, the primary instantiation of created grace, while the habitual grace and charity whereby we become adopted children of God is the secondary instantiation.[17] But what he reveals is that what catalyzes the transition to a new social situation is the authentically religious *word*, a word shot through with the soteriological differentiation[18] that acknowledges that the solution to the problem of evil is to render good for evil done. This dimension is progressively revealed by God, through the Israelite and Christian scriptures, as what really *is* holy and so sacred in human history. The word announcing the solution also increases the probability that the solution will be recognized and embraced.

Within the firm parameters set by the natural law of human interiority, by its supernatural fulfilment, and by the law of the cross as constituting the reality of what is genuinely sacred in human history, it may also be said that what is perhaps most intelligently regarded as a sacral domain at one stage of religious development can be secularized. There may, for instance, be a quite legitimate point to surrounding economies, polities, family arrangements, and legal institutions with sacral trappings when civilizations are in decline or when new civilizations are just beginning to emerge. But such a sacralization will be challenged as people grow and develop. Sacral domains can also be desacralized, and one wonders whether Jesus himself did not foster that process in many of the things he is reported to have said about the religious priorities of some of the teachers of Israel. Again, what seems to be secular activity can be given a genuine religious significance. "As often as you did it for the least of these, you did it for me" (Matthew 25.40). Finally, one style of religious development may be defective in comparison with another style. "When you pray, do not imitate the hypocrites, for they love to say their prayers standing up in the synagogues and at the street corners for people to see them … But when you pray, go to your private room and, when you have shut your door, pray to your Father who is in that secret place" (Matthew 6.5–6).[19]

The ultimate criterion has to be located in the authenticity of the person, understood both philosophically and theologically.

> … the authenticity of self-transcendence, measured by the standards of cumulative attentiveness, intelligence, reasonableness, and responsibility, with all of these preceded, accompanied, and transcended by a movement of life promoted and sustained by the grace

that is the gift of God's love, is the key to the authenticity of traditions, to collective as well as individual responsibility, and to both healing and creating in history. These social and cultural realities are objectifications of the concrete universal that is the normative subject. Again, since the gift of God's grace is required for sustained fidelity to these standards, the truly sacred is the source of all genuine development, even when genuine development entails a secularization of a domain of life that had previously been sacralized. The relations among the various levels in the scale of values are such that religious values condition personal authenticity, personal authenticity provokes cultural development, cultural development enhances the social good of order, and the social good of order promotes the equitable distribution of vital goods. Thus, no genuine secularization is an abandonment, only a refinement, of authentic religion.[20]

For Lonergan this context of development is best expressed in the language of (1) minor and major authenticity and unauthenticity, and (2) legitimate assurance regarding the genuineness of our religious convictions. Minor authenticity is measured by one's fidelity to one's cultural tradition; major authenticity is measured by the integrity of the tradition itself. In the long run, one must fall back on the criteria of personal authenticity promoted and sustained by the gift of God's love and revealed in the law of the cross. And I have attempted here to relate those criteria to the actual grace of divinely communicated insights and divinely effected transformations of fundamental options. More must be said about that connection, however, and I proceed to do so by revisiting first the Second Vatican Council and then Pope John Paul II commenting on one particular passage from the Council documents.

4   Questions Posed by Vatican II and Pope John Paul II

The structure just reviewed enables us, I believe, at least to begin to respond to questions explicitly raised by Vatican II's Pastoral Constitution on the Church in the Modern World ("Gaudium et Spes") and by Pope John Paul II regarding the presence of Christ's grace outside the formal bounds of the church. But again, this response also demands that we develop the theology of actual grace.

The Second Vatican Council raised questions that it did not answer. One of these was raised in section 22 of "Gaudium et Spes," the Pastoral Constitution on the Church in the Modern World. First, the text emphasizes the revelatory function of the visible mission of the Word. "It is Christ, the last Adam, who fully discloses humankind to itself and unfolds its noble calling by revealing the mystery of the Father and the Father's love." That revelatory mission is redemptive. "[B]y his incarnation the Son of God united himself in some sense with every human being" (GS 22). Second, however, if this is the case, the Council must admit, as it does, that it is not only Christians who receive "the first fruits of the Spirit" (Romans 8.23), which enable them to fulfil the law of love. Rather, "Gaudium et Spes" asserts, "This applies not only to Christians but to all people of good will in whose hearts grace is secretly at work. Since Christ died for everyone, and since the ultimate calling of each of us comes from God and is therefore a universal one, we are obliged to hold that the Holy Spirit offers everyone the possibility of *sharing in this paschal mystery* in a manner known to God" (GS 22, emphasis added).

The council is affirming a doctrine – "the Holy Spirit offers everyone the possibility of sharing in this paschal mystery" – but in the words "in a manner known to God" it is suggesting a systematic-theological question: How can this be?

The same combination of a doctrinal affirmation of the universal offer of the Holy Spirit and a systematic question as to how the doctrine is to be understood appears in two encyclicals of Pope John Paul II, "Redemptor hominis" and "Redemptoris missio." "This [the council's affirmation] applies to everyone, since everyone is included in the mystery of Redemption, and by the grace of this mystery Christ has joined himself with everyone for all time … Every individual, from his or her very conception, participates in this mystery … Everyone without exception was redeemed by Christ, since Christ is somehow joined to everyone, with no exception, even though the person may not be conscious of it" ("Redemptor hominis," §14). Again, "Universality of salvation does not mean that it is given only to those who believe explicitly in Christ and join the Church. If salvation is meant for all, it must be offered concretely to all … The salvation of Christ is available to them through a grace which, though relating them mysteriously with the Church, does not bring them into it formally but enlightens them in a way adapted to their state of spirit and life situation" ("Redemptoris missio," §10).

With some help from Thomas Aquinas, I hope to substantiate a response that I think can be given to the questions these texts raise. That response is expressed in our next thesis.

> **Thesis 64:** *The systematic understanding of the doctrine of the universality of salvation lies in a development in the theology of actual grace. At least some instances of actual grace as both operative and cooperative are also sanctifying graces in the strict sense of the term, in that they include the infusion of supernatural charity. This is particularly*

true of those instances in which insights into the law of the cross and horizon-elevating choices based in such insights offer what Vatican II calls the possibility of sharing in the paschal mystery.

5   Help from Aquinas

Valuable hints toward answering the question, How can this be? may be found in texts of Aquinas that Lonergan interpreted in his doctoral dissertation. In a sense, the breakthrough text for Lonergan in the history of Thomas's views on what would come to be called actual grace is the relatively early text *De veritate*, q. 27, a. 5. Here, in contrast with his position in the commentary on the *Sentences* and, it would seem, even with his position earlier in the *De veritate*, which we know was written over several years, Thomas does not limit *gratia gratum faciens*, the grace of justification, sanctifying grace, to the habitual grace infused in baptism. Consequent upon the discovery of the theorem of the supernatural, this baptismal grace, as Lonergan insists, was important in resolving difficulties in medieval theology. But Thomas writes, "The grace that makes one pleasing is understood in two ways: in one way for the divine acceptance itself, which is a gratuitous will of God; in another way for a certain created gift, which formally perfects man and makes him worthy of eternal life."[21] The second of these two ways is the habitual gift bestowed in baptism. But regarding the first of these two ways Thomas writes that "every effect that God works in us from his gratuitous will, by which he accepts us into his kingdom, pertains to the grace that makes one pleasing"[22] and so to sanctifying grace, the grace of justification. That these latter are to be acknowledged as "sanctifying graces" is explicitly affirmed by Lonergan.[23] There are other texts in Aquinas that make the same point, including the texts that Jacques Maritain relies on to argue that, in the first moral act of every individual, justification and elevation to a share in divine life are at stake.[24] But I am selecting this text because Lonergan emphasizes its importance in Thomas's development. Thomas is on his way toward a theology of what would later be called actual grace, and it is a theology that would acknowledge that at least some instances of actual grace as both operative and cooperative are also sanctifying graces in the strict sense of the term, in that they include the infusion of an elevating supernatural charity. Lonergan at least suggests that we might interpret Thomas's text precisely in this way. Supernatural habits, and especially of course charity, may not only be infused with baptism but also given as one assents to (cooperative grace) at least some of the inner promptings of the Holy Spirit (operative grace) by which a person is joined to God in the concrete circumstances of his or her own life; and they may be developed due to fidelity to such promptings.

In *De veritate*, these graces, in the form of "good thoughts and pious desires" ("bonas cogitationes et sanctas affectiones"), Thomas's expression for what Lonergan will call principal acts in intellect (insight) and will (willing of the end), are not yet "operans" but "cooperans," but in the later *Quodlibetum primum*, the grace of conversion, an actual grace that occurs before and independently of baptism, can be interpreted in no other way than as "gratia operans."[25] And in the *Prima secundae*, actual grace, like habitual grace, is both operative and cooperative, and to both habitual grace and actual grace may be assigned the term *gratia gratum faciens*. This may be argued from an exegesis of *Summa theologiae*, 1-2, q. 111, aa. 1 and 2, and especially from the connection between the two articles. Article 1 asks whether it is appropriate to distinguish grace into *gratia gratis data* and *gratia gratum faciens*, grace gratuitously given and grace that makes one pleasing. These two terms occur throughout the development that Lonergan is researching in *Grace and Freedom*, both prior to Aquinas and in Thomas's own work. But they constantly shift their meaning. The precise distinction in the *Prima secundae* (as contrasted with earlier references where the same terms are employed, both in Aquinas and especially in his predecessors) is a distinction between God's immediate action on the recipient (*gratia gratum faciens*) and God's use of other people as instruments to lead their fellow human beings to God; for instance, in the preaching of a sermon or homily. The latter is the exclusive meaning of *gratia gratis data* in article 1 of q. 111. God's immediate action on the person, on the soul, is *gratia gratum faciens*, and God's use of others is *gratia gratis data*. Over the course of the history of the use of these two terms, there can be discerned a broadening and differentiation of the meaning of *gratia gratum faciens* and a narrowing of the meaning of *gratia gratis data*. In Thomas's early commentary on the *Sentences* of Peter Lombard, as Lonergan emphasizes, *gratia gratis data* referred to every gratuitous gift of God other than the habitual grace infused with baptism, which alone merited the term *gratia gratum faciens*. But in article 1 of question 111 of the *Prima secundae, gratia gratum faciens* refers to every grace "per quam ipse homo Deo coniungitur" (through which a person is joined to God), while *gratia gratis data* refers exclusively to the gift of one person being provided by God to help another and lead that other to God. Obviously, both the habitual grace infused with baptism and the actual grace that is an interior movement caused immediately by God are instances of *gratia gratum faciens*, justifying grace, sanctifying grace. Moreover, article 2 goes on to ask whether both the habitual grace infused with baptism and the actual grace that in fact concretely joins a human being to God by a special interior movement are appropriately distinguished into operative and cooperative grace, and the answer is affirmative, with the addendum in the response to the fourth objection that operative grace and cooperative grace in either case, habitual or actual, are really the same grace but distinguished according to effects. In other words, the grace about which article 2 is asking includes every grace whereby human beings are joined to God by God's immediate action, whether that grace be habitual or actual. The history of Thomas's thinking about operative and cooperative grace moves, then, from the unity of *gratia gratum faciens* and the multiplicity of *gratia gratis data* in the commentary on the *Sentences* to the multiplicity of *gratia gratum faciens*, at least in terms of effects, and the extreme narrowing of the meaning of *gratia gratis data* in the *Prima secundae*. The God of the *Prima secundae*, it would seem, is much more prepared to invite human beings to participate in divine life, and does so in many more ways and with many more people, than was the case with the God of the commentary on the *Sentences*. At least this is a potential implication of what Aquinas is saying.

The issue would then be one of naming *which instances of actual grace qualify also as infusions of charity and thus of sanctifying grace*. I turn for at least part of the answer to the passage already cited from Vatican II. What the Holy Spirit offers everyone in a manner known only to God is "*the possibility of sharing in this paschal mystery.*" Paradigmatic of the instances of actual grace that are justifying, that are also sanctifying graces, are those in which the recipient is called to participate in the dynamics of what Christians know as the law of the cross, the dispensation whereby the evils of the human race are transformed into a greater good through the loving and non-violent response that returns good for evil. That dialectical posture is for the Lonergan of chapter 20 of *Insight* a function of supernatural charity. It is by no means limited to the baptized members of Christ's church or even to those outside the church who have in some way become heirs of the positive *Wirkungsgeschichte* of Christ's historical causality, an influence of which Girard makes so much.[26]

In his 1946 "De ente supernaturali," again, Lonergan proposed an original thesis on the meaning of actual grace. To repeat, "Interior actual grace essentially consists in vital, principal, and supernatural second acts of the intellect and the will."[27] The key word for my purposes is "principal." Principal acts stand as efficient causes of other acts. In the order of knowledge, principal acts are insights, acts of understanding, whether direct or inverse or reflective or deliberative. In the order of decision, principal acts are the willing of the end, which may be correlated with what the later Lonergan, following Joseph de Finance, will call acts of vertical liberty whereby one moves from one horizon to another, when this movement is a function of conversion.[28] Supernatural interior principal acts are acts produced by God immediately in us without any efficient causality on our part: acts of insight and the willing of horizon-elevating objectives or ends, where the insight and the willing are *gratia operans,* to which, by God's grace, we are enabled to assent (*gratia cooperans*). Among the principal supernatural acts that qualify as actual graces, then, are (1) the inverse insight that the violence that returns evil for evil solves nothing, (2) the direct, reflective, and deliberative insights entailed in concrete instances of non-violent resistance and the return of good for evil, and (3) the divinely proposed invitation to participate in a manner of living that concretely and, whether acknowledged as such or not, is patterned on the just and mysterious law of the cross. We are here moving into the territory staked out by charity, and charity and sanctifying grace are inseparable. There is never one without the other, just as there is never active spiration in the divinity without passive spiration. The grace-enabled assent to the promptings of the Holy Spirit regarding an act of charity that would return good for evil brings with it the justification that is meant by *gratia gratum faciens.* At least *these* actual graces are also sanctifying graces, and they are so by definition, because of the intimate relation of charity with sanctifying grace. When one takes seriously the theological doctrine that sanctifying grace and charity are participations in and imitations of, respectively, the divine relations of active and passive spiration, one easily grasps that they entail elevation to participation in divine life. The actual graces of insights that are invisible missions of the Word and of horizon-elevating intentions of the end that are invisible missions of the Holy Spirit are among the principal operators of such participation in divine active and passive spiration.

6   Lonergan on Actual Grace

We can strengthen our position by giving a more thorough interpretation of Lonergan's position on actual grace, just outlined.

First, then, there is the issue of the terminology employed in Lonergan's thesis.

Actual grace is really grace, but of course created grace, and so something in the so-called accidental or conjugate order that is conferred gratuitously on a person by God for the sake of the communication of participation in divine life, or, as Lonergan phrases it in the thesis, "in an order toward the possession of God as he is in himself" ("in ordine ad Deum uti in se est possidendum").[29]

"Actual" means not a permanent quality such as sanctifying grace but a transient operation. I am arguing, however, that there is an intimate relation between actual grace as transient operation and sanctifying grace as a permanent and habitual quality. This is something that is explicitly allowed by Lonergan, and probably even encouraged.[30]

"Interior" means, in Scholastic terms, something received in the so-called higher potencies of intellect and will, not as moved by their objects but as immediately governed by God.

To speak of "essentially consisting" means to specify that by reason of which there is had the object of inquiry, a systematic deduction of its properties, and all of this without any incongruity in the consequences and implications. Thus, Lonergan is saying (1) that what the tradition has called actual grace is at its core divinely given insights and acts of willing ends that elevate human beings to participation in divine life, (2) that from these two realities, one cognitional and the other existential, all other facets of actual grace can be derived, and (3) that all issues of coherence or congruity can be traced back to and resolved by appealing to this definition.

The thesis speaks of "second acts," that is, operations, as compared with the faculties themselves and their habits, which are "first act" still in potency to the operations.

The second acts are called vital, principal, and supernatural. While there is a whole history of disputes over what is and is not meant by "vital act" and its causality, Lonergan's meaning of the term is simple and straightforward: "pertaining to the order of living things precisely as living."[31] Thus being nourished, generating, feeling, understanding, assenting, and willing are instances of "vital acts."

The meaning of "principal acts" we have already seen. More fully, "a principal second act is one which, not on the side of the object but on the side of the faculty of a subject, stands as an efficient cause to the other acts received in that same faculty."[32] We should quote the examples that Lonergan cites, one with respect to the will and one with respect to the intellect.

> For example: two things have a causal influence upon the volitional act of willing the means to the end: (1) on the side of the object, the deliberation of the intellect which specifies the act, and (2) on the part of the subject faculty, the act of willing the end. In the will, therefore, the principal second act is the act of willing the end. Unless you will the end, you cannot will the means to that end.
>
> Similarly, the intellectual act that is an [inner] word, whether a simple word, a definition, or a compound word, a judgment, is causally influenced on the part of the object by a phantasm and also, in the case of judgment, even by external senses, but on the part of the faculty of a subject it is influenced by acts of understanding. In the possible intellect, therefore, the principal act is the act of understanding. Unless you understand something, you cannot define it or make a judgment about it.[33]

Next, the word "supernatural" in this definition can be taken either in a strict sense or in a broad sense. If taken strictly, "it means an act whose formal object is absolutely supernatural, as in the case of the infused virtues." And if taken broadly, "it is an act that is entitatively natural, but immediately and gratuitously produced by God." The example given of the latter is that we, despite being sinners, are enabled to observe substantially the whole of the natural law, or, as this would be transposed into interiority terms, that we are enabled to be consistently attentive, intelligent, reasonable, responsible, and loving.[34]

Lonergan proceeds to a succinct statement of the meaning of his thesis.

> … interior actual grace in the possible intellect is a certain act of understanding, such as the light of faith as a second act, or an illumination by the Holy Spirit as the source and font of understanding, knowledge, wisdom, and counsel; this act of understanding is a second act produced by God immediately in us without any efficient causality on our part. Again, interior actual grace received in the will is an act of willing a supernatural end (or, per accidens, willing a natural moral good not otherwise willed), which act is produced by God immediately in us without any efficient causality on our part.[35]

I wish now to argue that transposing this position on actual grace, as I have attempted to do, enables us to answer the question raised by Vatican II and Pope John Paul II: How can it be that the grace of redemption is present outside the explicit boundaries of Christian faith? How does the renewed theology of actual grace enable us to develop an understanding of the universal missions of the Holy Spirit and the Word? The answer will lie in correlating the divinely originated insights to which Lonergan refers with invisible missions of the divine Word, and the divinely originated willing of horizon-elevating ends with invisible missions of the Holy Spirit. This is a development beyond the relative limitation in *Missions and Processions* to the universal mission of the Holy Spirit. The missions of Word and Spirit are here more closely coordinated.

7   The Universal Mission of the Holy Spirit[36]

Thesis 65: *It is in terms of this theology of actual grace that the universal invisible missions of the Word and of the Holy Spirit are to be understood.*

The Holy Spirit is God's first gift. "Gift" is a personal, not appropriated, name for the Holy Spirit.[37] All other supernatural divine gifts, including the

Incarnation of the divine Word, are given "in" the Holy Spirit. This gift is universal: wherever there is human attentiveness, intelligence, rationality, and moral responsibility pursuing the transcendental objectives of the intelligible, the true and the real, the good, with these pursuits encased in a tidal movement that includes aesthetic and dramatic intentions of the transcendental objective of the beautiful, there is the offer of the gift of God's love, that is, the gift of the Holy Spirit, as the inchoate supernatural fulfilment of a natural desire for union with God, and as a pledge of the beatific knowing and loving that is our supernatural destiny. That fulfilment is experienced in the establishment, however precarious, of a level of consciousness beyond the levels of dreaming, waking attentiveness, understanding, judgment, and decision, but influencing all these levels from above downward. That level of consciousness created in grace is the conscious representation of the created consequent condition of the truth of the contingent statement "The Holy Spirit is sent by the Father and the Son to dwell within us."[38] In the transactions of God with us in ordinary living, the offer and inchoate conscious fulfilment result in insights from God into the demands of the exercise of charity, and in horizon-elevating willing of the ends that these insights propose. The insights themselves are instances of invisible missions of the Word, and the transformations of horizons are instances of invisible missions of the Holy Spirit. And there is never one divine mission without the other.

The mission of the Holy Spirit, the gift of divine love, was revealed, made thematic, in the visible mission of the incarnate Word, where it plays a constitutive role. Jesus, we are told, was conceived by the Holy Spirit in the womb of the Virgin Mary, baptized under the sign of the Holy Spirit at the Jordan, driven by the same Spirit into the desert for forty days, led back by the Spirit to preach the coming of God's reign, and raised to life from death by the Father in the power of the Holy Spirit. In the course of his public life he was constantly receiving not only the gift of the Spirit but also the insights that enabled him to utter the knowledge of God that in itself was ineffable.[39] That same Holy Spirit was then sent by the Father and the Son on the apostles and the other women and men gathered in the upper room on Pentecost, in what may be called a visible or palpable mission of the Holy Spirit, to fulfil the twofold mission of the Son and the Spirit, and to enable a public acknowledgment that what happened in Jesus was indeed the revelation of the triune God in history. The mutual interplay of divine and human freedom can now be carried on in explicit recognition of what, prior to the revelation that occurs in the mission of the incarnate Word, necessarily remained *vécu* but not *thématique*, implicit but not recognized, conscious but not known, present *in actu exercito* but not *in actu signato*.

If this is the case, Christians share religious community with other human beings, including people of the world's other religions. And yet this community is, at the present time, for the most part only potential. There is a shared *experience* of what Christians call the gift of God's love through the Holy Spirit who has been given to us, but shared experience is merely potential community. The principal task in front of us, it may be legitimately claimed, a task that it will take decades and perhaps centuries to work out, is to find ways to elevate potential community to formal and actual community through the elaboration in linguistic form of common meanings and values. We may better participate in the promotion of such community the clearer we are about the immanent constitution of life in God through the first gift, the gift of the Holy Spirit, the gift offered to all in the silent voice of grace. Even then, as Lonergan was well aware, we will have to forge a new language as we develop these common meanings in an explicit fashion,[40] and that effort will go through the vicissitudes of historical dialectic, much in the way Lonergan lays out in his spring 1963 course "De methodo theologiae," reported on in volume 24 of the Collected Works, *Early Works on Theological Method 3*.[41] But what follows is an attempt, using language familiar to Christians, to indicate precisely what it is that we will be expressing in that new language. The development of the requisite new language will be, I believe, a principal arena for cooperation, by theologians and others, with the invisible mission of the divine Word in our time.

What has been called sanctifying grace is, ontologically, nothing but a created term that serves as a supernatural base, in the form of the *gift* of a habit, for a created relation to the uncreated Holy Spirit. Its conscious reflection is found in the distinct level of consciousness created in grace as a function of the created term itself, a level beyond those that constitute human nature: in Lonergan's usual terms, experience, understanding, judgment, and decision. Since the Holy Spirit is an uncreated relation to the Father and the Son, however, to be in relation to the Holy Spirit must entail being related also to the Father and the Son, as distinct terms of a distinct created relation. The base of that distinct created relation is charity, the love of the God who has first loved us and bestowed divine love upon us in the Holy Spirit. The divine gift thus establishes created relations to each of the divine persons. Those relations share in and imitate the Trinitarian relations, and so bestow on us a distinct participation in the divine life of each person, in keeping with the distinct fashion in which each of them exercises the divine creative love. For Christians, these relations are thematic; but they exist even when they are not formulated in the Trinitarian terms that name for Christians what is going on.

While the ontological character of what we have known as sanctifying grace is that it is simply a created term that serves as consequent condition for the truth of a contingent predication about God, namely, that God has bestowed upon us the uncreated gift of the Holy Spirit, we are driven by theological exigence in our time to attempt as best we can to find psychological correlatives to such ontological terms, at least when this is possible. I have argued for some time that here we can be helped by one of the statements in Lonergan's so-called four-point hypothesis that links the four divine relations to four created participations and indeed imitations. In that hypothesis, the created base of a created relation to the uncreated Holy Spirit is understood as a participation in and imitation of the divine relation called active spiration, that is, a participation in and imitation of the Father and the Son as together, as one principle, they consciously "breathe" the Holy Spirit. Augustine found after much struggle that perhaps the self-presence of mind, *mens*, that he called *memoria* might function as a way of understanding the Father's role in this relation, while scriptural revelation itself gave grounds for understanding the Son's role in terms of *Verbum*, the Word that issues from the self-presence of divine Intelligence and Love. There is a transformed self-presence experienced on the part of one who finds herself on the receiving end of unqualified love, and from that transformed self-presence there issues an ineffable "yes" of value judgment, a word participating in the mission of the Word, a word that constitutes a universalist faith. From these two together, there issues charity as created participation in the passive spiration that is the Holy Spirit, as well as, I believe, the supernatural hope that constitutes the created relation to the Father. The triad of (1) self-presence in graced memory, (2) faith, and (3) charity-hope is the created participation in the Trinitarian relations that, while named in terms drawn explicitly from Christian doctrinal and theological sources, is really something that can be found unthematically just about everywhere, due to the promptings of actual grace and their consequences.[42] What I am suggesting is that it is the church's responsibility in our age to discern the presence of such participation in Trinitarian life wherever it may be found, and then to foster it and join hands with it in working for the establishment of God's reign in human affairs.

8   The Universal Mission of the Divine Word

Participation in the *Verbum spirans Amorem* that is the eternal divine Word takes place in part through the gift of insights from God into the appropriate responses to human situations, and then through a created supernatural judgment of value, an often ineffable "yes" uttered in response to the gift of divine love recalled in the self-presence of one who acknowledges his or her giftedness. Here I am putting Christian language to an experience that, more often than not, occurs without any such reflective objectification. The gift of God's love includes a participation in an invisible mission of the divine Word. The judgment or judgments of value that participate in the Word's role in breathing the Holy Spirit, our participation in the invisible mission of the Word, constitutes a universalist faith, a faith common to all who have assented to the reception of unqualified love. Faith thus grounds the proceeding charity that a Christian theology acknowledges as a created participation in and imitation of the passive spiration that is the Holy Spirit.

This universalist faith Lonergan distinguishes in his later work from the beliefs of particular religious traditions. The faith reflected in such judgments of value can be and is found in diverse traditions, and is responsible, it would seem, for Lonergan's hope that the religions of the world will find common ground and common cause in the gift of God's love. Such faith is the knowledge born of religious love, a knowledge contained in judgments of value consequent upon the reception of the gift of unqualified love. Articulating those common judgments of value represents, I believe, the locus of interreligious dialogue today. Christians will regard that locus as a share in the invisible mission of the divine Word. It is the articulation of common judgments of value that will raise our community with the people of the world's religions from the potential community constituted by a shared experience to the formal and actual state generated by shared understanding and affirmation, and because the judgments in question are judgments of value, also to the status of a community that can act in solidarity in the collaborative constitution of the human world. That elevation to articulate shared understanding will entail the emergence of a new language, and the work of developing that new language is a major arena of collaboration with the invisible mission of the divine Word in our time and for many years to come.

Most of what I want to say about the visible and invisible missions of the Word can be worked out by linking those missions as "religious values" with the remainder of the integral scale of values and specifying the relations among the other levels that obtain from above when divinely communicated insights are acknowledged and their implications pursued. That is to say, the heuristic structure for understanding that mission is already available in the scale of values that constitutes perhaps the central set of categories in my *Theology and the Dialectics of History*[43] and that remains central to the positions expressed in the first volume of *The Trinity in History*. The scale of values presents in effect the structure of what we may call social grace, where "social grace" is perhaps a contemporary way of talking about the kingdom of God. From a metaphysical point of view, social grace refers to the formal effects of actual and habitual grace in the creation of cultural values and the transformation of social structures. Social grace demands constitutive meaning, and the elaboration of that constitutive meaning will represent a major instance of human collaboration with the invisible mission of the divine Word. The discernment of social grace, of the presence of divine Truth and Love in cultural forms and social structures, is perhaps the central theological and pastoral challenge of our time. The scale of values, understood as the social objectification of the structure of authenticity due to the isomorphism of the scale with the levels of consciousness, will be central to that discernment. But a heuristic structure remains an upper blade. Even upper blades develop, and they do so in particular when they are brought to bear on the data of everyday living. Collaboration in the mission of the Word entails reorientation of human science and of myriad forms of common sense. This is one of the major theological challenges of the present century, along with the companion challenge of developing a systematic pneumatology.

9   The Multi-Religious Context and the Structure of Systematic Theology

What I am suggesting has important implications for the work of theology, and especially of systematic theology, whose objective is to express Christian constitutive meaning in terms that can be assimilated by contemporary women and men. Lonergan understood the massive shift called for in theological method in terms of the cultural factors of modernity: modern science, modern historical consciousness, and modern philosophy. To these must be added the deference to the other that constitutes the postmodern phenomenon. In particular, I stress the interreligious context within which systematic theology must be conducted from this point forward, as well as the vast call that both God and humanity are uttering for social and economic justice, for gender equity, and for a more empirically grounded notion of sexual differentiation. The triune God with which a contemporary systematics begins is a God whose gift of grace is offered to all women and men at every time and place. That gift calls for the transformation of cultural meanings and values and the elaboration of social structures that deliver the goods of the earth in an equitable fashion to all. The Incarnation of the Word of God is the revelation of that universal offer of grace and of the demands that come with it. Once meaning is acknowledged as constitutive of the real world in which human beings live and know and choose and love, soteriology can be phrased in part in revelational terms: the introduction of divine meaning into human history, which is what revelation is, is potentially redemptive of that history and of the subjects and communities that are both formed by that history and form its further advance in turn.[44] It is first and foremost the missions of the Word and the Holy Spirit that constitute the universal realm of religious values in the integral scale of values, and by and large the systematics that I envision would articulate the relation of that mission and of the revealing visible mission of the Word to realities at the other levels of value: personal, cultural, social, and vital. As the previous two sections have argued, the invisible mission of the Spirit is not isolated from an equally invisible mission of the Word. The elaboration of the gift of the Spirit enables us to develop a new variant on the Augustinian-Thomist psychological analogy for understanding the divine processions. As the gift of God's love comes to constitute the conscious *memoria* in which the human person is present to herself or himself, the summation, as it were, of life experiences as these constitute one's self-taste, it gives rise to a set of judgments of value that constitute a universalist faith, a faith that gives thanks for the gift, a faith that in fact is the created term of an invisible mission of the Word. Together this self-presence in *memoria* and its word of Yes in faith breathe charity, the love of the Givers of the gift and a love of all people and of the universe in loving the Givers.

Thus the theology that would move Vatican II forward, I believe, has to follow Frederick Crowe in understanding the visible mission of the Word in the context of the universal offer of divine healing and elevating grace in the invisible missions of the Holy Spirit and of the Word.[45] While I would now bring the invisible mission of the Word into greater prominence than did Crowe, his emphasis on the invisible missions of Spirit and Word introduces multi-religious advances on the theological situation, and these change everything in that situation. They do so in ways that are enriching but at the same time, for many, anxiety-producing. They also do so in ways that are as yet unforeseen. We do not know what God has in mind. As Crowe has insisted, there is no answer as yet to the question of the final relationship of Christianity to the other world religions. We are working that out. God wants us to work it out. We will work it out with divine assistance, with the actual graces of insights and horizon-converting intentions of the ends that God wants us to pursue. The relation of Christianity to the other religions is a set of future contingent realities, and nothing true can be said about them now. There will be no answer to that question until we have worked it out, and we are at the very beginning of that elaboration.[46]

It was with this in mind that I have also suggested that the functional specialties in which Lonergan elaborates the overall structure of theology, a structure in which systematics is but one set of tasks among many, need to be considered as functional specialties for a global or world theology.[47] The functional specialties, which I number as nine rather than eight,[48] are really functional specialties for a vast expansion of theology, and of every functional specialty in theology, beyond what even Lonergan had explicitly in mind. The data relevant for Christian theology become all the data on the religious living of men and women at every age, in every religion, and in every culture. For the Holy Spirit and the invisible Word are at work, on mission, everywhere, and not simply in the post-resurrection, Pentecostal context of Christian belief. It is the responsibility of Christians to discern the workings of the Holy Spirit and the Word on a universal scale, and in theology that responsibility will take the form of interpreting the religious data, narrating what has been going forward in the religious history of peoples, dialectically and dialogically discerning what is of God from what is not, discriminating genuine transcendence from deviated transcendence in the various religions of humankind including Christianity and Catholicism, and taking one's stand on what is of God wherever it may be found, articulating this in positions that all can accept, and understanding the realities affirmed in such judgments. At the heart of that discernment is the law of the cross that returns superabundant good for evil done. Everything that I have expressed in this chapter is built around the affirmation of the law of the cross as the key constituent in understanding what actual grace is.

10   Charles Taylor's Disjunctions

We may now relate these considerations to Charles Taylor's specification of four disjunctions. These disjunctions sometimes are phrased as found *in* the contemporary Catholic Church and sometimes are articulated as disjunctions *of* the church *from* the North Atlantic secular world in which Taylor lives and works.[49]

As disjunctions of the church from the world, they take the forms of, first, a disjunction of the official hierarchical dimension of the church from the spiritual seeking that prompts people to ask questions that some religious authorities do not want to entertain; second, a related disjunction of the very model of authority that some in the magisterium are holding on to from forms of authority respected in the secular world, where – and here is a point of convergence between Taylor and Lonergan – there is a sense that corresponds to Lonergan's definition of authority as legitimate power, with legitimacy conferred by an authenticity that is acknowledged by the community;[50] third, a disjunction from the sexual morality and gender equity that contemporaries, and especially younger contemporaries, increasingly accept as correct; and fourth, a disjunction from plural forms of spirituality.

When the disjunctions are articulated in order to highlight division *within* the church rather than alienation of the church from the secular world, the first disjunction is between "seekers" and "dwellers." Seekers "wish to realize in their life new, more personally authentic, ways of being Christian and Catholic," while dwellers "feel that in the Church all is already clear, well defined, and simply to be followed assiduously."

Second, again from an intra-ecclesial perspective, there is a disjunction between "those who bring a modern sense of personal responsibility to church teaching in search of critical convergence" with contemporary trends and exigences and, on the other hand, a conception of "the Church as a jurisdictional authority to which is due obedience" and from which little or no mediation with contemporary society is expected or to be expected.

Third, from the same perspective there is a disjunction between "ethical and moral praxis understood as a human, fallible, and historical or existential achievement" and a "natural law morality built on abstract, unchanging, and universal essences." Most of what Taylor and his students write about this third disjunction addresses divisions in the church over issues of artificial contraception, homosexuality, and the ordination of women.

Fourth, there is a disjunction between "a spirituality open to enrichment by the experiences and spiritualities of the many great religious cultures and civilizations, even the nonreligious" and "a stress on the completeness of the Christian spiritual tradition focused on the Second Person of the Trinity" become incarnate to save us from sin and death.

The situation that prompted Taylor to delineate these disjunctions is one in which "religious engagement and identity in a secular age is no longer expected but instead has become a difficult choice or option." Obviously, there are overlaps from one disjunction to another. Moreover, Taylor is quite clear that the alternatives in at least some of the disjunctions are ideal types, where the term "ideal types" seems to have much the same meaning as the term "models" has in Lonergan's later terminology: not descriptions about reality or hypotheses about reality but mental constructions that it might be helpful to have at hand when one is trying to describe reality or hypothesize about it.[51]

Taylor's delineation of these disjunctions has sparked a great deal of productive scholarly activity. Whether the disjunctions are phrased so as to highlight tensions within the church or in such a way as to articulate the alienation of the church from the secular ambience in which it functions in the North Atlantic context, the four disjunctions may be included under a more all-embracing category, one that names something very serious: the possible disjunction of the church from the very work of God in the contemporary secular world. Whether Taylor would modify his prognosis in the light of the papacy of Francis is not clear. In my view, the situation has changed quite radically on the global scene, but it remains much what it was in North America, where bishops, with few exceptions, are far behind the pope in assessing the situation and responding to it.

I would like to call for the church's attention to and discernment of invisible missions of both Word and Spirit, divine Truth and divine Love, as the source of the grace that would heal the all-embracing disjunction of the church from God. Grace is everywhere. The supernatural order is everywhere. The church is called to be its witness everywhere. "It is as though a room were filled with music though one can have no sure knowledge of its source. There is in the world, as it were, a charged field of love and meaning; here and there it reaches a notable intensity; but it is ever unobtrusive, hidden, inviting each of us to join. And join we must if we are to perceive it, for our perceiving is through our own loving."[52]

I confess that, until the election of Pope Francis, I felt a great deal of distrust over the programs that came under the umbrella of "the new evangelization." I regarded these, I think correctly, as instances of what Lonergan calls premature systematization,[53] desperate efforts to pin things down before all the relevant questions have been faced, and even as attempts to substitute another gospel for the gospel of God in Jesus Christ. The notion of premature systematization and closure, in fact, is in my estimation a more helpful way of understanding Taylor's second and third disjunctions. The issues of authority, gender equity, and sexual ethics are not closed, and they will remain open for some time to come, no matter what church officials say. But I see hopeful signs of a reorientation of the commitments to evangelization, at least with respect to the exercise of authority and with respect to social and economic justice, in both the elemental meaning of the pope's dramatic artistry in the exercise of his mission and in the linguistic meaning of many of his homilies and other comments, signs that "new evangelization" might not mean, as I had feared it would, a matter of substituting another gospel for the real one. But the task of reforming the church is enormous. There is much internal resistance to it, some of which is quite well organized and located in hierarchical circles. And there is required, I believe, an explicit if developing horizon for continued progress, for the step-by-step growth that Lonergan called for when he spoke of the perhaps not numerous center at home in both the old and the new, painstaking in working out one by one the transitions to be made, and strong enough to refuse half measures and insist on complete solutions.[54] One contribution to that horizon, I would propose, would be the acknowledgment of the universal presence of divine healing and elevating grace in the world, including the so-called secular world, through the invisible missions of Word and Spirit, of divine Truth and divine Love, both inside the church and beyond the explicit contours of ecclesial membership. In my view, it is in the realm of these instances of divine grace, of actual graces in the sense treated in previous sections of this chapter, actual graces that promote the law of the cross, that we must search as we find a way to a new evangelization; where the actual grace of insights may be understood as invisible missions of the Word, and the actual grace of horizon-elevating ends of the human spirit as invisible missions of the Holy Spirit, and where there is never one mission without the other.

The universal mission of the divine Word is affirmed in the prologue to John's Gospel. The Word that became flesh and dwelt among us in the man Christ Jesus, in the so-called visible mission of the Incarnation, that very Word through whom all things were made and in whom is the life that brings light to all, the real light that shines on all who are born into the world – the church is called to point to *that* Word, and especially to the presence of that Word in all efforts to speak truth in situations of injustice, poverty, and oppression, in attempts to formulate economic, social, and cultural meanings that address these situations with transforming power, and in efforts to mediate faith and contemporary science in the establishment of an intellectual discourse respectful of commitments in both arenas – and so in the advancement of secularizations to be welcomed as well as in the recognition of sacralizations to be fostered.

Next, the divine Love that was poured forth in a palpable mission on Pentecost is present everywhere in the world, as Vatican II and subsequent church teaching, including the teaching of Pope John Paul II, have made abundantly clear. The church is called to acknowledge and foster that gift of divine Love wherever it is found, and to call people together on the basis of a universal gift, a gift that is not restricted to explicit Christian belief but is found in a faith that is born of unqualified love.

The explicit acknowledgment of so-called visible missions of both Word in Incarnation and Spirit at Pentecost are, from this standpoint, the revelation of a divine Truth and a divine Love that are universally given. The genuinely "new" evangelization will be effected as the church has the humility and the discernment to acknowledge these divine gifts wherever they are found, call them for what they are, and encourage cooperation with them.

The issues that we have been raising cannot be theologically resolved simply in terms of the supernatural elements contained in Lonergan's four-point hypothesis. More specifically, in addition to the participations in and imitations of active and passive spiration that are, respectively, sanctifying grace and charity, there is also what the tradition has called "actual grace," which must be considered the predominant operative grace in bringing about participation in active and passive spiration. The issue of the presence of grace in traditions prior to and independent of the Christian heritage and the question of the openness of contemporary secularity to transcendence can be resolved only in terms of a very robust theology of actual grace.

We may take as expressing paradigmatically what is meant by the category "actual grace" this statement of Jesus: "When they bring you before the synagogues and the rulers and the authorities, do not worry about how or what you are to speak in your defense, or what you are to say; for the Holy Spirit will teach you in that very hour what you ought to say" (Luke 12.11). But that statement refers explicitly to experiences on the part of the disciples of

Jesus, and the reality of actual grace is far more universal than this. Moreover, I will argue that the theology of actual grace is required if we are to discover the relations even among the four created consequent conditions of divine missions named in the four-point hypothesis: the secondary act of existence of the Incarnation, sanctifying grace, charity, and the light of glory.

Again, actual grace consists of insights and radical shifts of horizon that are direct gifts of God in the course of concrete human historical experience. In the order of knowledge, principal acts are insights, acts of understanding, whether direct or inverse or reflective or deliberative. In the order of decision, principal acts are the willing of the end, the acts of vertical liberty whereby one moves from one horizon to another when this movement is a function of conversion. Supernatural interior principal acts are acts produced by God immediately in us without any efficient causality on our part: acts of insight and the acts of choosing horizon-elevating objectives or ends, where the insight and the willing are *gratia operans*, to which, by God's grace, we are enabled to assent (*gratia cooperans*).

Now I wish to suggest that principal acts in the order of knowledge, insights produced directly by God, wherever they occur, are instances of the invisible mission of the Word, and that principal acts in the order of decision, acts of willing the end that are produced directly by God, wherever they occur, are instances of the invisible mission of the Holy Spirit. As such, they are another instantiation of what our title calls "The Trinity in History." This chapter has been concerned largely with understanding this theological doctrine and drawing out its implications.

I close the chapter, then, with a thesis that sums up where we have come to.

Thesis 66: *The scale of values is the key to the notion of social grace. The invisible missions of Word and Holy Spirit are initially, and respectively, the actual grace of divinely given insights into the reign of God in concrete circumstances of human life and divinely prompted elevations of horizon to correspond to the ends dictated by supernatural charity. As the operative grace of these gifts becomes the cooperative grace that enables human assent, the justifying gift of God's love, a created participation in and imitation of divine active spiration, starts into movement the immanent constitution of life in God, the indwelling of the three divine persons. This constitution is the structure of the realm of religious values in the scale of values in the form of elevated* memoria, *faith, charity, and hope. It is the condition of the possibility of sustained personal integrity (personal value). Persons of integrity represent the condition of possibility of genuine meanings and values informing ways of living (cultural values). The pursuit of genuine cultural values is a constitutive dimension* *in the establishment of social structures and intersubjective habits (so-cial values) that would render more probable something approaching an equitable distribution of vital values to the human community (vital values). The integral functioning of the scale of values represents a set of formal effects of the gift of God's grace at the level of religious values. It constitutes in effect at least a heuristic anticipation of what the reign of God in human affairs would be. And all is marked by participation in the just and mysterious law of the cross.*

Before we can continue along these lines, however, we need to review Lonergan's theology of the divine relations and the divine persons, and to make it our own by adapting it to the specific goals of the present work.

4

The Relations That Are Imitated

The second new development to be introduced in the present volume is the appropriation for our present purposes of Lonergan's theology of the divine relations and the divine persons as presented in *The Triune God: Systematics.* The present chapter will interpret and adapt Lonergan's theology of divine relations and relate it to the theology of the divine missions that we are elaborating. The next chapter will begin to do the same with elements in Lonergan's theology of the divine persons.

The principal affirmation of the present chapter can be stated up front in a new thesis:

> **Thesis 67:** *Grace, both habitual and actual, effects participation in and graced imitation of the divine relations, and does so in such a way as to transform human relations with God and with one another, introducing human subjects into participation in divine circumincession.*

1 Doctrines and Systematics

Lonergan's theology of the immanent divine relations is presented in chapter 3 of *The Triune God: Systematics.* But the historical and doctrinal background to Lonergan's systematic theology of the divine relations is presented in thesis 3 of the companion volume, *The Triune God: Doctrines.* That thesis reads,

For an earlier version of some of the material in this chapter, see Robert M. Doran, "Bernard Lonergan's Treatment of the Divine Relations: A Commentary," in *Recerche Lonerganiane Offerte a Saturnino Muratore,* ed. Edoardo Cibelli and Cloe Taddei Ferretti (Naples: Istituto Italiano per Gli Studi Filosofici, 2017) 199–223.

"Thus, the Father and the Son and the Holy Spirit have one divinity, one power, one substance; they are, however, three hypostases or persons distinguished from one another by their proper attributes, which are relative; hence in God all things are one where there is no relational opposition."[1] The chapter on relations in *The Triune God: Systematics* is by and large a systematic attempt to understand the doctrine expressed in that thesis.

For Lonergan, then, the answer to the question of the reality to be attributed to what have been conceived as divine processions by the analogy of intelligible emanation (or what we have called autonomous spiritual procession) leads to four more assertions (assertions 4 through 7 in the book):

(4) "Four real relations follow upon the divine processions: paternity, filiation, active spiration, and passive spiration."[2]
(5) "These four relations are subsistent."[3]
(6) "Three real relations in God are really distinct from one another, on the basis of mutual opposition" – namely, paternity, filiation, and passive spiration.[4]
(7) "The real divine relations are conceptually distinct from the divine essence but really identical with it."[5]

We add to these doctrines the theological hypothesis that the divine missions are the divine relations joined to created external terms. The eternal divine relations of filiation and passive spiration have been sent into the world, into human history, visibly and invisibly, with the primary intention of effecting a completely new set of relations between human beings and God and among human persons.[6] Without the missions, visible and invisible, these relations – friendship with God and love even of enemies among human persons – would not exist.

The teaching concerning divine relations is part of the doctrinal tradition that comes to us from the patristic era and of the theological tradition established in the medieval period. Lonergan traced the patristic aspects of this teaching in the *pars dogmatica* of *De Deo trino*, now available as *The Triune God: Doctrines*. In his view, the medieval attempt to understand the divine relations, aside from early infelicitous attempts by Gilbert de la Porrée[7] and Joachim of Flora[8] and the later nominalist positions and the Scotist formal distinction,[9] reached unanimity on the positions that there are four real subsistent relations in God, that three of these are really distinct, and that only a conceptual distinction obtains between the divine substance, pure act, and the real divine relations. *Actus purus* is a set of relations.

We will not go into the details of the patristic and medieval history or even into every point in the systematic parts of Lonergan's treatment. We will limit ourselves to what is essential for our present purpose, which is to understand *the divine missions as the divine relations joined to their respective created external terms.*

From a dogmatic standpoint, the four theses that Lonergan proposes are theologically certain. These assertions are not hypothetical. First, that *there are real relations* in God follows from the use of the names "Father" and "Son." Second, that there are *four* real divine relations follows from the two divine processions.[10] Third, that *three* of these are really distinct follows from the Trinity of persons, whether one argues with the Fathers that consubstantial persons cannot be really distinct except by relations of origin,[11] or more briefly with the Council of Florence that in God everything is one except where there is a distinction by relational opposition (DB 703, DS 1330). Fourth, that the real divine relations and pure act are *not really distinct* follows from the doctrine that in God there is only Trinity, not quaternity (DB 432, DS 804). Fifth, from this it follows that the real divine relations are *subsistent* (DB 389, DS 745). And sixth, that they are *at least conceptually distinct* from pure act follows from the fact that, while it is not said of pure act that it begets or is begotten or proceeds, it is said of the Father that the Father begets, of the Son that the Son is begotten, and of the Holy Spirit that the Holy Spirit proceeds (DB 432, DS 804).

Full appreciation of the theology on which the present chapter draws depends on a careful reading not only of Lonergan's third chapter in *The Triune God: Systematics* but also of appendix 3 in the same volume, where a fuller presentation of the philosophical and metaphysical aspects of "relations" is offered. We begin here by studying Lonergan's appendix on relations and interjecting key elements from other facets of his thinking as well as applications to the realm of human relations. Relationality is so central to Lonergan's thinking about everything (even his thinking about scientific understanding, where the key explanatory elements are "terms *and relations*") that a clear presentation of this background cannot but aid us as we move forward.

2   The Metaphysics of Relations

Lonergan adds to his systematic treatise an entire appendix on relations, stating that, while the theological doctrine of real divine relations is clear enough without our having to go into the subtler questions of a general theory of relations to understand the essentials of the doctrine, further questions do spontaneously arise that, unless resolved, can disturb and distract us. I have chosen to begin this presentation of Lonergan's account of the divine relations with selected aspects of this more general theory of relations, emphasizing those aspects that are significant for my own purposes. It is especially to be hoped that engaging the general theory will help us eventually to specify *the relationality of the created external terms* that make of the divine relations historical missions, as well as *the character of integral and elevated relations of human beings to the three divine persons and to one another.*

2.1 Three Elements

Relation is an ordering of one to another. Every relation consists of three elements: a subject or base, a term, and that with respect to which the subject is related to the term. The *subject* or *base* of a relation is whatever is ordered to another. The *term* is that to which the subject or base is ordered. But in every relation there is a *tertium comparationis*, a third element comparing the base to the term, that with respect to which the subject is related to the term. The subject and the term may be "things" that simply *are*, that is, unities-identities-wholes. Things thus understood are given their major philosophical account by Lonergan in the evolutionary theory that emerges more fully in chapter 8 of *Insight* than it had appeared with the notion of emergent probability introduced in chapter 4. But the subject and the term may be characteristics "by which" these things are, that is (in the language of *Insight*), conjugates. The two are distinguished in the Latin text as "entia quae" (things) and "entia quibus."[12]

The divine relations, of course, display an identity of subject and relation. Only in God are the subject and that with respect to which the subject is related to the term really identical and only conceptually distinct. The Father *is* paternity, the Son *is* filiation, the Father and the Son together *are* active spiration, and the Holy Spirit *is* passive spiration.

2.2 Internal and External Relations

The most important distinction in Lonergan's theory of relations is that between internal and external relations. An internal relation is so intrinsic to the subject that, if the relation were negated, the subject itself would be negated. The relation belongs to the very formality or definition, the intrinsic intelligibility, the *ratio*, of the subject. An external relation is a relation that can be present or absent without such an ontological effect on the subject.

Thus, all quantified realities are internally related to all other quantified realities by internal relations, but to say that "this stone is exactly twice that stone" is to express an external relation that is constituted only by the existence of "that stone" and not by something intrinsic to "this stone." It is intrinsic to this stone that it have some quantitative relation to every other quantified reality, but not that this quantitative relation be "twice" or any other determinate proportion. The so-called external relation is constituted *only* by the existence of the quantified reality to which "this stone" is being compared. It is not intrinsic to the reality of "this stone."

Several arguments are proposed for the reality of internal relations. We need not cover them all, but the following instances are pertinent to our considerations.

(1) Accidents (conjugates), whose mode of being is to be in another, have a relation to that other; and that relation is part of the definition of an accident and so is an internal relation. Thus, if accidents or conjugates are real, there are real internal relations.

(2) Every finite nature is defined by its relation to accidents or conjugates that naturally result from it and to operations of which it is the remote or proximate principle. No nature can be real without that relation also being real, for that relation belongs to the definition of the nature. Thus, if there are real finite natures, there are real internal relations.

A corollary to this affirmation is that every finite substance when considered specifically – e.g., a human being – is also a finite nature and so possesses real internal relations. When considered specifically it can be defined only in relation to its accidents or conjugate forms and its operations or conjugate acts. Thus, in *Insight* things are defined in terms of sets of conjugate terms that through a series of correlations of correlations can be linked with concrete data.

(3) The reality that Aristotle defined as "the first act of a body capable of life" or "that principle whereby we live and sense and understand," that is, the soul in this technical Aristotelian sense of "central form," includes in these very definitions relations either to the body or to vital, sensitive, and intellectual operations; and these are real internal relations.

(4) The elements of Lonergan's intentionality analysis amply demonstrate the reality of internal relations: the ordering of questions to acts of understanding, of acts of understanding to inner words, of the inner words that are judgments of value to decisions; and the dependence of acts of understanding on questions, of inner words on acts of understanding, and of decisions upon the inner words that are judgments of value; etc., etc. What we have designated as autonomous spiritual processions are constituted by internal relations.

Lonergan asks whether external relations add another reality intrinsic to the subject besides the reality of the internal relation. That they add another reality is obvious; but this added reality is not intrinsic to the subject. The other reality that is proper to an external relation is extrinsic to the subject and is to be found rather in the term. "… if A is really and truly twice what B is, then that 'twice' has its truth-correspondence through the reality of an internal relation by which A really regards all quantified beings and, at the same time, through the reality of B which objectively determines that indeterminate internal relation."[13]

This discussion leads to our next two theses.

> **Thesis 68:** *Quantitative examples of internal and external relations, while easy to point to and understand, are of little existential, historical, or theological significance. The significant issue for our purposes will be to determine what constitutes internal relations between and among human beings. There are ideologies that would treat all relations among human beings as external, as depending only on the existence of the person to whom "this person" is being compared, and not on a primary internal relationality constitutive of what it is to be a human being.*

Thus, whatever Margaret Thatcher meant when she said, "There is no such thing as society; there are only individuals," it can be and often is taken to mean in effect that there is no such thing as internal relationality among human beings (except in nuclear traditional families, which even Thatcher conceded). Neo-liberal economics, the varieties of political options that exist only to promote it, and the practices that implement it function as if this were the case. Such theories, options, and practices also deny the entire structure of the scale of values, where the relations that obtain among the levels of value constitute the immanent intelligibility of what we have called social grace. The breakdown of the scale of values is itself the defining characteristic of the later stages of decline that the contemporary human world has entered upon.

Thus, we may propose thesis 69:

> **Thesis 69:** *It will be crucial for the expansion of the theology of divine missions to argue for primary internal relationality as constitutive of the subjects of autonomous spiritual processions. Radical individualism, philosophies of selfishness, and the embodiment of such intellectual inauthenticity in political and economic theories, systems, and budgets display a denial of internal human relationality.*

2.3 Internal Relations and Science

For Lonergan, explanatory knowledge of internal relations is on the way; it is not something securely achieved. But explanatory scientific understanding is required if we are to understand a real internal relation. All explanatory understanding of real internal relations will be found in the sciences, in proportion to the extent to which the sciences have achieved their goals. The knowledge of internal relations will not be had before the sciences are so evolved that they can set forth the objects of their analytic reflection and investigation. This does not mean that we are to doubt that all things are fully intelligible just because we do not understand everything. But it will not do to substitute external relations known by common sense for internal relations known only hypothetically by the sciences in their present state of development. An external relation arises not from the subject alone but from the comparison between the subject and the term of a relation. In particular, as Lonergan repeatedly argued, Aristotelian "predicamental" attribution in terms of the ten categories is purely descriptive knowledge and will vanish with the development of explanatory scientific understanding.

But a question arises in this regard with respect to *human* science. If one accepts the argument of chapter 11 of *Insight*, which I do, one will affirm that there are some terms and relations in human science that are not subject to basic revision, namely, those specified in generalized empirical method, that is, those that one has affirmed in making the self-affirmation of the knower, in the expansion of that judgment to other levels of consciousness, and in the isomorphism between those levels of consciousness and the scale of values. May we also reach, on the basis of these terms and relations, some firm explanatory understanding of primary internal relationality *between and among* human beings? The terms and relations of generalized empirical method, as they have been worked out to date, are constitutive of individual subjects in their authenticity. But do they also ground explanatory relations between and among human subjects? Can they be used to provide foundations in the realm of general categories for a theology of *collective* responsibility and *social* grace?

The fact that we have already begun such a theology with a scale of values that is isomorphic with the constituents of individual authenticity might argue for the possibility of an affirmative answer, but, if so, that answer remains to be worked out. It will be the point of the third volume in this project to begin that elaboration. We may, however, propose a thesis 70.

> **Thesis 70:** *The social objectification of the terms and relations constituting the normative source of meaning and value in history is provided by the integral scale of values. From the grasp of internal relations in the normative source we may hope to proceed to a grasp of internal relations obtaining in the realm of cultural and social values in which the normative source is objectified.*

2.4 *Simply Absolute, Simply Relative, and Absolute and Relative in a Qualified Way*

Some of the questions that Lonergan raises in the appendix are important for our considerations. The first major area of questions subdivides into four interrelated matters: Are there in creation (1) any simply absolute realities, (2) any simply relative realities, (3) absolute realities in some qualified sense, and (4) relative realities in some qualified sense?

Lonergan's answer to the first two questions is No, and to the second two Yes. As usual, his argument is complex. It proceeds through eight steps.

First, every relation is either internal or external, either so intrinsic to the subject that it cannot be removed without removing the subject, or not.

Second, every subject of a real relation, whether it be a "thing" or something attributed to a thing, has an absolute reality – it *is*.

Third, the subject of a real internal relation, however, is not *simply* absolute, since by the definition of internal relation what the subject is includes such relation, without which it would not be what it is.

Fourth, however, because every subject of a real relation *is* absolute, a real internal relation does not posit any *simply* relative reality.

Fifth, a real external relation does not posit some *simply* relative reality, for it adds no reality intrinsic to the subject beyond that of internal relation.

Sixth, among created things there exist things that are absolute and relative, both in a qualified sense: namely, the subjects of internal relations. These are absolute insofar as they are subjects of internal relations but relative insofar as relations are of their essence.

Seventh, in creation there does not exist anything that is simply relative. If there did, it would be a relation. But a relation is either internal or external, and neither of these posits a simply relative reality.

Again, whatever is real can be affirmed; whatever can be affirmed participates in the *ratio* of absolute, since it already stands in itself, independent of its causes; and so every relative, insofar as it is real, is absolute in this qualified sense of being contingently unconditioned.

Eighth, there does not exist in creation anything that is simply absolute, for what is simply absolute has no real causes, either extrinsic or intrinsic, and what has no extrinsic causes is not created, while what has no intrinsic causes is not finite.

Moreover, every created thing is a nature, every nature is an intrinsic principle of operations, and every such created principle is really related to something that is really distinct from it.

Again, if anything in created things were simply absolute, it would be at least a substance; but it is not the concrete entity of substance but the generic intelligibility of substance that is simply absolute, since every substance is also a nature and every nature is a principle really related to something else.

Again, we know nothing unless we affirm it; we affirm nothing unless we conceive it; and we conceive nothing without relations; therefore, we know nothing without relations.

That we conceive nothing without relations is clear a posteriori and a priori: a priori, since every finite act of understanding is synthetic, so that many are apprehended *per unum*; a posteriori, since by going through all primitive concepts there is found analogy, proportion, and comparison, as of essence to existence, potency to act, matter to form, nature to operation, part to whole, accident to substance, sensible to sense, appetible to appetite, intelligible to intellect; similarly in mathematics, rules determine operations, and operations generate numbers of every kind; in physics, objects are defined through the laws by which objects are connected with one another; in chemistry, elements are defined through the series of relations contained in the periodic table; in physiology, organs are defined through the functions which they exercise within the whole, etc., etc., etc.

To this discussion perhaps we may add another thesis.

> **Thesis 71:** *Social, political, and economic theories or practices that would in effect deny internal relationality to human subjects would tend to affirm individuals as simply absolute realities. On the other hand, without the breakthrough beyond the primordial mimetic interdividuality analyzed by René Girard to the capacity for autonomous spiritual processions, one is in fact living as if it were the case that one is a simply relative reality, with a center that does not hold. Again, while individualism is in effect a denial of internal relationality in human beings, primal interdividuality prior to any individuation on the part of the subject of autonomous spiritual processions is an existence as if there were a simply relative reality on the part of the subject.*

Girard and I would maintain that for this breakthrough beyond interdividuality to become systematic and consistent, for it to set up schemes of recurrence, the operation of God's grace is a requirement. And I would add that this involves introducing into the reality of the subject the created participations in Trinitarian relations that are at the heart of the theology of the Trinity in history.[14]

2.5 *Toward the Real Divine Relations*

Next, can several real relations be internal to one and the same absolute? Are they really distinct from the absolute? Are they really distinct from one another? With these questions, we come closer to considerations that will remain important when we discuss the divine relations.

First, then, there can obviously be several real relations internal to one and the same absolute. Lonergan's examples are presented in Scholastic terms. "… the soul is really related to the body as well as to vital, sentient, and intellectual operations; and these relations are internal, for they are in the very definitions of soul. Also, action and passion are one and the same act, differing by relation in that action is the act of this as from this, while passion is the act of this as in this … Further, since every effect produced by a creature is necessarily really from the agent and really in the patient, these relations are both real and internal to the effect. Besides, the Trinitarian relations are both real and internal to God."[15]

Next, real internal relations cannot be really distinct from the absolute to which they are internal. But real internal relations can be really distinct from one another if they also imply mutual opposition. Real relations that are mutually opposed necessarily involve a real distinction; otherwise these relations themselves would cease to exist. But real relations internal to one absolute that are not mutually opposed are distinct only conceptually. Each relation regards a different term, and the terms are really distinct, and so there is a foundation in reality for the conceptual distinction. But the difference in the relations is not a real distinction.

> … the more perfect each one is, the greater is its power; and the greater its power is, the more things there are to which its power extends. Thus, one and the same act of understanding relates simultaneously (1) to the agent intellect from which it exists as from its principal cause, (2) to the phantasm from which it exists as from its instrumental cause, (3) to the phantasm in which it beholds its species illumined, (4) to the acts of sensing from which the phantasms were derived, (5) to the objects of sensation which were known through the acts of sensing, (6) to the simple inner word which proceeds from the act of understanding, (7) to the compound inner word by which the objectivity of the simple word is judged, (8) to the real beings that are known in the word, (9) to the goods that are known through judgments of value, (10) to the acts of the will that are consequent upon the intellect, (11) to the operations that are directed and carried out by the intellect and will; finally (12), the more perfect the act of understanding, the more it comprehends as a unified whole; and thereby it extends to more sensible objects, more acts of sensing, more phantasms, more simple and compound words, more goods, more acts of the will, and more operations. These relations are internal, since they belong to the very formality of an understanding that is joined to the body and directs the will and operations. These relations are also real, since the act of understanding itself is real, and there can be no real thing which does not really include whatever belongs to its essence.[16]

But these real internal relations are conceptually distinct, not really distinct, because they do not entail mutual opposition. The conceptual distinctions have a foundation in reality in that each relation regards a really distinct term. But, as we anticipated in *Missions and Processions,* real relations are distinguished by orderings, not by terms.[17] This will be clarified further as we discuss the theology of the divine relations.

3   The Four Divine Relations[18]

Lonergan's fourth systematic Trinitarian thesis, and the first of his theses on the divine relations, is the following: "Four real relations follow upon the divine processions: paternity, filiation, active spiration, and passive spiration."[19]

The link (*sequuntur,* "follow upon") to which Lonergan refers is conceptual. It lies in the *via synthetica* ordering of ideas in systematics. The *via analytica* or way of discovery, in contrast, concludes from the distinct *persons* to *relative* properties and from these to *processions,* and then identifies the relations with the processions. The *via synthetica* goes the other way, beginning with processions, moving to relations, then on to persons, and ending with missions.[20]

The terms in the thesis are relatively clear. A *procession* is an origin of one from another, and a *relation* is the ordering of one to another. A *real relation* is an ordering of one to another that is not only conceived but is truly affirmed to exist. *Paternity* is the real ordering of what begets to what is begotten. *Filiation* is the real ordering of what is begotten to what begets. *Spiration* is the term used to speak of the procession of love from the one uttering and from the word uttered. *Active spiration* is the real ordering of the spirating act of uttering and word uttered to the spirated love proceeding from them. And *passive spiration* is the real ordering of the spirated proceeding love to the spirating act of uttering and the word uttered.

The argument of the thesis is presented in five steps, the fifth of which simply repeats the thesis. The argument is followed by a *scholion,* where the relations are identified with the processions. It seems essential to the building of our own argument that we first repeat Lonergan's.

3.1   Steps of the Argument

The steps are as follows.

(1) "From the real procession of the Word there follows a real relation of the Word to the principle that utters the Word, and since this procession is generation in the proper sense of the term, this real relation of the Word to its principle is filiation."[21]

(2) "From the real procession of Love there follows a real relation of the Love that is spirated to the principle that spirates Love; and since this procession is not generation properly so called,

this real relation is not filiation, and can fittingly be called passive spiration."[22]

(3) "The intellectually conscious procession of the word is from the grasped intelligibility of whatever is to be uttered; moreover, from this grasp of intelligibility there emerges in the intellect that grasps it an intellectual necessity to speak the word. Since this necessity to speak the word really exists in the intellect, it is a real relation to the word to be spoken and, once the word is uttered, a real relation to the word spoken. Finally, since in God to speak the Word is to generate the Son, the real relation to the eternally spoken Word, the eternally generated Son, is the real relation of paternity."[23]

A fuller exposition of this material will have to consider two other starting points: not simply the Father as act of understanding, but also the Father as *agapē*, as in the later Lonergan, and the Father as understood by analogy with *memoria*, as first in Augustine and most recently in *Missions and Processions*. But for now, I limit myself to Lonergan's presentation in *The Triune God: Systematics*, which fills out that found in the *Summa theologiae* and adds a good deal more detail regarding cognitional process. Here the analogy for the Father is the human act of understanding from which an inner word proceeds: more precisely, the relevant act of understanding for Lonergan is a reflective act in the existential order, an evaluative insight grasping *the sufficiency of evidence for a judgment of value*, and the word that proceeds from the reflective grasp is *the judgment of value* grounded in the grasp. While this reference to a judgment of value as most appropriate to the analogy is explicitly mentioned only twice in *The Triune God: Systematics*,[24] suggesting, I believe, that Lonergan's position on judgments of value was still developing, the affirmation is crucial to his position, and even more so to my own. I will extend the discussion to my own version of the analogy below, at p. 90.

(4) "The intellectually conscious procession of love is from the grasp and affirmation of the goodness of whatever is to be loved; moreover, from this grasp and affirmation of goodness there emerges in the one who grasps and affirms it an intellectual or moral necessity to spirate love; since this necessity really exists in the one who has grasped and affirmed goodness, it is a real relation to the love that is to be spirated, and, once the love has arisen, a real relation to the love spirated; finally, this real relation of the spirator to what is spirated is fittingly termed active spiration."[25]

(5) It follows from the real divine processions that there are four real relations in God, namely, paternity, filiation, active spiration, and passive spiration.[26]

We proceed to our own thesis 72.

> **Thesis 72:** *The four-point hypothesis expresses the created participation of created realities in the four real uncreated relations; the participation is grounded in four created terms that are consequent conditions for these uncreated relations to become "the Trinity in history." These four created terms are also four created bases of created relations to the four uncreated relations in which the four terms participate. As such, their relations to one another participate in the order of the divine relations themselves. As paternity is to filiation, so the secondary act of existence of the incarnation is to the light of glory. As active spiration is to passive spiration, so sanctifying grace is to the circle of operations that constitute the habit or set of schemes of recurrence that constitute charity.*[27]

3.2 *The Relations Are the Processions*

The scholion that follows the fourth assertion in Lonergan's text establishes the identity of the relations with the processions. It states, "The processions are conceptually distinct from, but really identical with, the relations."[28] The conceptual distinction follows from the fact that it is not the same thing to *conceive* the origin of one thing from another as to *conceive* the ordering of one to another: a father does not have his origin from his son, but he does have an ordering to his son. The real identification is established in a metaphysical statement: where there is a procession without any motion, the procession is in reality nothing but a relation, as is also the case even in creation, which occurs without any motion.[29]

There is a question, however. Each procession is marked by two relations. With which relation is the procession really identical? A set of distinctions is required. If the procession is conceived as an origination, the origination and so the procession really exist in that which is originated, and so the divine processions are really identical with filiation and passive spiration. But if the procession is conceived as an action, then a further distinction is to be made. In one sense action is conceived as in or from the agent, and then the processions are really identical with a real relation of the agent, and so with paternity and active spiration; but in another sense action is conceived as in the patient, and then again the processions are really identical with that which is originated and so with filiation and passive spiration.

The Trinitarian import of the question is grasped when we ask whether in God the procession of the Word and the procession of Love are really or only conceptually distinct. If "procession" here means origin or action *as in the recipient*, the answer is that they are really distinct, since filiation as origination and passive spiration as origination are really distinct. But if "procession" means action *in or from the agent*, the answer is that they are only conceptually distinct, since paternity and active spiration, as we shall see, are not really distinct, nor are filiation as *spirans Amorem* and active spiration really distinct. To generate the Word *is* to breathe the Spirit. To be generated as the Word *is* also to breathe the Spirit. Active spiration is paternity and filiation together. But Lonergan is concerned to argue against the view that "there is only a virtual, not a real, distinction between generation and spiration."[30] And his solution is that the real distinction arises because the procession of word and the procession of love are distinct as origin or action *in the recipient*.

Thus, the important thesis 73:

> **Thesis 73:** *To say "yes" and to be the "yes" uttered together breathe love. The implication regarding the relation of the terms of the missions to one another, that is, the relation of the secondary act of existence of the Incarnation to sanctifying grace, the gift of God's love, will re-establish in a quite new and thoroughly Trinitarian context that all grace is really the grace of the Son, and is revealed as such in Jesus. To beget the Son and to be begotten of the Father are together also to breathe the Spirit, who would not be breathed without the mutual relations of Father and Son. In this sense, while all mission is in the Spirit, it remains that nothing would be "in the Spirit" were it not the case that the Father eternally begets the Son and the Son is eternally begotten of the Father. For it is only in and through those relations of paternity and filiation, which together are active spiration, that there even is a Holy Spirit. Moreover, just as there is not one procession without the other, so there never is and never can be one mission without the other.*

We must return to these matters later.

4   Subsistent Relations

The *via synthetica* argument moves from relations to subsistent subjects: from paternity to Father, from filiation to Son, from active spiration to Spirator, and from passive spiration to Spirit. Thus, Lonergan's fifth systematic Trinitarian thesis, and the second on divine relations, is that these four relations are subsistent.[31]

The conclusion is simple, and derived from divine simplicity: if there is paternity, there is something by which someone is Father, and so on for each of the relations; and if God is totally simple, there can be no distinction between *id quod* and *id quo*, between "that which" and "that by which." By the very fact that there is divine paternity, there is not only that by which there is a Father, there is that which is the Father, and so on. As Aquinas said, "Just as divinity is God, so divine paternity is God the Father."[32]

The thesis itself, Lonergan says, is theologically certain as to what it affirms, while the mode of affirming it is the common and certain opinion of theologians.

Lonergan treats the matter in the following order: first, he addresses the issue of the meaning of subsistence; then he applies this notion to the divine; third, there is a brief discussion of issues once thought to belong to the decrees of the Council of Rheims; and fourth, the argument for the assertion is presented. In the interest of completeness, we will discuss each of these points.

4.1 *The Notion of Subsistence*

This notion will be important for much of what follows, especially in the treatment of persons.

A subsistent being is something that exists *simpliciter*. In contrast, (a) a chimera is just a conceptual being, existing just in the mind; (b) possible beings exist only in the potency of an agent or of matter, and therefore are what can be rather than what are; (c) the mode of being of accidents is to be in something else, and so they "are in" rather than simply "are"; (d) none of the constitutive principles of being, that is, the metaphysical elements, can be said simply to be; rather, *by* them something is. But besides all of these, which *are* in a qualified way, there are realities that are simply said to be. Examples are minerals, plants, animals, human beings, angels, God, the Father, the Son, and the Holy Spirit. These are "subsistent" because they simply and truly *are*. "A subsistent, then, is whatever simply is that which is. It is distinguished from conceptual beings, possibles, accidents, and the constitutive principles of being."[33] In the created order, it is equivalent to what in *Insight* are called "things."

4.2 *Subsistence in God*

Consequently, whatever in God is "that which is" subsists. But God is completely simple. Everything composite must have a cause of its composition, and since God is the first principle of everything, God admits no real composition at all. In an utterly simple reality there can be nothing that is not the totally simple being itself. And so whatever in God really is, is the same as God, the same as that which is, the same as that which subsists, and therefore must itself be said to subsist.

This forces some clarification regarding predications with respect to God. All names that we use to speak of God have a mode of signification appropriate to creatures that are composite beings, and so we need to distinguish in the divine names between what they signify and our mode of signifying.

What they signify is always the absolutely simple supreme being. The way they signify, though, is better suited to composite creatures. Thus, for example, "Whether we say 'God' or 'divinity,' we mean the same utterly simple supreme being; but in saying 'God' we seem to be emphasizing that which is, while in using the term 'divinity' we seem to be emphasizing that by which God is."[34]

4.3 *The Council of Rheims*

The *Professio fidei de Trinitate* which was once attributed to this council (DB 389–92) was not issued by the council itself (DS 745). What *does* emerge as dogmatically significant was defined by Pope Eugene III in regard to the position of Gilbert de la Porrée. According to Gilbert, the divine essence, substance, nature, which is called divinity, goodness, wisdom, the greatness of God, and similar things, is not God, but the form by which God is. The pope's clarification is that "no theological formality is to divide nature and person, nor in the phrase *Deus divina essentia* are the last two words to be understood in the ablative case only [God is by the divine essence] but also in the nominative [God is the divine essence]" (DS 745). The meaning is that, if there is no formality that divides a divine person and the divine nature, then there is no real distinction between the Father and deity. Moreover, since God is said to be the divine essence not only in the ablative sense (that by which) but also in the nominative sense (that which), not only is God *by* or *by reason of* deity (as a human being is *by* or *by reason of* humanity) but also God *is* deity, even though a human being is not humanity.

But this brings us back to what has already been said. For even if, in their mode of signifying, words like "divinity," "paternity," "filiation" say *id quo*, that by which, nonetheless, as to the reality signified, "God" and "divinity," "Father" and "paternity," do not denote different realities; and so just as "God" and "Father" denote an *id quod*, so too "divinity" and "paternity" also denote not a reality whereby some other is, but a reality which itself is or which itself subsists.

4.4 *The Argument*

All of this has been necessary to build up to the argument for the assertion.

Id quod est and *id quo est* in God are the same; the real divine relations are at least *quo est*; and so they are *quod est*. But *id quod est* subsists; and so the real divine relations are subsistent. Divine paternity is God the Father, divine filiation is God the Son, divine active spiration is God the Spirator, and divine passive spiration is God the Spirit. "… although there is a distinction in their way of signifying between those words that name that which is (God, Father) and those that name that by which it is (divinity, paternity), still what they signify is in each case the very same reality, so that divinity really is God and paternity really is the Father."[35]

4.5 Scholion

In created reality, there is a difference between "man" or "woman" and "humanity," "father" and "paternity," "son" or "daughter" and "filiation," both with respect to the way they signify and with respect to what they mean. For in created reality the subsistent which is differs from the essence or form or relation whereby it is. But in God, "God" and "divinity," "Father" and "paternity," "Son" and "filiation," "Spirator" and "active spiration," and "Spirit" and "passive spiration" differ only with respect to the way they signify, and not with respect to what they mean.

Moreover, in creatures a subject that is related by a relation is distinguished from the relation whereby the subject is related; there is in creation no simply absolute reality, as we have seen; but in God the subject that is related and the relation by which the subject is related are the same. When a real relation is posited in God, not only is there posited that whereby some subject is related, but there is also posited the very subject that is related. A real relation in God *is* that which is related. Thus is clarified the difference between "relation as relation" and "relation as subsistent." The relations as relations are paternity, filiation, active spiration, and passive spiration. The relations as subsistent are Father, Son, Spirator, and Spirit. Only the *modus significandi* is different, not the *id quod significatur*. This does not happen in created realities. Thus Lonergan refers to and quotes Thomas Aquinas, *Summa theologiae*, 1, q. 40, a. 3: "For the properties of the persons are not to be understood as coming to the divine hypostases as form comes to a preexisting subject; rather, their own supposits come with them [literally, they bring their own supposits with them], since they are the subsistent persons themselves, as, for example, paternity is the Father himself."[36] That the personal properties are the same as the relations is stated by Aquinas in the introduction to q. 40, "Deinde quaeritur de personis in comparatione ad *relationes sive proprietates.*"

This brings us, however, to our own next thesis, since, while the distinction between relations and personal properties is merely conceptual, still the meaning attached to the conceptual distinction is important in the context of our considerations and priorities.

> **Thesis 74:** *Despite the real identification of the divine relations, and so of the divine missions, which are the relations joined to created contingent external terms, with the divine processions, persons, personal properties, and notional acts, it remains crucial that the four-point hypothesis speaks of the created contingent external terms as participations in and*

imitations of the divine relations. This makes "participation" and "imitation" more than purely metaphysical terms. They signify interpersonal relations of knowing and loving between the recipients of divine life and the three divine persons, each of whom is received in a unique manner in accord with the order of the divine relations: the terms are created interpersonal communications of divine life. Because of the secondary act of existence, the assumed humanity of the historical Jesus of Nazareth is related to the divine Word in a manner analogous to the way in which the Father is eternally related to the same divine Word: as the one who speaks the Word of God the Father. Because of sanctifying grace, the elevated central form or identity of the historical human person is related to the Holy Spirit in a manner analogous to the way in which the Father and Son together are eternally related to the same Holy Spirit: as the Father and Son together are the single principle of the One who does the eternal truth that God is love, so the human being who loves with the love of Father and Son breathes a proceeding love for Father and Son that consciously shares in that same Holy Spirit. Because of charity, which is that created proceeding love, the circle of operations of the historical person who loves with divine love is related to the Father and the Son in a manner analogous to that in which the Holy Spirit is eternally related to the same Father and Son: as the One who receives the eternal love that is then "done." Because of the light of glory the enduring personal identity even of the one who lives after death still awaiting life after life after death, the resurrection of the body, is personally related to the eternal Father in a manner analogous to that in which the Son is eternally related to the same Father: as child of God into whose conscious intelligence and love the divine reality has insinuated itself as primary object or, in metaphysical terms, intelligible species.

It may be that this thesis really should be several. But I have chosen not to break the four-point hypothesis prematurely into its several components, but to try to treat them as one, primarily in order that we may advance toward our goal of attempting to understand the relations among the four created terms of the divine relations.

Let us begin, then, with the first sentence in the thesis: "Despite the real identification of the divine relations, and so of the divine missions, which are the relations joined to created contingent external terms, with the divine processions, persons, personal properties, and notional acts, it remains crucial that the four-point hypothesis speaks of the created contingent external terms as participations in and imitations of the divine *relations.*"

There is a purely conceptual distinction between the principal items or elements of Trinitarian theology: divine processions, relations, persons, missions, personal properties, and notional acts. Everything in God is one except where there is relational opposition. Thus: "… there are in God four real relations and … these are really identical with the processions."[37] "… a divine person is a subsistent relation."[38] "… the relation of origin of the person sent is included in the formality of mission."[39] "When the sense is that a divine person is really and truly sent by a divine person … a real relation *who from another* is included in the very formality of mission; and since this sort of real relation in God is not really distinct from the relation of origin it necessarily follows that a divine person is not sent except by the one or by those from whom that person proceeds."[40] "… 'properties' means the same as 'relations.'"[41] "The notional acts are the proper divine attributes expressed not by nouns or adjectives but by verbs: for example, to generate, to be generated, to speak, to be spoken, to spirate, to be spirated, to love notionally, and to proceed as love."[42] Etc., etc., etc.

The terms "participation" and "imitation," then, as these are employed in the four-point hypothesis, are misunderstood if they are taken in a purely metaphysical fashion. The participation in question is a participation in the divine *relations constitutive of conscious circumincession*. The terms are understood in relational fashion, purely and simply, that is to say, as created bases of created relations to the divine subsistent relations or persons. The created relations themselves are conscious relations of experiencing and loving, and if they are known, then they are conscious relations of knowing and loving. Thus to "participation" and "imitation" we must add "communication." The created terms are created communications of divine life.

One of the four participations or communications, the secondary act of existence of the Incarnation, affects directly only the assumed humanity of Jesus. It establishes the base of a conscious created relation of the assumed humanity to the divine Word, and thus it participates, precisely because of that conscious relation, in the divine relation of paternity, of speaking the divine Word. John 7.17: "Anyone who resolves to do the will of God will know whether the teaching is from God or whether I am speaking on my own." 12.49: "I have not spoken on my own, but the Father who sent me has himself given me a commandment about what to say and what to speak." 14.10: "The words that I say to you I do not speak on my own; but the Father who dwells in me does his works." 8.26: "… the one who sent me is true, and I declare to the world what I have heard from him." 8.28: "I speak these things as the Father instructed me." 8.38: "I declare what I have seen in the Father's presence." Etc., etc., etc.

Again, two of the four participations or communications, sanctifying grace and charity, affect the rest of us in this life (as they affected, of course, Jesus himself).[43] Sanctifying grace is the base of a conscious (though not necessarily known) relation of the "I" of the person to the uncreated Holy Spirit, who dwells within the person precisely as the term of this conscious relation. Charity is the base of a conscious (though not necessarily known) relation of the person's conscious transcendental notion of value, the existential consciousness of the person touched by divine love, to the Father and the Son, who precisely as terms of this relation come with the Holy Spirit to dwell within us.

Finally, the light of glory is the base of a conscious *and* known relation of the "I" awaiting bodily resurrection to the divine Father to whom the Son leads us home in eternal life. Precisely as the base of a conscious relation to the Father, the light of glory is a participation in the Son, a created communication of filiation, where the entire identity of the Son is subsistent relation to the Father.

Hence the next two sentences in the thesis: This makes "participation" and "imitation" more than purely metaphysical terms. They signify interpersonal relations of knowing and loving between the recipients of divine life and the three divine persons, each of whom is received in a unique manner in accord with the order of the divine relations. They signify, in short, created interpersonal communications of divine life.

The remainder of the thesis simply spells out in a new set of terms what we have already seen about each of these receptions of divine life.

5   Three Really Distinct Relations

Lonergan's sixth systematic Trinitarian thesis, and the third on the divine relations, is to the effect that three of the real divine relations, namely, paternity, filiation, and passive spiration, are really distinct, because of mutual opposition.[44] Active spiration is really identical with paternity and filiation together, and so is only notionally or conceptually distinct from them. But it is of course really distinct from passive spiration, as the Father and the Son, who, together precisely as Father and Son, *are* active spiration, are really distinct from the Holy Spirit. Mutually opposed relations are relations the subject of each of which is term of the other: father-son, son-father; spirator-spirit, spirit-spirator.

5.1 Preliminary Points

The argument here is more complex, perhaps the most complex in the whole of Lonergan's Trinitarian theology. A certain number of presuppositions or preliminary points (*praemittenda*), six to be exact, are dealt with before the argument itself is presented. Not only are these points not discrete and unrelated, but also their impact is cumulative.

The first two points head to the conclusion that *if mutually opposed relations are real, they are necessarily distinct from each other.* Or again, if they are not really distinct from each other, they are not real relations but only conceptual relations. This is what gives us ground for speaking about relations that are really distinct, that is, for specifying what it is that constitutes a distinction of relations as a real distinction: there is a real distinction of the relations if the relations are themselves real relations that are mutually opposed. (This is not the only ground, of course. Relations not in the same ordering are also really distinct.)

If mutually opposed relations *are* real, then, they must be really distinct. If paternity and filiation are real relations, they must be really distinct relations. If active spiration and passive spiration are real relations, they must be really distinct relations. This is the conclusion to which the first two points are heading. What constitutes a real *distinction* of mutually opposed relations is precisely that these mutually opposed relations are themselves real, not conceptual. What makes the distinction between active spiration and both paternity and filiation not a real but a conceptual distinction is that there is not a real mutual opposition between active spiration and either paternity or filiation. While the upshot of this is simply an elaboration of what Lonergan has himself said, its emphasis is sufficient for it to qualify as a distinct thesis of my own.

> **Thesis 75:** *If it is true that for the Father to beget the Son and for the Son to be begotten of the Father is for them together to spirate the Spirit of love, or that for the Father to speak the Word and for the Word to be spoken is for them together actively to breathe Love, then the mutual opposition of Father-Son actively spirates the Spirit, and that active spiration, itself constituted by this mutual opposition, itself stands in mutual opposition to the proceeding Holy Spirit, who is passive spiration.*

The question of the identity of active spiration with paternity and filiation taken together is addressed in the third of Lonergan's *praemittenda*, and is explained by asking what constitutes the multiplication of real relations. We saw earlier that real relations internal to one absolute that are not mutually opposed are distinct only conceptually if they are in the same ordering. Paternity and active spiration are not mutually opposed relations. Each regards a distinct *term*: paternity the Son, and active spiration the Holy Spirit. The terms are really distinct, and so there is a foundation in reality for the conceptual distinction between paternity and active spiration. But the difference in the relations themselves is not real. The per se reason for the multiplication of relations lies in the multiplication, not of subjects, nor of terms, but of orderings. True, the real relations of a father to his son and of a son to his father are distinct because the father and the son are distinct subjects and distinct terms. But this does not provide the *per se reason* for their distinction; that reason lies in the *distinct orderings* of paternity and filiation, since "ordering" is what relation *is*.

What has been said of paternity and active spiration may also be said of filiation and active spiration. The terms are distinct, since the term of filiation is the Father and the term of active spiration is the Holy Spirit. But the ordering is one: *for the Father to beget the Son and for the Son to be begotten of the Father is for the two together to breathe the Holy Spirit.* The entire system of exchanges in God is an eternal blaze of love.

Real relations, again, are not multiplied by the multiplication of terms. This is Lonergan's fourth presupposition. If the relations of a single subject to multiple terms stand in a single ordering, they are conceptually distinct relations, but really one relation binding the entire order together, because they constitute one ordering. A relation is an ordering, and the many that stand in a single order make for but a single order.

Examples can be drawn from other fields besides Trinitarian systematics. Thus, in Scholastic terms that can easily be transposed into intentionality analysis, it is by one real relation that a substantial nature is related to its accidental potencies, to the forms received in these potencies, to the acts to be elicited through these forms, and to the effects produced by the acts. A substantial nature is not ordered to its accidental potencies without *eo ipso* being ordered to the forms received in these potencies, to the acts to be elicited through these forms, and to the effects produced by the acts; nor is it ordered to accidental forms without being ordered to the potencies, and so on. Besides, in the same way, the individual potencies, forms, acts, and effects are ordered by a single real relation to everything else that is interrelated in one and the same system. It is one ordering with multiple terms.

This raises an existential question that Lonergan does not raise or answer in this context but only in his treatment of such matters as moral impotence, evil, and sin. Can the ordering be interrupted or broken? Obviously yes, in the case of human intentional operations; but in this instance that interruption or break would be due to the underdevelopment or the inauthenticity of the "substantial nature," in this case the human subject.

The two mutually opposed relations of Father and Son together stand in one order to the Holy Spirit, who proceeds precisely from the Father-Son pair of mutually opposed relations. The relations of Father to Word and of Father to Proceeding Love may be conceptually distinct, but they are really only one relation. And the relation of Word to Father and of Word to Proceeding Love may be conceptually distinct, but they are really only one relation. The relation of what utters to what is uttered, and the relation of what utters to the love that proceeds from or through what is uttered, are conceptually distinct, and the conceptual distinction has a ground in the distinction of terms, but they are really one relation. Again, the relation of what is uttered to the speaker that utters it is conceptually distinct from its relation to the love that proceeds from or through it, again with a similar ground in the distinction of terms, but these two conceptually distinct relations are really one. Active spiration is conceptually distinct from paternity and filiation but really one with these two relations taken together in their mutual opposition. To utter the Word and to be uttered by the Father *are* actively to spirate Proceeding Love.

The analogy in this case is very remote, however, because in us there are two distinct acts actively spirating love: understanding as uttering a judgment of value and the judgment of value thus uttered. In God there is but one infinite act by which God understands and speaks and conceives and judges. In God the relation of understanding as uttering a word to the word uttered is *conceptually* distinct from the relation of understanding as uttering a word to the love that proceeds from or through the word just uttered, but they are *really* one relation. The Father cannot utter the value judgment that is the divine Word without love proceeding from or through the utterance and the judgment. In us, on the other hand, there is an *exigence*, not a necessity, that the value judgment that is spoken from the grasp of sufficient evidence also breathe love. The ordering can and often does break down. Again, in God the relation of the word uttered to the speaker that utters it is *conceptually* distinct from the relation of the word uttered to the love that proceeds from it, but these two conceptually distinct relations are *really* one. In God the value judgment as an inner word proceeding from the grasp of sufficient evidence *necessarily* breathes love. In us there is an *exigence* that the value judgment breathe love, but that exigence can be violated.

Thus, in God active spiration is conceptually distinct from paternity and filiation but really one with these two relations taken together. *To utter the Word of value judgment and to be the Word of value judgment uttered by the Father are together actively to spirate Proceeding Love.*

> **Thesis 76:** *An upshot or implication of this for the divine missions is that there is never Spirit without Word or Word without Spirit, whether in the immanent Trinity or in the missions, and whether the mission be "visible" or "invisible." If it is the case that for the Son to be uttered by the Father is also for the Father and the Word actively to spirate the Holy Spirit, then because the missions are the processions and relations joined to created external terms, it follows that for the Son to be sent by the Father is also for the Father and the Word to send the Holy Spirit. This holds for both "visible" and "invisible" missions.*

This fills out what might correctly be viewed as something incomplete in *Missions and Processions.* In that book there are acknowledged both invisible and visible missions of both the Son and the Holy Spirit. But in its treatment of the order of the missions, the book states clearly only the following: (1) invisible mission of the Holy Spirit, (2) visible mission of the Son, (3) visible mission of the Holy Spirit. But the order of the missions must be the order of the divine processions, since the missions are the processions joined to an external term. There must, then, be acknowledged an invisible mission of the Son ontologically prior to the invisible mission of the Holy Spirit. Its created term is the universalist faith already described in *Missions and Processions*, the knowledge born of religious love, while the created term of the invisible mission of the Holy Spirit is the charity that proceeds from faith thus conceived.

In the human analogue, of course, as we have said, the order can break down due to the inauthenticity of the subject. One can correctly judge what is good and refuse to follow through in decision and action. The grasp of evidence sufficient to ground a judgment of value may lead to the judgment, but love, authentic decision, may not follow. Then the one relation that binds together the entire order has been violated. With us this is possible, but not with God.

The *sixth* step moves to an expansion of the analogue in human consciousness that would help us understand this. To start with Lonergan's analogy in the work under consideration, consider in human consciousness (1) the reflective grasp speaking (analogue for the Father) the word "yes" (analogue for the Son) because of sufficient evidence for an affirmative judgment of value, (2) the word "yes" that is uttered, and (3) the act of love (analogue for the Holy Spirit) that proceeds from the uttering and from the word uttered. It is by one real relation that the speaking is really related *both* to the "yes" that is spoken *and* to the love that proceeds from the speaking and the word spoken, and it is by the *same* real relation that the "yes" is really related *both* to the speaking *and* to the love. That real relation makes both speaking and spoken at once and together the principles of the proceeding love. Here is the analogue for active spiration in the divinity. Because the speaking and the word in us are really distinct acts in an absolute sense, whereas in God speaking and the word spoken are one act internally differentiated by relations, there is a difference. And this difference has the existential implication just mentioned: we can distort the one ordering by not following through in the exercise of autonomous spiritual processions demanded for the integrity of our performance as subjects. But such difference is precisely what analogy is all about.

Again, it is by a distinct and opposed real relation that the love that proceeds is really related to *both* the speaking *and* the "yes," and that distinct and opposed relation is the analogue for passive spiration in the divinity.

Suppose that the single object of reflective grasp of evidence as speaking, of the word spoken, and of love is some good. First, then, the reflective evaluative understanding that speaks grasps sufficient evidence to affirm the goodness of the object in a true word and so to love it with a proper love. Second, because of the grasped evidence the goodness because of which the object is to be loved is uttered in a true judgment of value, an inner assent. Third, there is spirated the love on account of the evident goodness that is grasped by the uttering understanding and that is affirmed in a true word. Thus, insofar as they regard one object, the understanding uttering, the word uttered, and love are related to one another in a single system of relations, and so it is by one real relation that the understanding that utters is related both to the word and to love, it is by the same real relation that the word is related both to the "speaker" and to love, and it is by one distinct and opposed real relation that love is related both to the one uttering and to the word. The one uttering does not utter an abstract truth such that the one uttering it could utter a word without simultaneously spirating love, but a concrete truth and good such that it cannot (or should not) be that the word be uttered without love being spirated. Nor is an abstract truth uttered in the word, such that it depends on the one uttering and nonetheless does not spirate love, but by the word there is uttered the truth by which goodness is affirmed, and so the dependence of the word on the one uttering is such that it cannot (or should not) be separated from the spiration of love. Finally, love is rational and good, not only on account of the affirmed goodness, not only on account of the grasped sufficiency of the evidence for affirming goodness, but on account of both of these together, the goodness which is affirmed because sufficient reason has been grasped.

One of the most interesting things about this analogy is that two really distinct mutually opposed relations together make up one relation that is mutually opposed to the love that proceeds from them. So the relations of speaking to "yes" and to love, and of "yes" to speaking and to love involve (1) the mutually opposed relations of speaking to "yes" and "yes" to speaking, and (2) the mutually opposed relations of speaking-and-"yes" to love and love to speaking-and-"yes." The two mutually opposed real and distinct relations posited in (1), taken together, are one subject of the mutually opposed real and distinct relations posited in (2), namely, speaking-and-"yes," and are the analogue of active spiration in the Trinity; and the other subject of the relations posited in (2), namely, love proceeding, is the analogue of passive spiration. Thus in God, the Holy Spirit as Proceeding Love is really distinct from the Speaker and the Word spoken, from whom together the Spirit proceeds, and that real distinction is a really distinct relation of passive spiration. But the Speaker and the Word spoken, paternity and filiation, while really distinct from each other as Speaker and Word, Father and Son, are only conceptually distinct from the combined principle of active spiration from which the Proceeding Love proceeds. Paternity and filiation, which themselves are really distinct and mutually opposed relations, taken together really *are* active spiration *precisely in their real mutual opposition.* Active spiration is constituted by their mutual opposition. Divine Love proceeds as the Father speaks the Word and the Word is spoken by the Father, as each acknowledges the lovableness of the other.

We must now relate this to the version of the analogy that we are suggesting.[45]

As I have insisted from the beginning, the structure of the psychological analogy is the same whether the analogy be that proposed by Augustine, by Aquinas, by the early Lonergan, by the later Lonergan, or by myself. What differs is principally the analogue for the Father, the Speaker of the divine Word. In Augustine, that analogue is called *memoria.* In Aquinas, it is *intelligere,* understanding precisely as *dicere,* as speaking an inner word. In the early Lonergan, it is the same as for Aquinas, but in a much more fully articulated and differentiated expression, with two mentions in *The Triune God: Systematics* that the analogue for the Word is a judgment of value. In the later Lonergan, the analogue for the Father is *agapē,* being in love, uttering a judgment of value. In the analogy that I am suggesting, it is again *memoria,* now understood as *the retrospective appropriation of the state of mind in which one finds oneself gifted by unconditional love,* with this appropriation *grasped* (reflective understanding) as sufficient evidence for a judgment of value. From that fundamental disposition grasped in evaluative insight as sufficient evidence for a judgment of value, there emerges the judgment of value, faith as the knowledge born of love, perhaps in the form of a word of gratitude. And from the disposition and word, the silent "yes" of gratitude, there flows the love of God in return, coalescing through repeated acts of self-transcendent generosity into a habitual universal willingness, that is, into charity as state of mind emanating from the original giftedness. Here too, the initial *memoria* and the word that emanates ineffably from it are themselves the terms of mutually opposed relations, but they operate together as a single principle to which the love that flows from that single principle is opposed. The analogue for the eternal Father is the *memoria* of lovableness revealed, the analogue for the eternal Son is the silent "yes" that is the knowledge born of being gifted and loving with that gift, and the analogue for the eternal Holy Spirit is the love-in-return that proceeds at once from the retrospective appropriation of the gift and from the word acknowledging the gift.

By way of a parenthesis, and also by way of illustration, let me add that the opening words of Pope Francis's Apostolic Exhortation *Evangelii Gaudium* express this analogy in words that all can identify. "The joy of the Gospel (the evangelical disposition or state of mind) fills the hearts and lives of all who encounter Jesus. Those who accept (the 'yes' of faith) his offer of salvation are set free from sin, sorrow, inner emptiness and loneliness. With Christ joy is constantly born anew. In this Exhortation I wish to encourage the Christian faithful to embark upon a new chapter of evangelization (love manifest as mission) marked by this joy, while pointing out new paths for the Church's journey in years to come." Furthermore, in a subsequent paragraph Pope Francis expands this structure to communal dimensions: "Memory is a dimension of our faith which we might call 'deuteronomic', not unlike the memory of Israel itself. Jesus leaves us the Eucharist as the Church's daily remembrance of, and deeper sharing in, the event of his Passover ... The joy of evangelizing always arises from grateful remembrance: it is a grace which we constantly need to implore ... The believer is essentially 'one who remembers.'"

5.2 *The Argument*

We return to Lonergan's text, and specifically to his argument for the assertion.

The argument proceeds by considering, not directly the four real relations already affirmed, but six comparisons. "Since in God there are four real relations, we can determine which ones are really distinct from one another only by making six comparisons, namely (1) of paternity with filiation, (2) of active spiration with passive spiration, (3) of paternity with active spiration, (4) of paternity with passive spiration, (5) of filiation with active spiration, and (6) of filiation with passive spiration."[46]

> (1) Paternity and filiation are really distinct, for they are real, mutually opposed relations.
>
> (2) Active spiration and passive spiration are also real and mutually opposed relations, and so they too are really distinct.
>
> (3) Paternity and the active spiration of the Father are real relations of the Father as speaker (*Dicens*) to, respectively, the Word and Proceeding Love. But relations of the same, if they are one in order, constitute only one order and so one real relation. The relations of Speaker to Word and to Love are one in order. This is the key to the identity of paternity with active spiration. The Father in one Word utters a true good, and so (1) speaks the Word and (2) by so doing, through the Word, breathes Proceeding Love. The terms are distinct but the order is one.
>
> (4) Passive spiration is really distinct from paternity. It is a relation of love to the one uttering, and is opposed to the real active spiration that is only conceptually distinct from paternity.
>
> (5) Filiation and the active spiration of the Son are real relations of the Word to, respectively, the Speaker and Proceeding Love.

> They are conceptually and not really distinct from each other.
> For again, relations that are one in order constitute only one
> order and one real relation, and the relations of the Word to the
> Speaker and to Proceeding Love are one in order: in one Word
> there is uttered the true good which as true proceeds from the
> Speaker and as good is ordered to the spiration of Love. So filia-
> tion and the active spiration of the Son are conceptually distinct
> but really constitute one intelligible order.

Thus paternity and filiation, which *are* really distinct, together and in their real distinction from each other *are* the active spiration of the Holy Spirit.

> (6) Passive spiration is really distinct from filiation. It is a relation of
> Proceeding Love to the Word, and it is opposed to the real ac-
> tive spiration of the Word that is only conceptually distinct from
> filiation.

So three of the real relations in God are also really distinct: paternity, filiation, and passive spiration. Active spiration, while it is really distinct from
passive spiration, is not really distinct from paternity or from filiation.[47]

5.3 Scholion

A scholion follows, and it takes up a question that obviously remains unan-
swered in the six comparisons (though I have already indicated how it is
to be answered), namely, Is the active spiration of the Father really distinct
from that of the Son? Is the breathing of Proceeding Love by the Father
really distinct from the breathing of Proceeding Love by the Son?

In favor of an affirmative answer are the following considerations: Father
and Son are two really distinct subjects; each really spirates love; and two
really distinct subjects are not really related by what numerically is one real
relation. Father and Son are really related by (in fact, *as*) two really distinct
relations.

But in favor of a negative answer is the following: Everything in God is
one except where the opposition of relation dictates otherwise; the active
spiration of the Father and that of the Son are not mutually opposed, and
so must be one. What *are* mutually opposed are their relations as Father
and Son, but *it is precisely in that mutual opposition as Father and Son, in their
mutual acknowledgment of each other's lovableness, that the active spiration of the
Holy Spirit resides.*

While Lonergan's response, in my view, could fruitfully have highlighted
this last point, it has the advantage of pointing to the difference between
the relation of "speaking" and word in us and in God. "*We* understand
in one act and conceive or judge in another act. But in God there is but

one infinite act by which God understands and speaks and conceives and judges. Hence *in us two real active spirations are really distinct,* since spiration proceeds from two really distinct acts. But in God, where there is but one act that is both speaker and word, there is but one principle of spiration; and since only one love is spirated from this one principle, there can be only one active spiration."[48]

This explains why the ordering can be and often is interrupted and distorted in us, and why this is impossible in God. The two acts in us are bound by an exigence, but the connection remains contingent. In God the generation of the Word and the spiration of the Holy Spirit are necessary. We can be said to approximate the divine relations more fully the more it is true, that our "yes" flows habitually from its principle, whether that principle be understood as Augustine's *memoria* or as Aquinas's and the early Lonergan's *intelligere* or as the later Lonergan's *agapē* or as the retrieved Augustinian *memoria* that I am suggesting. But in us these will always remain two really distinct acts, bound by an exigence that can be violated, whereas in God we are speaking of two really distinct relations in the one pure act that God is.

Again, Father and Son *are* really distinct as Father and Son, but not as what Thomas calls their *notionaliter diligere* spirating *Amor procedens.* As they are really one God, so also they are one principle of spirating, one Spirator, just as, while Father, Son, and Spirit are three persons, nonetheless they are one God and one principle of creating, one Creator. Again, what Lonergan might have emphasized more in the present context is that it is precisely in being the mutually opposed relations of paternity and filiation that they are *active loving* (*notionaliter diligere* in Aquinas's phrase) and so *one* principle of Proceeding Love (*Amor procedens*).

6   Divine Relations and the Divine Essence

Lonergan's seventh Trinitarian thesis, and his fourth on the divine relations, asserts that the four real divine relations are conceptually distinct from the divine essence but really identical with it.[49] They are what God *is.* Pure Act *is* four real relations, three of which are really distinct, while the fourth is really identical with and conceptually distinct from the first two considered together.

The four relations are paternity, filiation, active spiration, and passive spiration.

By "the divine essence" is meant God as common to the three persons, God as Father, Son, and Holy Spirit.

Things are conceptually distinct if the concept of one is not the concept of the other. They are really distinct if one as real is not the same as the other as real. They are really identical if they are really not distinct.

6.1 The Argument

The argument begins with a logical step, based in the principle of non-contradiction: the divine essence and a real divine relation cannot be the same both in reality and in concept. The second step is that they are the same in reality. And the third is that they are conceptually distinct.

First, then, the divine essence and a real divine relation cannot be the same both in reality and in concept. We predicate contradictories of the divine essence and of real divine relations. We say, for instance, (1) that the Father is not the Son, and (2) that God is the Son.[50] "Son" and "not Son" are contradictories. But contradictories cannot be predicated of the same both in reality and in concept, and so "Father" (a divine relation) and "God" (the divine essence) cannot be both really and conceptually the same. They can only be *either* really the same or conceptually the same, but not both. This is a straightforward application of the principle of contradiction, which applies to the same thing (reality) in the same respect (concept). The same follows as well for comparing the Son and the Spirit, filiation and passive spiration, with the divine essence.

Second, the divine essence and the real divine relations are really identical. Three arguments are given. First, divinity and, e.g., paternity are either "(1) really different and not a composite, or (2) really different and a composite, or (3) really the same." But if the divine essence and paternity were really distinct and not a composite, the Father would not be God. And if they were really distinct and a composite, God would not be simple and would have a cause of composition, and so would not be the first principle. So the divine essence and paternity must be really identical. The same holds for the divine essence and the Son and for the divine essence and the Holy Spirit.[51]

Again, in God all things are one except where there is no relational opposition. Paternity and the divine essence are not mutually opposed relations: the divine essence is not a relation, much less a relation opposed to paternity. And so paternity and the divine essence are one. And the same follows for filiation, active spiration, and passive spiration, as compared with the divine essence.

Again, in God there is only trinity, not quaternity. There are three real divine relations that are really distinct. If these were again really distinguished from the divine essence, there would be quaternity in God. So there cannot be admitted a real distinction between the divine essence and a real divine relation.

Third, finally, the divine essence and the real divine relations are conceptually distinct. If they are really the same, yet cannot be the same both in reality and in conception because of contradictory predications, then they must be conceptually distinct. Again, a conceptual distinction obtains when the concept of one is not the concept of the other, and the concept of paternity or of filiation or of active or passive spiration is not the concept of divinity.

Lonergan concludes the chapter on the divine relations with four notes and with the consideration of five questions. These are mentioned briefly above. We do not need go into them here. They are not relevant to our concerns. His own text may be consulted.[52]

I have presented my understanding of Lonergan's chapter on the divine relations. I have derived several theses of my own from this understanding. And I have begun to tease out an answer to the question, How are the created contingent external terms that make of the divine relations also divine missions related to one another? We must turn now to the issue of the divine persons, with an emphasis on the divine person of the incarnate Word.

5

Mission and Person

1   Introduction: Four Theses

From processions and relations Lonergan moves to the divine persons.

In his order of proceeding in *The Triune God: Systematics*, where he follows Aquinas's *ordo doctrinae*, the Father, the Son, and the Holy Spirit are considered first as *distinct* persons (chapter 4), then as *related* to one another (chapter 5), and finally in terms of their relationship to us, that is, in terms of the divine missions of the Son and the Holy Spirit (chapter 6).

I am suggesting the possibility of a new ordering of Trinitarian systematics, precisely because of Aquinas's and then Lonergan's identification of the divine missions with the divine processions and relations joined to created external terms. I have been attempting to use that identification, offered clearly and emphatically in the final chapter of Lonergan's Trinitarian systematics, as a key to an analogical understanding of the divine processions and relations.

In other words, I am proposing that one may now start one's attempt to reach an analogical understanding of the divine processions and relations from one's understanding of the missions. A new starting point has been made available. If one regards as a permanent theological achievement the identification of mission with procession and relation joined to a created term that is the consequent condition of the procession and relation being also mission, then one may begin one's Trinitarian systematics with the divine missions, provided one has correctly understood the best contributions that have been made in the history of theology to the theology of the divine processions and relations and has decided, on the basis of that understanding, which of these contributions one intends to carry forward: in other words, provided one has worked one's way through the results of the best work in the functional specialties that lead into systematics.

Then, when one begins with the missions one will not fail to begin also with the processions and relations precisely as they have come to be understood in the theological tradition that enabled one to make the identification. The missions give access to the processions and relations. The divine processions and relations, when joined to created external terms, are missions. Because of this identification, we have begun our systematics with the missions without failing to begin as well with the processions and relations. The processions and relations are revealed in the created external terms that are the consequent conditions of processions and relations being also missions. Indeed, once that identification has been accepted, the divine missions can provide perhaps the most fruitful analogies of faith for understanding the processions and relations. Once the theological identification of mission with procession and relation joined to a created term has been made and accepted as one's own theological doctrine, the missions give one theological access to the processions and relations. The necessary divine processions and relations, when joined to created external terms as consequent conditions, *are* contingent historical missions. The processions and relations are then made accessible to theological understanding through the created external terms that are the consequent conditions of the processions and relations being also missions.

This brings us to an important question about theological method, one that perhaps Lonergan was asking in his first writings on this question. In three articles commenting on Lonergan's seminal first chapter on method in *Divinarum personarum* and on the changes to that chapter found in *De Deo trino: Pars systematica*,[1] I pointed to a problem: advances in theological method, and in particular on the various orderings of theological ideas, that Lonergan suggested in *Divinarum personarum* (1957, 1959) were not picked up on in *De Deo trino* (1964) but rather seem to have been silently abandoned. They had to do with the thorny problem of relating system and history. We are encountering one of these problems in our present remarks.[2] The *order of discovery* in the history of Latin Trinitarian theology moved from the missions to the persons, from the persons to the relations, and from the relations to Augustine's efforts to provide what has since come to be known as a psychological analogy for the processions. But centuries later *the order of teaching* in Trinitarian theology, as presented in Aquinas's *Summa theologiae*, 1, qq. 27–43, moved from the processions to the relations, then to the persons, and finally to the missions. But Lonergan's first version of a methodological chapter in his Trinitarian systematics, that found in *Divinarum personarum*, allows us to speculate that the movement from the order of discovery to the order of teaching may not be the end of the history of the ordering of theological ideas, since the order of teaching, which in Trinitarian theology ends with the missions, can then start over with the *systematic* position on the missions as its starting point, where the missions are identical with the processions joined to a created external term. But in the second version of the same chapter, that found in *De Deo trino: Pars systematica*, Lonergan does not pick up on his suggestion regarding the speculative appropriation of history. In fact, to one already familiar with the first version of this chapter he would seem to have abandoned this suggestion. I am proposing, and have been for some time, that once the order of teaching has arrived at a *systematic* understanding of what was the starting point in the order of discovery – in this case the divine missions – a new Trinitarian systematics can begin with that starting point as it has come to be understood in the order of teaching, without losing any systematic rigor or precision and in fact without failing simultaneously to begin with the processions, privileged access to which is provided precisely through the missions. We can return to history as it actually occurred, understand it in the light of *later* systematic developments, and offer a systematic theology that aims to be every bit as precise as Thomas's or Lonergan's Trinitarian systematics. That has been one of the options I am attempting to begin to carry off in this work. And this is only a beginning. Implementing these suggestions throughout systematic theology will take quite some time.

Supporting my position is the fact that it was in Lonergan's treatment of the divine missions that I found the formula that I have adopted as the core, indeed as the starting point, of a systematic theology and as an essential part of its unified field structure, namely, the four-point hypothesis linking immanent divine relations to their created external terms. This I regard as one dimension of the unified field structure of a contemporary systematics, the other dimension being the theory of history presented in *Theology and the Dialectics of History* and the developments that may be offered on that theory. What in a medieval theoretical theology were called sanctifying grace and charity, as created participations in active and passive spiration, and so as related to the invisible missions of the Word and the Holy Spirit, constitute the fifth level in a Christian theological understanding of the scale of values, namely, "religious values." As invisible missions of Word and Spirit, as grace both actual and habitual, they also constitute the transformation or conversion of the fifth level in Lonergan's schema of consciousness, consciousness as relationality. In that transformation, the transition from the natural to the supernatural in the vertical finality of conscious intentionality occurs.[3] The structure of consciousness and the scale of values are isomorphic. The scale of values is the collective objectification of personal authenticity. In my view it provides the structure of the collective responsibility that Lonergan is searching for in his seminal paper "Natural Right and

Historical Mindedness."[4] In turn, the movement from above in the schemes of recurrence of values in history moves from the grace that establishes and confirms the authenticity of personal value to the formal effects of grace in the cultural meanings and social structures – effects that I call social grace – that promote the equitable distribution of vital goods to all.[5]

So we are proceeding from a new starting point, one that enables our systematics to be a theological theory of history. That new starting point has already yielded an analogical understanding of the divine processions that follows the structure of the analogies employed by Augustine, Thomas Aquinas, and the earlier and later Lonergan, but that also moves that structure explicitly into the order of grace, and indeed grace precisely as it operates in history. In the briefest terms, graced memory, recollected self-presence, gives rise to the faith (the knowledge born of religious love) that breathes charity. Graced memory stands as an analogue for the Father. Faith stands as an analogue for the Son. Memory as the fruit of the gift of God's love and faith as the knowledge born of that gift stand together as an analogue for Father and Son in active spiration. And charity stands as an analogue for the Holy Spirit. *Missions and Processions* works out the implications of that analogy in detail, including a specification of hope as our current relation to the Father. The theological possibility of interreligious mutual self-mediation is grounded in the realities that I attempt to name in this analogy, since those realities are universal; they are offered everywhere, to everyone, and can be found in many quite distinct religious traditions. Christian theologies of religion have the task of specifying how these elements are found in various traditions.

Then, after beginning with missions and processions, we moved in the preceding chapter of the present volume to the divine relations. There we sublated Lonergan's considerations of the relations into the context established by our starting point in the missions.

In the present chapter I wish to begin to extend that attempt to the systematics of the divine persons. We are now moving to an understanding of the divine persons from the standpoint of the missions. The present chapter is concerned above all with the person of the Son. While the mission of the Holy Spirit was the central focus of our efforts to establish the core analogy (even though the analogy also names an invisible mission of the Son), we now move to the mission of the Word Incarnate as a locus for exploring the divine persons understood precisely in relation to mission.

Hans Urs von Balthasar has already contributed to reflection on the link of person and mission, working from the mission of the Word Incarnate. The theological notion of *person as mission* found in Balthasar's work, once it has been refined in the fire of Lonergan's intentionality analysis, Trinitarian theology, Christology, and method, will make an input into the outcome of this exploration. Balthasar's mission emphasis is salutary, indeed important, and must be promoted. But his theology needs to pay more attention to (1) the significance and importance of the Augustinian-Thomist-Lonerganian psychological analogy, (2) the relations between the ontological and psychological constitution of Christ, and (3) the significance for Christology of the metaphysics of the real distinction between essence and existence (a metaphysics that Balthasar clearly accepts but whose relevance to Christology is not clear in his work). I will have more to say on (1) later in this chapter. As for (2), Balthasar writes, "… we cannot ascribe a twofold consciousness to the Logos-made-man."[6] In the same context, he calls Aquinas's position on the divine act of existence as the *unicum esse* of the incarnate Word an "extreme theory"[7] that "unwittingly comes close to Monophysitism."[8] This same theory is said to be inconsistent with the doctrine found at least in Aquinas's *De unione Verbi incarnati* of the *esse secundarium* of the humanity of the Word made man.[9] And as for (3), Thomas, says Balthasar, has made "the application to Christology of the philosophical (Neo-Thomist) doctrine of the real distinction between esse and essentia, importing into Christology all its inherited problems."[10]

Aside from the problem of understanding how Aquinas could possibly have applied to his own thirteenth-century Christology a neo-Thomist doctrine, these statements clearly conflict with Lonergan's Christology. For Lonergan the theological doctrine of two consciousnesses in Christ is an implication of the Chalcedonian dogma and of the later dogma from the Third Council of Constantinople on two operations and two wills in Christ. Moreover, Lonergan tells us that it was in a course in Christology from Bernard Leeming at the Gregorian University that he became convinced of the importance for the hypostatic union of the real distinction between essence and existence.[11] Finally, Lonergan will identify "secondary act of existence" as the best expression in a metaphysical theology of the created consequent condition of the procession of the Son being also a mission of the Son incarnate.

I am now prepared to state up front the first four theses of the present chapter. What I now express in these theses will become clear, I hope, from the ensuing elaboration of these issues.

> **Thesis 77:** *In contrast with the position of Hans Urs von Balthasar, person is not precisely mission, even in Jesus, whose person is the divine relation of filiation, but in whose human consciousness procession, relation, filiation, person become mission because of the created external term without which they could not be mission. Procession, relation, and person in Jesus are divine and necessary. But mission is contingent, conditioned by the created external term consequent on divine freedom, namely, what Aquinas calls the secondary act of existence. The absolutely supernatural created gift of the secondary act of existence is the condition*

consequent upon divine decision that makes it possible to say truly, "The second person of the Blessed Trinity is this man Jesus of Nazareth." This contingent "is" is the secondary act of existence.

Thesis 78: *The divine consciousness of Jesus is the consciousness precisely of the One who proceeds eternally as Son and Word from the Father, while his human consciousness is the consciousness of the One who has been sent in time as Son and Word made flesh.*

Thus, to begin. I want to extend to mission and to the human consciousness of Christ the features of divine consciousness affirmed in assertion 12 in *The Triune God: Systematics*: "Father, Son, and Holy Spirit through one real consciousness are three subjects conscious both of themselves and of each of the others, as well as of their own act both notional and essential."[12] Lonergan explains this thesis:

> Without doubt, the Father, the Son, and the Spirit alike *know* on the side of the object *that* the Father consciously generates the Son, and *that* the Son is consciously generated by the Father, and *that* the Father and the Son consciously spirate the Spirit, and *that* the Spirit is consciously spirated by the Father and the Son. But what the Father, the Son, and the Spirit know on the side of the object, theologians *conclude to* on the side of the object. But the very same reality that is *known* by the divine persons and *concluded to* from faith by theologians is not only known or concluded to, but also *exists*. And *as existing*, it is *on the side of the subject,* namely, on the side of the subject that is the Father in consciously generating the Son, *on the side of the subject that is the Son in being consciously generated by the Father, on the side of the subject that is the Father and the Son in consciously spirating the Spirit,* and on the side of the subject that is the Spirit in being consciously spirated by the Father and the Son.[13]

The divine consciousness of the incarnate Word, then, would be the consciousness "on the side of the subject that is the Son in being consciously generated by the Father" as well as "on the side of the subject that is the Son who with the Father consciously spirates the Spirit." The incarnate Word is present to himself through divine consciousness in this way, conscious as well of the Father from whom he proceeds and of the Holy Spirit whom, together with the Father, he spirates. He must be conscious of the Father and the Holy Spirit in being conscious of himself, for he *is* relation to the Father and the Holy Spirit. This is the significance of Lonergan's words "as existing" ("prout existit").

What about his human consciousness? His human consciousness is ontologically grounded in the secondary act of existence that makes it true to affirm that the second person of the Blessed Trinity *is* this man Jesus of Nazareth. This human consciousness is the mission consciousness of the Eternal Word become flesh. It is *the consciousness on the side of the subject that is the Son in being consciously sent by the Father.* The mission is the procession joined to the created external term. Thus if, as proceeding, the Son is conscious of proceeding from the Father, then as sent, he must be conscious of being sent by the Father. This is consciousness, not knowledge, in a manner similar to that in which the divine consciousness "on the side of the subject that is the Son in being consciously generated by the Father" is consciousness: not knowledge *that,* but consciousness *of* self precisely in relation. His divine consciousness is procession consciousness, and his human consciousness is mission consciousness. This affirmation is rooted in the position common to Aquinas, Lonergan, and Balthasar that the divine missions are the divine processions joined to created terms that are consequent conditions of the processions being also missions.

The two consciousnesses – procession consciousness and mission consciousness – are continuous, connected, and communicating, but also distinct. The divine consciousness is eternal, uncreated, and necessary. The human consciousness is temporal, historical, created, and contingent. They are united both ontologically and psychologically in the person of the eternal Word become flesh, who is the subject of both a divine procession consciousness and a human mission consciousness. That is my thesis. The remainder of this chapter spells it out in greater detail.

Let me emphasize that I want to insist on a continuity and not, as Balthasar (may I say "characteristically"?) would have it, an abyss or chasm.[14] The continuity is due to the grace of union or, in Aquinas's late hypothetical formulation, to the secondary act of existence of the Incarnation, enabling the participation of the assumed human nature of Jesus in the divine act of existence of the eternal Word. The participation is a participation of mission in procession, of secondary act of existence in divine act of existence as exercised by the Son and so as filiation. Again, the eternal Word of God, the second person of the Blessed Trinity, *is* this man Jesus of Nazareth. The theological doctrine of the secondary act of existence names this "is," precisely as *this* unique "is."

The same secondary act of existence is the ontological ground of a human subjectivity, a human consciousness, distinct from the eternal procession consciousness of the divine Word. The human consciousness of Jesus is the consciousness, the self-presence, of one contingently sent in history, where the consequent condition of that sending is the secondary act of existence, while the divine consciousness is the consciousness, the self-presence, of the one who eternally and necessarily proceeds from the same Father who also contingently and freely sends him to announce the reign of God in history. He is a person *on* mission, but his person cannot be identified *tout court* with his mission. His human subjectivity *can* be so identified, but his human subjectivity is not his divine identity, not his person. The two are distinct by what an ontological Christology calls a real inadequate minor distinction, the same kind of distinction as is drawn in theological explanations of Chalcedonian doctrine between the person and each of the natures of the incarnate Word.

As for the psychological analogy (problem 1 above), I propose thesis 79.

Thesis 79: *Only spiritual subjects in whom there occur autonomous spiritual processions can possibly be persons on mission.*[15]

Unless one grasps the structure of these autonomous spiritual processions, in both their natural and their supernatural dimensions, precisely as images of, and indeed, in the graced order, conscious participants in, receivers of the communication of, the Triune processions and missions, one lacks the basis for pursuing the theological notion of person on mission.

Balthasar and Joseph Ratzinger, to whom Balthasar appeals, were reluctant to acknowledge the significance of this strand in the Western theological tradition. I will address these concerns with the help of Lonergan, but I will also have to acknowledge the advances that Lonergan himself made with regard to the understanding of person beyond the characteristics of person explicitly acknowledged in his Latin theological treatises. The earlier notion of person in Lonergan's work, which is not wrong but incomplete, was advanced after he recognized significant dimensions of consciousness beyond the intellectual and rational, dimensions indeed that are part of my reason for changing "intelligible emanation" or "intellectual emanation" to "autonomous *spiritual* procession."

The same reason lies behind the suggestion I make in thesis 80:

Thesis 80: *Lonergan's discussion of person in his Latin works on the Trinity and Christ must be sublated into a notion that takes more explicitly into account the developments subsequent to Aquinas's definition and to Aquinas's reliance on Boethius's definition as well as the developments in Lonergan's own thinking. As the cognitive levels of consciousness – experience, understanding, and judgment – are sublated by the fourth, existential level, and as these four are sublated by being in love in an unqualified fashion, so the objective of authentic subjectivity sublates being (the objective of the desire to know) into the full range of the scale of values, which is the objective that serves to define what is meant by "person." A person can be defined as a distinct subsistent in a spiritual nature. A human person, then, is a distinct subsistent potentially oriented to commitment to the integral scale of values, and an authentic human person is a distinct subsistent actually oriented to the same commitment.*

> *This definition, which is also open to what is meant by "personal value"
> in the scale of values, really does take into account the developments on
> the notion of person reached by the turn to the subject in modernity, by the
> turn to the other in postmodernity, and by the expansions of conscious-
> ness beyond cognitional levels in Lonergan's own work.*

Much of the remainder of this chapter will be devoted to providing the
background and the argument for these theses. The procedure is as follows. After tracing the respective histories of the notion of person found
in Lonergan and Balthasar, I will trace the development of Lonergan's theology of person before attempting to advance the position in Balthasar's
notion of person understood as mission. Such is the overall outline of the
remainder of the present lengthy chapter, which will introduce two more
theses and then conclude with comments on the transition to soteriology.

Moving in this way, of course, might also reveal that Lonergan's treatment
of the divine persons as related (his chapter 5) might perhaps better have
preceded the treatment of the persons as distinct (his chapter 4). Part of
Lonergan's and Balthasar's problem with the Thomist heritage in Trinitarian
theology is that the emphasis on "substantia individua" in Boethius's definition of person, which was used by Aquinas, blurs the acknowledgment of the
fact that divine persons *are* relations. That Aquinas cannot be so charged, however, seems to me to be clear from *Summa theologiae*, 1, q. 29, a. 4. One expert
in Thomas's Trinitarian theology has persuaded me that Boethius's "substantia individua" is interpreted by Aquinas in a way that allows it to be identified
with the "subsistens distinctum" that was part of Aquinas's original definition
of person: "subsistens distinctum in natura intellectuali," a distinct subsistent
in an intellectual nature (*Super I Sententiarum*, d. 23, a. 1, q. 4 c.). This is the
definition that Lonergan prefers, precisely because "subsistens distinctum" is
more ready, he says, to be qualified as relational than is "substantia individua."

Nonetheless, Balthasar's caution is salutary, even if he downplays or simply
misses the subtleties of Aquinas's Trinitarian positions. In the present work,
we have already seen that chapter 3 of Lonergan's *The Triune God: Systematics* established that the reality to be attributed to the divine processions was
the reality of relations. We must ask, then, why Lonergan's treatment of the
persons as distinct precedes his treatment of the persons as related. Toward
the end of the chapter on the persons as distinct he admits that "divine
person" could be defined as the divine essence differentiated by relations.
But he did not begin the treatment with that definition of divine person.
This is probably explained very simply: he is following Aquinas in moving
from the relations (for Aquinas, *Summa theologiae*, 1, q. 28) to the persons
as first distinct (q. 29) and then as related to one another. It is in that context that Aquinas continued to use Boethius's incomplete definition of the

person, "rationalis naturae substantia individua," an individual substance of a rational nature, and in the same context that Lonergan indicates his own preference for Thomas's earlier definition, "subsistens distinctum in natura intellectuali," a distinct subsistent in an intellectual nature. But perhaps another and more complete definition of what constitutes at least a divine person could have been proposed had Lonergan begun by defining the divine persons through the differentiations of the divine essence by relations.

However that may be, the danger of the alternative that would abandon the psychological analogy altogether, the alternative preferred by Ratzinger and, following Ratzinger, by Balthasar, contains a different problem, and one that I find more serious, namely, the collapse, in the very notion of person, of personal responsibility and legitimate autonomy under God. What is at stake here is not only the abandonment of the positive fruit of the anthropological turn that is responsible first for the axial shift that moved humanity intellectually beyond mythic consciousness and into philosophy, science, and theology, and then practically and politically beyond collectivist societies and into democratic institutions collaborating for the advancement of the human good. There is also potential jeopardy to the primacy of conscience contained in these suggestions. Such a move becomes especially questionable if it would link itself to a notion of person, even of Trinitarian person, that misses the most essential ingredient in the analogy, namely, autonomous and responsible freedom under God adopting and assenting to a vocation for mission, where the vocation is *gratia operans* and the assent *gratia cooperans*. At the heart of any valid psychological analogy for Trinitarian processions must be the autonomous spiritual processions that in human beings constitute the interiority of authentic subjects precisely in their responsibility for their own human acts vis-à-vis the human good, and so for the human community to which they are internally related.

Thus I am heading toward a higher viewpoint on the theological notion of person, one that sublates the work of Balthasar and Lonergan into a more complete position. I will begin with comments on the respective histories of the notion of person provided by Lonergan and Balthasar. This will lead me to suggest that Balthasar's insistence on beginning with a Christology of consciousness and following that with a Christology of being or a treatment of the ontological constitution of Christ is problematic. Only after one has worked out the psychological constitution of Christ on the basis of Christ's ontological constitution may one turn the tables and proceed in the reverse direction. For then one's position on the consciousness (indeed consciousnesses, something that Balthasar does not seem to want to admit) of Christ will be correct, and on that basis one's full Christology can follow an order that roots Jesus concretely in the historical details of his life: the One who proceeds eternally and necessarily is, in the Incarnation, also contingently sent into human history, with a very precise mission, a mission to be uncovered in the work of critical-realist exegesis. The *esse secundarium* of the Incarnation is the created external term that is the consequent condition of the procession of the Son in eternal filiation also being the visible mission of the Son in Jesus of Nazareth. The historical details of the life of Jesus reflect both dimensions.

In all these instances I am trying to point toward a third step beyond the twofold ordering of ideas that can be found in the doctrinal and theological tradition to this point. Moreover, despite the relative adequacy of Lonergan's position on Christ's consciousnesses, there still remain questions that must be answered. I hope to begin to resolve at least one of those questions in the inquiry that I am beginning here, namely, the question of the conscious relation of the divine and human consciousnesses of Christ. As I have already indicated, I wish to express that relation as the intimate relation between *processio* consciousness (divine) and *missio* consciousness (human), joined in the one person of the eternal divine Word become flesh. Lonergan's thesis on the two consciousnesses of Christ[16] is the last in a series of theological conclusions drawn from his understanding of the scriptural and conciliar doctrines. Such conclusions are theological doctrines. They are not yet systematic theology, whose province it is to offer a hypothetical understanding of what one has already affirmed in faith. Lonergan has established *that* "there are in the incarnate Word two distinct consciousnesses, a divine and a human consciousness; by these two, nevertheless, one and the same divine person is present to himself in both a divine and a human way."[17] The task of the systematic theologian remains: How is this to be understood?[18]

2   Lonergan's History of the Notion of Person

Before moving to an assertion that affirms that the divine relations studied in the previous chapter are the distinct persons we know as Father, Son, and Holy Spirit, Lonergan treats in a question (10) many things that have been said about "person," beginning with treatments of person in the history of Western Christian theology and, extending in modern times beyond theology, in philosophy. He reduces these to a unity that he finds first in Augustine's heuristic question "Three what?" and then in a definition of person that appears as such in a single text of Thomas Aquinas, and in modified form in a few more.

Lonergan reviews the history of the notion of person beginning with Augustine and extending into the twentieth century. Thus he begins with a theological notion that itself has been taken over in philosophical circles with or without acknowledgment of its theological roots. He concludes that five components have been differentiated in Western thought, all of which, he says, must enter in one way or another not only into the contemporary notion of person but also into the notion that will be employed when it is affirmed that the real divine relations are indeed themselves distinct persons. Moreover, none of these five components is sufficient on its own or in isolation from the others.

Despite the open admission of the insufficiency of any of the components on its own, however, Lonergan claims that Aquinas's definition of person as "subsistens distinctum in natura intellectuali," "a distinct subsistent in an intellectual nature," is indeed sufficient to account for all five components, even those that emerged into the discussion after Thomas. I find this claim questionable, at least in the manner in which Lonergan defends it in his systematics of the Trinity. It represents an overestimation of, or perhaps better an exclusive attention to, the cognitional dimensions of the person, something characteristic of the so-called "early Lonergan." It is a claim that was made before Lonergan acknowledged a distinct fourth level of intentional consciousness, a level whose operations are not simply an extension of intellectual and rational activity. For the Lonergan of *Insight*, "deliberation and decision, choice and will" are an "extension of intellectual activity."[19] That position obtains also in his working out of the meaning of "distinct subsistent in an intellectual nature" in both *The Ontological and Psychological Constitution of Christ* and *The Triune God: Systematics*. The emergence of the transcendental notion of value, the recognition of feelings as the locus of the apprehension of values, and the distinction of a new set of operations often involved in existential issues took some time to unfold in Lonergan's development. From my experience of editing most of his Collected Works, I am not sure that the position that is clearly set forth in *Method in Theology* was firmly in place until around 1967 or 1968. However that might be, Lonergan admits the development: "In *Insight* the good was the intelligent and reasonable. In *Method* the good is a distinct notion. It is intended in questions for deliberation: Is this worthwhile? Is it truly or only apparently good? It is aspired to in the intentional response of feeling to values. It is known in judgments of value made by a virtuous or authentic person with a good conscience. It is brought about by deciding and living up to one's decisions. Just as intelligence sublates sense, just as reasonableness sublates intelligence, so deliberation sublates and thereby unifies knowing and feeling."[20] In *Insight*, on the other hand, existential issues, issues that are aesthetic and dramatic, ethical and religious, are sometimes constrained to fit into the narrower confines of strictly cognitional operations alone.

Thus, the notion of "intellectual nature" in the Latin texts where Lonergan discusses "person," namely, *De constitutione Christi ontologica et psychologica* (1956, unchanged in subsequent printings)[21] and *Divinarum personarum* (1957, and unchanged in this section in the 1964 *De Deo trino: Pars*

systematica), remains almost exclusively at the level of cognitional operations. No matter how essential Lonergan's notion of the cognitional subject
may be – and without it we could have no further development on these
key issues – I don't believe we can leave the notion of the person there and
assert that it is sufficient to account for later developments in the evolution
of the notion itself. If cognitional operations were not sufficient to account
for Lonergan's own development beyond cognitional theory to a fuller intentionality analysis, then they certainly are not sufficient to account for
historical developments in the notion of person beyond the limitation to
cognitional operations found in the definition "distinct subsistent in an intellectual nature," at least as Lonergan explains this definition. If the self-
affirmation of the knower in chapter 11 of *Insight* is not sufficient to account for the other dimensions of the conscious subject highlighted not
only in Lonergan's later works but even in the final chapters of *Insight* itself,
then a notion of the person purely as knower cannot account for the person as existential agent and as lover.[22]

It did not take Lonergan long to acknowledge this quite explicitly. It may
be the case – and as I study this material I am more and more convinced
that it *is* the case – that Lonergan's development on notions related to the
understanding of what a person is, which are closely related to the successive expansions or enlargements of his notion of conscious intentionality,
is more important than some realize. The sections on person in *De constitutione Christi* and *De Deo trino: Pars systematica* cannot be taken as expressing
his definitive position on the issue. They are at best steps along the way to a
much more inclusive viewpoint that shifts the basic meaning of some terms
and relations, and so that is precisely what in *Insight* he calls a *higher* viewpoint. That more inclusive viewpoint could be honored very simply, as I suggested above in thesis 80, by changing "distinct subsistent in an intellectual
nature" to "distinct subsistent in a spiritual nature": a change that parallels
the movement that I suggested in *Missions and Processions*, for the same rea-
sons, from "intellectual emanation" to "autonomous spiritual processions."

At any rate, the five components treated by Lonergan in the history of
reflections on person are

(1) Augustine's heuristic notion of person;
(2) the medieval definitions of person, among which Thomas's
"distinct subsistent in an intellectual nature" is, says Lonergan,
to be preferred;
(3) various accounts by theologians of the ontological constitution
of a person;
(4) the turn to the subject and consequent accounts of the person
from the standpoint of consciousness; and
(5) a more contemporary insistence on the person as interpersonal.

2.1 Augustine's Heuristic Notion of Person

For Augustine, "person" is what there are three of in God. "Person" is a common name: what singly we call Father, Son, and Holy Spirit commonly we name persons. What are there three of in God? Augustine proposed the generic term "person" as signifying neither diversity of essence nor singularity of distinction. His intention was that, as the divine unity would be understood by speaking of one essence, so also the Trinity would be understood by speaking of three persons. The notion of divine person is the very question, Three what? With as simple a question as that, a heuristic structure is established. But little more than perplexity occurs by way of response to the question seeking a more specific term.[23]

2.2 Definitions

Second, efforts were made at defining what a person is. The best known are those of Boethius, Richard of St Victor, and Thomas Aquinas. For Boethius a person is an individual substance of a rational nature ("rationalis naturae substantia individua"). For Richard of St Victor a *divine* person is an incommunicable existence of the divine nature ("divinae naturae existentia incommunicabilis"). And for Aquinas, a person is a distinct subsistent in an intellectual nature ("subsistens distinctum in natura intellectuali"). Here there is an effort at answering not just the particular question "Three what?" but the general question "What is a person?" For Lonergan, the definitions of Boethius and Richard are steps along the way to that of Aquinas, and yet even for Lonergan the definition of Aquinas does not contain *in an explicit manner* all of the requisite elements in the notion of person, even though Lonergan claims it is capacious enough to incorporate them.

Now it must be noted that the definition that Lonergan cites from Aquinas, "subsistens distinctum in natura intellectuali," is found in these precise terms only in the early work *Super I Sententiarum*, d. 23, a. 1, q. 4 c. This does not mean that Aquinas abandoned the definition in later works: it is drawn upon in *De potentia*, q. 9, a. 4 c., where a human person is "subsistens distinctum in natura humana" and a divine person "subsistens distinctum in natura divina," but where Boethius's definition is also accepted without question. Moreover, in the *Summa contra Gentiles*, book 4, chapter 35, Aquinas writes, "omne quod subsistit in intellectuali vel rationali natura habet rationem personae," "whatever subsists in an intellectual or rational nature has the formality of person." And in q. 29 of the *Summa theologiae*, it is likely that Aquinas treated Boethius's definition as if it really meant precisely what he meant by "subsistens distinctum in natura intellectuali." Thus in article 3 he speaks of person as meaning what is most perfect in the whole of nature, namely, "subsistens in rationali natura," "what subsists in a rational nature."

2.3 Metaphysical Theories

Third, a number of more or less metaphysical theories were put forward –
by Scotus, Capreolus, Cajetan, Suárez, Tiphanus, and others – in an effort
to compare the definitions clearly and distinctly with one another. These
theories proceeded by clarifying such metaphysical questions as: What is an
intellectual nature? a substance? an individual? existence? incommunicable? a subsistent? something distinct? While Lonergan will find difficulties
with each of these theories, he does not deny the need for an account of the
ontological constitution of a person. Lonergan's position on the issue will
begin from the affirmation that a divine person is "a subsistent relation or
a subsistent that is distinct by reason of a relation."[24]

2.4 The Turn to the Subject

Fourth, in modern times a person was said to be defined as consciousness,
or conscious individuality, as a distinct center of consciousness, or in some
other psychological way. This was all part of the general modern movement,
which concerned more than simply the notion of person, to treat matters
epistemologically and psychologically rather than or at least prior to treat-
ing them metaphysically. "Person" also had to be treated in this way.

2.5 Intersubjectivity and Interpersonal Relations

Finally, the epistemological theories proved to be as many as the metaphysical, and so "person" came to be explained in a way that would enable it
to be apprehended concretely: a person is one with whom one enters into
interpersonal relationships, one to whom one says "thou," one simply distinct from "things," one naturally ordained to communication with other
persons, and so on. Here it is not a matter of definitions, but of descriptions
of what each of us should recognize from our vital personal experience.
There is a movement away from all speculation and a return to concrete
life, where one who says "I" and one to whom one says "thou" are persons,
and something of which one says "it" is not a person but a thing. If I may
add a bit to what Lonergan says here, this development acknowledges that
internal relationality, as discussed in thesis 68 in the previous chapter, is a
dimension in the constitution of a person.

2.6 Unity from the Question

There is a unity to be found in this manifold of approaches. It derives from
the question itself "What is a person?" and even more basically from the

question "Three what?" The dynamic orientation of the wondering and inquiring mind constitutes heuristic structures that preserve a unity grounded in the original question even as different responses are offered. So it is with the history of the meaning of "person." But this one heuristic structure also evolves in the course of time, and the evolution enables us to see how the five approaches can be related to one another.

Thus, the particular question of Augustine is not discarded by those who sought a general definition. The definitions need not be overlooked when a deeper inquiry into metaphysical foundations is made, yet that deeper inquiry is necessary because the various definitions cannot be related clearly and distinctly to one another unless the various metaphysical notions are clarified. The metaphysical knowledge of things according to the ultimate causes of being does not exclude a consideration of *conscious* being, and in fact because metaphysical disputes raged on, philosophers had recourse to gnoseological questions and attempted psychological explanations of everything, including the notion of person. Nor does a general consideration of conscious being prevent an investigation of self-conscious being in its concrete relations with other self-conscious beings.

And so, Lonergan concludes, Father, Son, and Holy Spirit can be called persons, first in name, then by definition, then in terms of metaphysical constitution, then in terms of consciousness, and finally in terms of their relations both to one another and to us. The systematic-theological treatment of the divine persons must include and integrate the five factors.

3   Balthasar's History of the Notion of Person

Balthasar presents a distinct understanding of the history of the notion of person. Balthasar and Lonergan agree that the notion of person was greatly enriched when it received its unique theological meaning, first in Trinitarian matters and then in Christology. But there are differences between them that must also be adjudicated, both with respect to the evaluation of moments in the history and with respect to the theological identification of person with mission.

Balthasar's presentation of the history of the notion of person is more complex than Lonergan's, but it also does not contain some important ingredients that Lonergan emphasizes. Thus it does not grant any significance either to Augustine's heuristic notion or to Aquinas's early definition of person, the definition that Lonergan prefers.

Lonergan's history, as we have seen, begins with the theological enrichment, where for him the first step is Augustine's use of the word "person" to designate what there are three of in God. For Lonergan this question sets up the heuristic structure that has guided reflection on "person" ever since, whether by theologians or by philosophers, and in doing so begins the course of theological enrichment of the notion of person.

Balthasar speaks not of a heuristic structure governed by a question but of a string that might guide us through the "mazelike garden" of complexity in the use of the word "person."[25] The two major features of the string are more than a question originating a heuristic structure. They consist in *content* that is more than heuristic: (1) the distinction between individual and person, and (2) the vacillation of the meaning of the word "person" between a commonsense meaning that was already operative before the theological enrichment and the subsequent Christian theological meaning.

Balthasar thus stresses that the theological question already had a content that presumably – even though Balthasar does not address Augustine's question – would have encouraged Augustine to use the word "person" rather than some other term for what there are three of in God. Lonergan, in contrast, does not tell us *why* Augustine chose to use the word "person" rather than some other word. Surely, however, he presumes it must have been because of something about the meaning of that word as it already functioned in more or less ordinary discourse and in the earlier theological tradition. The heuristic anticipation structured by Augustine's "Three what?" is not the same as the mathematician's "Let *x* be the unknown number." "Person" already had a content that made it a worthy candidate for designating what there are three of in God. What that might have been is at least suggested by Balthasar's use of a study by Carl Andresen in which the literary method of allotting parts of a text to several *characters* or *roles* is applied to the doctrine of the Trinity. "In Justin, Tertullian, Hippolytus, Clement and Origen, we frequently find that a passage of Scripture is said to be uttered '*ex persona Patris*' or '*Filii*' or '*Spiritus*'; this comes from the Stoic interpretation of Homer, later adopted by Platonists in order to denote the 'characters' who, in the Platonic dialogues, put forward Plato's own views … what we have here is the prelude not only to the concept of 'person' but also to that of a person-in-dialogue."[26]

On individual and person (the first part of Balthasar's "string"), he writes, "If one distinguishes between *individual* and *person* (and we should for the sake of clarity), then a special dignity is ascribed to the person, which the individual as such does not possess … [W]e will speak … of 'individuals' when primarily concerned with the identity of human nature, to which, of course, a certain dignity cannot be denied insofar as all human beings are spiritual subjects. We will speak of a 'person', however, when considering the uniqueness, the incomparability and therefore irreplaceability of the individual."[27] The difference may be understood in Aristotelian-Thomist-Lonerganian terms as that between prime potency as the principle of individuation in a purely material or empirical fashion and the inevitability of form emerging or failing to emerge in the *dramatic* history of one's life. "Individual" obviously is being used here not in the positive Jungian sense of "individuation" nor in the sense of Karl Jaspers' axial emergence of the significance of the individual but in a manner closer to the purely meta-physical sense of prime matter or prime potency. Balthasar uses "individual" to refer to "the conscious subject" who "knows *that* he is such ... that he is human in a unique and incommunicable way," but who does not "also know *who* he is," how he is "not only quantitatively but also qualitatively different from all other conscious subjects."[28]

For Balthasar this qualitative difference cannot be provided "either by the nonpersonal, empirical world nor by our fellow men" and women. It can only be given "by the absolute Subject, God."[29]

Just a word of caution, to indicate where I am heading: that Balthasar's insistence on the role of God in the emergence of personhood must entail the explicit knowledge of a vocation or mission remains to be demonstrated. Grace is always operative in the emergence of a genuine person, whether or not those affected by it *know* that this is the case. That the emergence into *genuine or authentic* personhood, into what Lonergan calls "personal value" in the scale of values, demands grace seems to me to be clear. But that the grace must also entail the personal *cognitive recognition* of a vocation or mission explicitly from God is questionable.

At any rate, Balthasar's history of the notion of "person," while it starts with pretheological sources, prescinds from earlier cultures – what in *Theology and the Dialectics of History* I called cosmological cultures – in which personal incomparability was limited to select individuals or a select few. It begins "at the point in [humankind's] development when the human being ... stands in the tension between the individual and the person."[30] While he does not say as much, Balthasar would thus begin his history with what Jaspers has called the axial period, which could be understood as marked by a transition from cosmological to anthropological and/or soteriological constitutive meaning.[31] Even Israel had not reached this point prior to the emergence in the major prophets of an insistence on personal responsi-bility in history under God. In Israel this emergence did not pass through, but rather set up the possibility of, anthropological constitutive meaning, which emerges on its own in the wisdom literature, after being prefigured in the later prophets and perhaps especially in the book of Ezekiel. Israel went directly from cosmological to soteriological constitutive meaning under the power of divine revelation and in fact of divine liberation not only from slavery but also from the exclusively cosmological constitutive meanings of ancient Egypt, and only then to anthropological components, under the influence of Greek philosophy. The extent to which other ax-ial cultures enjoyed an analogous soteriological moment on their way to the acknowledgment of "person" remains to be studied. Moreover, even in Israel there is a history that shows some variation in the emphasis placed on the significance of the person's own choices. Many have proposed that this stress is emphasized more in Ezekiel than in previous literature.[32]

As for the vacillation in meaning, Balthasar writes, "the concept of person acquires a completely new sense [new in contrast to an earlier general or philosophical meaning] first in trinitarian doctrine and then in christology."[33] Moreover, "the unique trinitarian or christological content that the concept acquires in theology casts its light back upon the general (or philosophical) understanding without the latter having, therefore, to leave the realm of what is generally human."[34] Thus, "the word *person* in the sense of a human being, and in contradistinction to mere individuality, receives its special dignity in history when it is illuminated by the unique theological meaning. When this is not the case ... the human person sinks back into the sphere of mere individuality."[35]

In the light of Lonergan's cognitional theory and intentionality analysis, we might say that what Balthasar is calling "mere individuality" is known at the level of experience and thus is simply potency for status as person, while human personality is best appropriated by a movement from above so that "person" is defined in terms of potentiality for and exercise of interpersonal, existential, rational, and intelligent activity, that is, influence from what Lonergan would come to acknowledge as a fifth level of consciousness "down" through the fourth to the full cognitional levels of judgment and understanding and then to a decisive enrichment of the level of presentations or "experience." The scale of values that is so central to my own theological vision is this structure writ large, objectified in history. Lonergan's presentation in *De constitutione Christi* and *De Deo trino* has not yet reached this rich fullness of meaning, a fullness signalled more by the definition "distinct subsistent in a spiritual nature" than by "distinct subsistent in an intellectual nature."

Further, in terms of what we have already said in commenting on Lonergan's notion of relations, we might link an exclusive regard of others in terms of "mere individuality" with the neo-liberal assumption, more or less explicit, that all human relations are purely external – "There is no such thing as society; there are only individuals" – while the word "person" with its connotations of human dignity connotes the realization of constitutive internal relationality. What is important for our own considerations is that both Lonergan and Balthasar point to the theological influence that lies behind the development of such a notion of person. What Balthasar is calling incomparability and irreplaceability is also the condition of possibility of interpersonal relations. It is persons, not individuals, in Balthasar's sense of these terms, who relate to one another.

Despite the fact that he began his history earlier than Lonergan did, the central elements in Balthasar's development of the notion of person match some of those of Lonergan. This is the case even with regard to the reason Lonergan prefers the early definition of Aquinas to that of Boethius (even if Aquinas himself seems to have interpreted Boethius's definition in the light of his own). "Subsistens *distinctum*" replaces "substantia *individua*," which at least for Lonergan suggests three gods. Distinction, *distinctum*, is not known at the level of sensitive experience, as is individuality, but at the level of judgment. Moreover, the ground of interpersonal communication for Lonergan is the "incommunicability" of personal identity that Balthasar expresses in terms of incomparability and irreplaceability. Lonergan does not put as much stress on this in his initial presentation of the notion of person as perhaps he should, but it stands out clearly when he turns his attention to the divine persons precisely in their relations to one another, and then in his later extensive enrichments of the notion of the human person as incarnate subject functioning as intermediary in the scale of values between divine grace and the cultural meanings and values that would inform a flourishing set of social relations in the economic and political orders.

The postaxial but pre-Trinitarian history of the word "person" that Balthasar traces is familiar.

> The derivation of *persona* from the Etruscan *phersu* is almost universally recognized today. *Phersu* evidently denoted a mask, or the wearer of the mask, at festivals in honor of P(h)ersephone. On the stage, *persona* could denote both the actor (the one who puts the masks on), or the role (hence generally the "assignment") as well as the character represented – Oedipus, for example – or by extension that which is essential, the personal character, that which carries meaning (the "legal person"), or simply "this particular one." With these origins we are close to a philosophy influential today once again that each individual human life has the character of a role.[36]

Balthasar goes on to trace a set of gradual transpositions that led right into the Trinitarian and Christological implications found in Ambrose and Augustine. Augustine, again, was drawing on already sedimented meanings when he chose the word *persona* to designate what there are three of in God. Thus, while Balthasar overlooks this heuristic aspect of the Augustinian step in the history of the notion, he does call to our attention an earlier statement of Tertullian's, which indicates that the theological enrichment began earlier. "Tertullian could already have drawn on a concept of person prepared in various ways when he wrote about Christ that amazing sentence which seems to have anticipated everything that was to come later. *Videmus duplicem statum non confusum sed coniunctum in una persona deum et hominem Jesum.*"[37] The precise sense of "persona" in this statement is disputed, says Balthasar, but whatever it meant the statement itself remained without effect, which might explain why Lonergan did not mention it. Still, "the concept of person emerges almost at the same time in other church authors, and the Latin meaning of *persona* as a real spiritual subject (and not only as 'role') gains increasing importance in theology."[38] Again, there is a content already available to Augustine that makes it more than simply a heuristic notion of an unknown.

Still, Balthasar wonders, to what extent did "real spiritual subject" include relationality in a sufficiently explicit fashion? In particular, Balthasar asks, did Chalcedon's "establishing that in Christ two natures, the divine and the human, are united in one (divine) person ... [pay] sufficient attention to the fact that *this divine person can, as such, exist only in a (Trinitarian) relation,* for otherwise we would end up with a doctrine of three gods?"[39] Most importantly for Balthasar, this inattention might have been "the prelude to the famous first philosophical definition of *person* by Boethius (480–524): *persona est naturae rationalis individua substantia.*" Balthasar's translation of this definition is telling of his evaluation of it: "A person is the individual *standing-in-itself* of a spiritual nature."[40] Clearly, Balthasar, like Lonergan, finds it extremely difficult to apply the term thus understood to God. Lonergan stresses that the difficulty lies in the danger of ending up with three substances in God because of a lack of relationality in the definition, whereas for Balthasar the problem is precisely that lack of relationality in the very definition of person. On this they are in agreement.

But Lonergan's preference for Thomas's early definition, "subsistens distinctum in natura intellectuali," removes the difficulty, precisely by leaving open, even if not affirming, the possibility of three subsistent *relations* (not *substantiae individuae*) in one substance. Internal relationality can be constitutive of the one who is defined as "a distinct subsistent in an intellectual nature," especially if that intellectual nature is the divine nature. I have not found Balthasar referring to this early definition of Aquinas. He says simply that Thomas "holds to Boethius's" definition or makes only minor changes. But he insists that Thomas had "all sorts of difficulties" in applying Boethius's definition to God. Part of Balthasar's difficulty is that for him Boethius's definition levels the difference between person and individual, a difference that should have been established by the time of Boethius. "Person" had already taken on a relational significance with the identification of the Trinitarian persons as subsistent relations, but Boethius's definition, at least for Balthasar, overlooked this significance, and perhaps carried forward a neglect of this significance that might, Balthasar suggests, already have been lurking in the Chalcedonian statement of Christological faith. Even if I would prefer to raise this question, not about the Chalcedonian meaning in its original context, but as regards its effective history, Balthasar's basic question is sound: did Chalcedon's definition of two natures in one person sufficiently stress that the one person of Christ is himself a subsistent *relation?*

The next step that Balthasar takes, however, is one that I believe must be strongly challenged. For this question leads him to relate his discussion to Joseph Ratzinger's description of Augustine's "unfortunately decisive abbreviation" of the concept of person, an "abbreviation" that occurs when Augustine places the image of the Trinity in "the single individual" (memory, understanding, and will). Note the language: "the single individual," not the person. At this point, in my estimation, Balthasar reveals his own (and Ratzinger's) under-appreciation of what became the so-called psychological analogy. Even Balthasar seems to applaud "the Latin meaning of *persona* as a real spiritual subject (and not only as 'role')."[41] But the psychological analogy that is prefigured in Augustine emphasizes "real spiritual subject" much more than does any Ratzingerian alternative. Far from being an "unfortunately decisive abbreviation," it is a decisive advance toward maturity. It does not exclude relationality from the definition of person but rather grounds authentic relationality. Nobody who has read Lonergan's mature appropriation of the psychological analogy could make the charge of non-relationality, but I also do not believe it can be made against Augustine himself or against Aquinas. All that Balthasar will concede to Augustine is that he "certainly understood the relational and dialogical character of the persons in God," even as "he placed the image of the Trinity in created man completely in the single individual."[42] In contrast, let us listen again to the later Lonergan: "*The psychological analogy, then, has its starting point in that higher synthesis of intellectual, rational, and moral consciousness that is the dynamic state of being in love.* Such love manifests itself in its judgments of value. And the judgments are carried out in decisions that are acts of loving. *Such is the analogy found in the creature.*"[43] Nobody can call this "non-relational" or "individualistic," even if it is centered in the spiritual subject who alone makes such judgments and decisions.

But what about Aquinas? Balthasar criticizes *Summa theologiae*, 1, q. 29, a. 3, ad 2m, to the effect that "the concept [of person] is applied to God solely on the basis of the idea of dignity. The relation of the divine persons to one another is not mentioned here at all but only when the unity of the divine essence must be defended."[44] From this comment on a single passage, Balthasar moves to the very strong statement, "High Scholasticism is no longer aware that the dignity, which it here ascribes to the person (in distinction to the mere individual), is ultimately indebted to the light shed by theology" on the meaning of person.[45]

To this I would reply that the concept of person is applied to God in this response solely on the basis of the idea of dignity because Thomas is responding to a particular objection. There is no intention to make that restriction universal. Balthasar has chosen one passage and used it to convey the impression that q. 29 itself and even "High Scholasticism" (by which he means primarily Thomas) is skewed in this direction. Such an interpretation is hard to defend in light of the fact that Thomas introduced question 29 with the explicit connection of what will be said about the divine persons with what has already been said about the divine processions *and relations,* and even more in light of the fact that in precisely the next article, q. 29, a. 4, the relational quality of person, even when person is defined in Boethian terms, is stressed.

What I wish to highlight, though, is (1) that Aquinas is also aware of yet another characteristic of person, one that is not opposed to relationality but is rather the source of authentic relationality in the autonomous spiritual processions that characterize the authentic person, and (2) that Balthasar and Ratzinger might not want to go there with Thomas. True, article 1 of question 29 defends Boethius's definition. But it does so because individual substances of a rational nature, as understood by Aquinas, "habent dominium sui actus et non solum aguntur, sicut alia, sed per se agunt," "*exercise dominion over their own acts and not only are acted upon, as are other beings, but also act on the basis of their own resources*": precisely the emphasis I have tried to convey in the expression "autonomous spiritual processions" and in defending existential autonomy as the proper sphere of the analogy, in contradistinction to the lack of self-possession acknowledged in Girardian mimetic theory, where individuals "aguntur," are acted upon, and do not "per se agunt," act on the basis of their own resources. "Non solum aguntur sed per se agunt" is an attribute of irreplaceable persons, not of replaceable individuals. Having "dominium sui actus" is a condition of the possibility of authentic interpersonal relations, not a denial of them. This is, I believe, an important qualification that must be made to the steps that Balthasar, following Ratzinger, is taking at this point.

Before we comment on what Balthasar says about the modern understanding of person, we should mention that Balthasar pays fuller attention than does Lonergan to the definition of person proposed by Richard of St Victor. Lonergan mentions without much comment Richard's definition of a *divine* person as "divinae naturae existentia incommunicabilis," an incommunicable existence of a divine nature, but he fails to note that Richard also gives a more generic definition of person: incommunicable existence – period. "… nihil aliud est persona quam incommunicabilis existentia."[46]

Now, on Balthasar's interpretation Richard is attempting to go beyond Boethius's purely philosophical definition to emphasize that a person is "a spiritual subject that earns the name *person* only by going out beyond itself (*ex*), and that when this is applied analogously to God the going out beyond itself is purely relative." Balthasar cites Richard: "per adjunctam 'ex' prepositionem notari potest quod (persona) pertinet ad aliam" ("through the *ex* in *ex-sisten-tia* let it be noted that person refers to, is ordered to, another").[47]

Another interpretation of Richard's ordering to another has been given, however, and it seems preferable. According to this alternate interpretation, the "ex" in "ex-sistentia" means "to be *out from*," to be *with regard to the origin of one's being*. One is a *distinct* divine person *solely* by the way in which one can be considered to be "out from" another. This is precisely what is meant by divine personhood. A divine person is an incommunicable "being out from." Or more precisely, a divine person is defined in relation to the manner in which that person is "out from." The Father is "out from" no other. The Son is "out from" the Father. The Holy Spirit is "out from" the Father and the Son. Precisely because the way of standing in relation to being "out from" is different for each of the three, a divine person is an incommunicable "being out from" in the divine nature or substance.

The only unfortunate aspect in this interpretation is the word "out." "Being from" would be sufficient, I believe. The insistence on "out," whether in Balthasar's sense or in this other interpretation, possibly conveys the same problems that are included in Balthasar's insistence on "distance" as marking the divine relations. Procession *is* conveyed by "being out from," whereas it does not have a place in Balthasar's "going out beyond oneself." But it is also conveyed, and perhaps better, simply by "being from," which also sufficiently captures the meaning of "ex" without the spatial connotation of "out." And procession is precisely what characterizes the personhood of the Word who became incarnate in Jesus.

At any rate, Balthasar is correct that Richard refused to use the Boethian "substantia" for a divine person. "Substance" is properly used only of the divine being that itself is constituted by three quite distinct instances or ways of "being from." "It is common to two alone [Father and Son] to give all plenitude. It is common to two alone [Son and Holy Spirit] to receive plenitude. It is common to two alone [Father and Holy Spirit] not to have both. For the property of one [Father] is in giving alone; the property of another [Holy Spirit] is in receiving alone; while the property of a third [Son] is in receiving and giving. It is common to two alone [Father and Son] to have a person proceeding from them. It is common to two alone [Son and Holy Spirit] to proceed from another. It is common to two alone [Father and Holy Spirit] not to have both. For the property of one [Father] is to have another proceeding from him; the property of another [Holy Spirit] is to proceed; while the property of a third [Son] is to proceed from another as well as to have another proceeding from him."[48] Thus the "reference to another" implied by the preposition "ex" is not, as Balthasar seems to say, a "going out beyond" oneself *to* another but rather a "being from" another. They are incommunicable in that each stands in a unique way to that characteristic of "being from."[49]

Finally, for Richard the key unifying factor in the divine relations having to do with "being from" is not knowledge but love. The three distinct ways of being with regard to "being from" are three distinct ways of "being in love," in fact of *being* "being-in-love." The Father's love is purely gratuitous. It receives from none, and it gives to the other two. The Son's love is mixed. It receives from the Father, and it gives to the Holy Spirit. The Holy Spirit's love is purely indebted. It receives from the Father and the Son, and it gives to none. The three share love, each in a unique way. Each love is equal to the others, for each loves the other two because of or for the unique way of loving proper to the other two.

This interpretation of Richard supports my contention that Jesus' divine consciousness is the consciousness of the One who is eternally "from" the Father, and his human consciousness is the "mission consciousness" of the Word become flesh and contingently "sent" by or from the Father, a consciousness grounded in the created external term, the secondary act of existence, which is the consequent created condition of this procession being also a mission. This is why I have introduced Richard into the conversation. There are other riches in Richard's expression that I regret I have to omit here. But I do wish to indicate that this interpretation of Richard bears a great deal of similarity to Lonergan's efforts to formulate a new expression of the analogy in an aborted seventh chapter of *De Deo trino: Pars systematica.*[50]

At any rate, Balthasar's history continues on the basis of his view that the option for the Boethian definition shows what was lost in so-called High Scholasticism. And so his reading of what for Lonergan was the fourth step in the history, namely, the turn to consciousness, is far less benign than Lonergan's. "… the philosophical 'independence' of the person sought first to define itself as subjective self-consciousness (Descartes), and this independence then absolutized itself very soon (Spinoza, Hegel) so that the individuals had to give themselves up to this Absolute. Kant's attempt to save the dignity of the person could not halt this drift. For even though it was demanded that the other person be respected, the absoluteness of the person was anchored simply in his ethical freedom. Thus there was nothing preserved of a fundamental interrelatedness of persons – as a meaningfully understood *imago Trinitatis* would have demanded."[51]

Moreover, how the evolving notion of person moved to what Lonergan would have called its fifth stage – interpersonal relations – was, says Balthasar, "paradoxical": "… after a personless idealism met its end in Hegel, the popular atheistic materialism of a Feuerbach had to rediscover the elementary fact that there simply cannot be a single person, existing within himself, but that existence as a person comes about only in the relationship between the I and Thou." So strong is Balthasar's opposition to the psychological analogy that he proposes that "the atheistic materialist was the one who reached *beyond Augustine* to the insight about what man is, in Christian terms, as the personal *imago Trinitatis*."[52] Only after a century of Jewish and Christian attempts to draw from the biblical heritage with regard to the meaning of "person," "[f]irst with Guardini, then more strongly with Mounier, Gabriel Marcel, and Denis de Rougement does something of a true image of the Trinity appear – in any case, the connection of the I, which is open to the Thou and the We and which realizes itself only in self-giving, with the image of man in Scripture, and above all in the New Testament."[53] But a passage from de Rougemont that Balthasar cites implicitly appeals to the individuation that in fact is reflected in the "dominium sui actus" of those who "agunt, non solum aguntur." The choice recommended by de Rougement is to "accept an always urgent *vocation* that distinguishes the human being and binds him at the same time to his neighbor and founds the church." But that acceptance can be done only in the exercise of one's autonomous spiritual identity. The necessity of the step that insists on "dominium sui actus" is overlooked if one views the Augustinian position as simply an "unfortunately decisive abbreviation" or if one holds, as Balthasar implies at least in the passage quoted above, that we must move (with Feuerbach!) *beyond Augustine* to discover how the human person is an *imago Trinitatis*.

Nonetheless – and here we come to the aspect of Balthasar's thought from which we will attempt to distill a real and genuine position that can be integrated into a higher unity with Lonergan's view – while for de Rougemont person is "concrete obedience to a transcendent vocation," what de Rougement calls "vocation" Balthasar names "mission." The meaning is explicitly Trinitarian, as Balthasar's citation of John 20.21 shows: "As the Father has sent me, so I send you." In a statement entirely in agreement with what we have seen in Lonergan and Thomas, Balthasar writes, "in a Trinitarian sense *missio* is the economic form of the eternal *processio* that constitutes the persons of the Son and of the Spirit in God. Participation in the mission of Christ (or that which in the building up of the church Paul calls 'charisma' and which is given to each as his eternal idea with God and his social task) – that would be the actual core of the reality of the person."[54] In terms that match my own concerns, he adds, "The world situation today shows clearly enough that whoever discards this Christian or at least biblical view (in theology or philosophy) must in one way or another find in a personless collectivism or individualism (which converge upon one another) his downfall."[55]

4   Lonergan on Person

We have treated the respective histories of the notion of person offered by Lonergan and Balthasar. I have indicated the direction in which I plan to take the discussion. Now, despite my view that the theological notion of person as mission proposed by Hans Urs von Balthasar will find its way in a trans-formed fashion into my treatment of these issues, I begin with Lonergan as I move toward filling out the details of my own definition of person: *a distinct subsistent in a spiritual nature.* Part of the reason for doing so is precisely to avoid the danger mentioned above, one to which Balthasar's thought, including his notion of mission, is prone: the danger of (1) overlooking the significance of existential autonomy under God in the spiritual processions that are identical with what Thomas and Lonergan call intelligible emanations, and (2) moving too quickly to a variant of *communio* theology that I regard as ideological. The church is *communio on mission,* yes, but it is not *communio* alone. Our volume 1, *Missions and Processions,* involved a close reading of much of the material in Lonergan's chapter on the processions of Word and Holy Spirit and offered what I hope is a careful restatement of some of that material in the light of accepting the theological doctrine that the missions are the processions joined to created external terms that are participations in the divine relations. The previous chapter in this volume involved a similarly close reading and careful restatement of Lonergan's chapter on the divine relations in light of a similar identification of the missions and the relations. Now our treatment of the theology of the divine persons must express an appropriation but also an adaptation for present purposes of elements from Lonergan's two chapters on the divine persons, again from the standpoint of specifying *how and under what conditions we might identify the missions of the Word and the Spirit with the persons of the Word and the Spirit joined to appropriate created external terms.* Balthasar will be drawn upon to help in this undertaking, since he has in a sense forced into the open the issue of the relation of person and mission. But again, I am going to follow Lonergan's order, partly in order to point to, but also to move beyond, the shortcomings of his early notion of person, which still governs the discussion in *The Triune God: Systematics,* but even more to enable us to meet the shortcomings in Balthasar's procedures. Just as one has to accept as a permanent contribution Lonergan's work in the *ordo doctrinae* in Trinitarian theology before realizing that, on the basis of that work, one may now compose a Trinitarian theology that starts from the missions precisely as created reflections of the divine processions, so too one has to accept Lonergan's understanding of the ontological constitution of Christ before beginning anew with what Balthasar calls "a christology of consciousness."[56] This, I fear, is what Balthasar has not done, and I hope to show that it is what has to be done if we are to reap fully the benefits of his position on the relation of person and mission.

There are two major sections to Lonergan's treatment of the divine persons considered in themselves, that is, as distinct persons. In the first, the notion of person is clarified and applied to the divine persons. In the second, the attributes and properties of the divine persons are investigated, along with the notional acts. In the present chapter I address only part of the first of these sections. I treat only the clarification of the notion of person. This, plus the material from Lonergan's chapter 5 that I have already mentioned regarding the three subjects of one divine consciousness, will be sufficient for our present purposes.

But I will also indicate briefly how Lonergan's notion of person eventually was expanded beyond what appears in *The Triune God: Systematics*. Lonergan's own notion of the person developed beyond what he says on the issue in his systematic work on the Trinity, even if the basis of the expansion is already provided there, and it has been developed further by others, including, I hope, by myself. All of that must be put forward here, however briefly.

I will then conclude the chapter with some exposition and critique of Balthasar's way of appealing to Christology to ground his own notion of person. Person for Balthasar already is mission. I question his way of making this identification, but I also find in his work a procedure that will enable us to salvage from him an element very important for the unfolding of my own position. Lonergan will be partly supplemented by Balthasar, but Balthasar also by Lonergan. In any event, mission will enter into our discussion and decisively influence it.

4.1 Resuming Lonergan's History of the Notion of Person

We can best move toward the explicit notion of person advanced by Lonergan in *The Triune God: Systematics* if we begin with Lonergan's recognition that more must be said about the history of the notion of person. The heuristic structure set up by Augustine's question "Three what?" evolved. But it evolved only because *questions* emerged at each stage of the process.

4.1.1 Boethius's Definition

Lonergan begins with the problems found in Boethius's definition, "rationalis naturae substantia individua." As we have seen, the difficulty Lonergan finds in applying this definition to the Trinity (although it can be properly done, as Lonergan indicates Aquinas showed in *Summa theologiae*, 1, q. 29, a. 1)[57] is that the three persons would then seem to be three substances. Since we acknowledge only one substance in God, Boethius's definition, at least in the words it employs and the meaning they spontaneously communicate, poses more problems than it solves.[58] From the period in which definitions were offered, the early definition of Thomas alone remains for Lonergan without objection precisely because it is not as prone to fall victim to this mistake: "subsistens distinctum in natura intellectuali," a distinct subsistent in an intellectual nature. It avoids the problems Lonergan finds in Boethius's definition, since "subsistent" does not necessarily mean "individual substance." It is open to being applied to relations, and in fact to three relations constitutive of one substance. A divine person can be thought of, then, as "a subsistent that is distinct by reason of a relation."[59] In fact, Aquinas himself comes close to his earlier definition in q. 29, a. 3, where person is defined as "subsistens in rationali natura." He seems to be identifying what Boethius means with what his own definition means, even as he continues to employ Boethius's definition most of the time.

Still, I would like to propose that the definition "subsistens distinctum in natura intellectuali," precisely as Lonergan appropriates it in *De constitutione Christi ontologica et psychologica* (to which he refers the reader at this point in *The Triune God: Systematics*), is more of an incremental step along the way than it is a secure base into which the historical developments on the notion of person that occurred after Aquinas, developments in terms of consciousness and interpersonal relations, can easily be fitted. *De constitutione Christi* was written in 1956 and reissued thereafter as needed, without change. But in 1956 Lonergan had yet to expand securely his notion of the subject beyond the first three levels of consciousness. His unfolding of the definition that he prefers from Aquinas still manifests this limitation.

4.1.2 Consciousness

The question about the role of consciousness in the notion of the person represents Lonergan's distinct and major contribution to the notion of person. It is a serious question from a theological point of view. The fourth step in Lonergan's history of the notion of person, the move to consciousness or turn to the subject, contained potential doctrinal pitfalls. While Balthasar fastens almost exclusively on the negative aspects of this modern turn to the subject, Lonergan proceeds first to advance the position or positions contained in this turn. His clarifications with regard to consciousness – whether human consciousness or divine consciousness or the consciousnesses of Christ – are in my view all but necessary if we are going to avoid the pitfalls, but these clarifications would not have been possible had it not been for the history of the turn itself. Lonergan finds the turn itself to be a response to questions that could not be answered in any other way, rather than an arrogant claim to an individual autonomy independent of communion with others or with God.

The doctrinal pitfalls connected with identifying person with consciousness may be expressed quite succinctly. If there are as many consciousnesses as there are persons, then three persons would mean three consciousnesses, and three separate consciousnesses would mean three gods. Again, if from divine unity it follows that there is one consciousness in God, and if the number of persons is the number of consciousnesses, then there is only one person in God; modalism would replace Trinitarian theology. Similarly in Christology, without further clarifications either the unity of the person of Christ would lead to monophysitism or the distinction of two natures to Nestorianism. Two natures in one person means two sets of operations and two wills. This was already dogmatically decided at the Third Council of Constantinople. What Lonergan concludes from this definition is that there must also be two consciousnesses in Jesus and two sets of cognitive operations. Moreover, the consciousness and the knowledge of Christ are distinct questions, as distinct as are consciousness and knowledge themselves. Balthasar appears loath to go in the direction of two consciousnesses in Christ, and his failure to do so is one of the most serious lapses in his presentation of Christology, in my view.[60] But it is doubtful as well whether he has grasped the distinction of consciousness and knowledge. The subtlety of the question of consciousness arises from the very meaning of consciousness. It is one thing to be conscious and another to know one is conscious, in the proper sense of "to know." As Lonergan once pointed out, German-speaking/writing authors will have difficulty with the distinction, since *Bewusstsein*, the German word for "consciousness," literally means "to be *known*."[61] Consciousness is the very presence of the subject to oneself. That presence is effected for human beings whenever our sensitive or intellectual nature is actuated by apprehending or desiring. It matters nothing to our being conscious what object is apprehended or desired; a conscious self consciously apprehends and desires different objects. Nor do we become conscious because of the fact that we turn our attention to ourselves, since consciousness is found on the side of the subject turning, not on the side of the object to which we turn, even if that object is ourselves. With such a turning, however, there begins something else, which we call knowing oneself to be conscious. For the conscious subject sets himself or herself up on the side of the object insofar as he or she understands and conceives consciousness and truly affirms himself or herself to be conscious. Therefore the conscious subject, the consciousness of the subject, precedes and accompanies all understanding and conception and affirmation of oneself as conscious, and remains even if these are lacking or erroneous. But unless we define what consciousness is and truly affirm that we are conscious in the sense intended in the definition, we do not attain to knowledge properly so-called regarding our own consciousness. And then, if we insist on emphasizing the psychological dimensions of the person, we will go astray. A great deal of the controversy surrounding the consciousness of Christ in twentieth-century Thomist circles reflects these problems.[62] And it may be that Balthasar's position is not immune.

Properly human knowledge is accomplished in three steps: first, we experience externally or internally; then by inquiring about data of sense or data of consciousness we come to understand and conceive; and third, by reflecting and weighing the evidence we proceed to affirm the true and, through the true as through a medium, to know what is. But it is one thing to accomplish this process of knowing by these three steps, and it is quite another to know by this same threefold process that our knowledge is accomplished in a threefold process: to experience one's experiencing, understanding, and judging, and then to understand the relations that obtain among one's experiencing, understanding, and judging, and finally to judge that one has understood these matters correctly. This judgment is what Lonergan in *Insight* calls "the self-affirmation of the knower."

If one comes to acknowledge only the first step, one is an empiricist, one for whom nothing is knowable except sensible external things and, perhaps, an empirical internal "ego." While this position is manifestly at variance with the respective philosophers' own inquiring intelligence, still it is defended in many philosophical positions: materialism, sensism, empiricism, phenomenalism, positivism, and some variants of pragmatism. Others, however, clearly and distinctly recognize not only the first but also the second step, but since the same or similar sensible and conscious data are understood differently by different persons, those who acknowledge only the first two steps in the process easily fall into relativism – nothing intelligible can be pronounced true – or immanentism – being is reached only through the true, but the true cannot be known – or idealism – to know anything as true depends upon perfectly understanding everything – or instrumentalism (a form of pragmatism) – each intelligible is true only inasmuch as it leads to favourable consequences. Finally, others not only know by the threefold process but also grasp the nature of those three steps. These are critical realists.[63] In addition, they affirm that, as our knowing is accomplished by experiencing, understanding, and judging, so the being proportionate to it is composed of potency, form, and act.

Lonergan's point is that discussions of consciousness require a subtle grasp of philosophic differences. The positions on consciousness and on knowing are not easily attained, and in fact reaching them demands something along the lines of an intellectual conversion. Minus that, whoever speaks of human consciousness will easily go astray, and if error is so easy concerning human consciousness, all the more easily is it incurred when one proceeds by analogy from human consciousness to a conception of divine consciousness or for that matter to an understanding of the consciousness of Jesus.

Still, the issue cannot be overlooked. Twentieth-century philosophies have emphasized that one can grasp what kind of person one can be, and one can either will to become precisely that or turn away in inauthenticity. The grasping and becoming of the person is, for all practical purposes, the person's "existing," in the existential sense of *Existenz*. And this existing is accomplished not in some ideal solitude but in the concrete circumstances of human life and together with other persons. Even so, it is not an easy step to go from this quite true conception of personal authenticity to an analogical grasp of what a divine person might be. Moreover, writes Lonergan, "far more serious, there is such an emphasis on the subject and such disdain for anything that has the formality of object that this doctrine is incompatible with both faith and traditional theology. Since our faith is an assent to the true ... so that through the mediation of the true we arrive at the divine reality that has been revealed to us, one cannot oppose the whole notion of object and objectivity without at the same time rejecting our faith itself ... [S]ince the Catholic theological tradition is founded upon truth and being, to despise the object is necessarily to despise traditional theology as well ... *[T]o the extent that one ignores rational reflection, the grasp of the virtually unconditioned, the autonomous intellectual necessity whereby the uttering of a true word emanates from reflective under-standing, and the similarly autonomous intellectual necessity consequent upon it, in which moral obligation and the spirating of volition consist – to that extent one surely ignores those features that are most proper to and distinctive of a person.*"[64]

Note how Lonergan, precisely after pointing to the pitfalls in the modern turn to the subject, has very subtly but decisively advanced the position in the same turn, precisely in the words I have emphasized. Advancing the position counteracts ignoring "those features that are most proper to and distinctive of a person." As I argued above, this "ignoring" constitutes the principal problem also in Ratzinger's and Balthasar's criticisms of the Augustinian psychological analogy, despite their correct insistence on the dogmatic necessity of the objectivity of truth. The issue has to do with how one reaches that objectivity. One does not reach it by surrendering dominion over one's own acts in favor of being acted upon by the guiding forces of some ersatz *communio*, however religious the latter may seem. "Genuine objectivity is the fruit of authentic subjectivity,"[65] and authentic subjectivity is named by correctly objectifying the autonomous spiritual processions that constitute the essential ingredients in every valid presentation of the psychological analogy. "Authenticity" is not Heidegger's amoral self-assertion (which may or may not have influenced Balthasar's and Ratzinger's reluctance to use such language) but Lonergan's self-transcendence in cognitive, ethical, and religious operations and processes.

4.1.3 Interpersonal Relations

The final stage in the evolution of the notion of person as it has been traced by Lonergan has to do with interpersonal relations, and similar considerations apply here. They are phrased in *The Triune God: Systematics* in such a way as to criticize an exaggerated personalism that would overlook the formalities of the true and of being and attend solely to the experience of intersubjectivity, in contrast with a personalism that insists on and adheres to the true in such a way that the true is always the measure and revealed truth is never diminished but is all the more clearly and easily made to accord with concrete, vital, and personal experience. All of this is, of course, valid, and yet much more needs to be said. On this point, I will eventually move with John Dadosky into a discussion of a fourth stage of meaning.[66] But at the moment I wish simply to continue my critique of the tendencies that would bypass the psychological analogy in favor of *communio* considerations.

The interplay of the dialectic of the subject with the dialectic of community is complex. It can be rephrased in terms of the movements among the levels of value in the scale of values from below, where the dialectic of community exercises a relative dominance over the emergence into authenticity of the subject's own dialectical development, and from above, where the conversion of the subject to authenticity is an essential ingredient in the transformation of culture and, through transformed cultural meanings and values, of social structures so as to see to the equitable distribution of vital goods. Until persons change, nothing else changes. And the psychological analogy draws attention to the constitution of personal authenticity under God, to the autonomous spiritual processions that are the condition of the possibility of authentic communion.

4.1.4 Summary and Transition

So much for what Lonergan says on this issue at this point in chapter 4 of *De Deo trino: Pars systematica.* He uses his history of the notion of person to sum up what is understood by the word "person": "The answer is that we understand five things. To begin with, 'person' is a common word that answers the question, Three what? Next, a person is, according to St Thomas's definition, 'a distinct subsistent in an intellectual nature.' Third, a divine person is a subsistent relation, or a subsistent that is distinct by reason of a relation. Fourth, a divine person is a distinct subject and is conscious of himself both as subject and as distinct. Fifth, by reason of their interpersonal relations the divine persons are not only related to one another but are also constituted as persons."[67]

But the movement to the issue of authenticity as self-transcendence eventually forced an expansion of the notion of person beyond what Lonergan was able to offer at the time he put these Latin treatises together. He was not quite there yet. His detailed and very accurate portrayal of "intellectual nature" in *De constitutione Christi,* to which he refers the reader in *De Deo trino,* but where "intellectual" means "cognitional," does not meet the demands that he placed upon himself when he insisted in chapter 2 of his 1964 Trinitarian text that it is in the realm of *existential autonomy* that the appropriate analogy for understanding the divine processions must be found. In that 1964 text the analogue for the divine Word is referred to as "iudicium valoris," a judgment of value, but that reference occurs only twice in the book. And it is clear from other writings at the time that his notion of judgments of value has not yet reached the point of incorporating the deliverances of affectivity, which is a major emphasis in his post-1965 writings on the fourth level of consciousness. I have attempted to draw attention to the expansion that occurred even by the time of the 1964 text by suggesting that the Thomist term "intelligible emanation" be sublated into the broader term "autonomous spiritual procession." It is true that in the chapter on processions in the 1964 *De Deo trino: Pars systematica,* as I emphasized in *Missions and Processions,* thesis 53, the relevant processions in the order of human nature for an analogy for divine procession have to do explicitly with our existential autonomy. The procession of a judgment of value emerges from existential-ethical grasp of sufficient evidence regarding what it would be good for one not only to do but also and more importantly to *be.* This procession of a judgment of value provides the analogue for the procession of the Son, an analogue that is called, twice in *De Deo trino,* a judgment of value. But the model of the procession is still that proposed in chapter 18 of *Insight,* where decision and choice are an extension of intellectual activity. From that grasp and judgment operating together, there proceeds loving decision to do and to be precisely what has been affirmed; this provides a natural analogue for the procession of the Holy Spirit. By 1964 Lonergan prefers to find the natural analogue for the divine processions in this realm of existential autonomy, and in this he is, I believe, quite correct. But he had not explicitly reached this position by the time he wrote his sections on person either in *De constitutione Christi* (1956) or in *Divinarum personarum* (1957), and unfortunately the relevant sections from *Divinarum personarum* on person migrate in their entirety into *De Deo trino: Pars systematica,* chapter 4, even though their relatively narrow context, that of cognitional theory alone, with its limitation to three levels of consciousness, had been transcended not only by his own movement to the emphasis on existential autonomy but also by his explicit and continually developing acknowledgment of a quite distinct fourth level of consciousness. The fact that, even in chapter 2 of the 1964 text, explicit mention of a judgment of value as the natural analogue for the Son occurs only twice, and the first time when he is giving a definition of "spirans," indicates that we are at the very beginning of a movement that will take off in Lonergan's last years of writing on these subjects.

Nonetheless, the development does begin even by the time of the 1964 text, and the affirmation is clearly related to the emphasis on existential autonomy that is new with the 1964 *De Deo trino: Pars systematica;* that material is not provided in *Divinarum personarum*. My present point in rehearsing these details is that the reflections on person in Lonergan's chapter 4, transported verbatim from the 1957 and 1959 *Divinarum personarum*, and relying on the 1956 *De constitutione Christi*, have not caught up with chapter 2's new, distinct, 1964 acknowledgment of a judgment of value as analogue for the Son and of existential autonomy as the context for constructing the appropriate psychological analogy. Chapter 4 is still implicitly stuck in a three-level conception of the person – "I am a knower" – or at best straddling the fence between the three-level conception and the four-level understanding that we know from other writings Lonergan had already reached. Yes, I am a knower, but the psychological subject, the person, is more than a knower. Lonergan has explicitly recognized this by this time. But he has not brought this recognition to bear on the discussion. And the issue here is not simply a matter of making Lonergan's articulations catch up with his own development.

It is part of my present task to bring these reflections up to date, not only in the sense of making them more pertinent in our own time but even in the sense of harmonizing them with Lonergan's own development not only in *Method in Theology* but even by the time he published the 1964 edition of his Trinitarian systematics.

This is not to deny a continuity in Lonergan's development. In 1957 – and this comes over into the 1964 *Pars systematica*, as we have seen – he correctly stresses that the insistence placed on the subject in the historical unfolding of the notion of person can be joined with contempt heaped on what has the formality of "object." In that case one's Trinitarian doctrine cannot be reconciled with faith in the sense of an assent to the true in which we attain by the medium of the true something about the divine reality revealed to us. This insistence was not to change, nor must it be allowed to. As Lonergan emphasized toward the end of the 1968 lecture "The Subject," the concreteness offered by the wealth of existential reflection cannot eliminate the issues of cognitional theory, epistemology, and metaphysics. "I have no doubt," he writes there, "I never did doubt, that the old answers [to questions of cognitional theory, epistemology, and metaphysics] were defective. But to reject the questions as well is to refuse to know what one is doing when one is knowing; it is to refuse to know why doing that is knowing; it is to refuse to set up a basic semantics by concluding what one knows when one does it. That threefold refusal is worse than mere neglect of the subject, and it generates a far more radical truncation."[68] In particular, the point that Lonergan is making throughout his development is that the truth grasped by existential reflection cannot neglect the cognitional level of judgment, as is frequently the case in existentialist thinking, where a leap can be made from understanding to decision. This is one of Lonergan's criticisms of Bultmann, for example.[69] The move to decision must not be accompanied by a failure to move cognitionally beyond experience and understanding to the third step in cognitional process. There is indeed an omission of what is especially proper and distinctive of the authentic human person if one omits rational reflection, grasp of the virtually unconditioned, and the autonomous intelligible necessity whereby a true judgment emanates from an act of reflective understanding. Only then can the consequent equally autonomous and intelligible necessity in which moral obligation and the "spiration" of will consists be placed in its proper context. Lonergan's insistence on this in the first chapter on the divine persons is not offset by his later much more explicit affirmation of the primacy of the existential.

Moreover – and here we are commenting again on the 1964 text that was originally published in 1957 – while "objectivity" and "object" are complex notions because of the diversity of steps through which our knowledge proceeds, the other meanings of these words – Lonergan is referring here to what in *Insight* are called "normative objectivity" and "experiential objectivity" – are reduced to the principal meaning, where by objectivity is simply meant truth, and object is what is made known through the mediation of the true. This is *Insight*'s "absolute objectivity."[70] This, of course, is not lost on one who has grasped that the supreme perfection of person consists in intelligible emanations in accord with truth and goodness ("secundum veritatem et honestatem"), nor is any other meaning of objectivity required for conformity with faith and traditional theology.

Lonergan is appealing here in more traditional language to dimensions of the reality that in *Missions and Processions* I attempted to understand in terms of autonomous spiritual processions. But in the 1956 *De constitutione Christi* and the 1957 *Divinarum personarum*, these spiritual processions are still framed in a context in which cognitional theory has not yet been adequately sublated by existential ethics, to say nothing of existential ethics being sublated by a theology that begins with the operative grace of God's love poured into our hearts by the Holy Spirit who has been given to us.

The qualifications that I am introducing in the light of Lonergan's later developments do not in any way minimize the significance of what he writes in the earlier works. There is a meaning of reality, objectivity, evidence, and knowledge that arises from an animal faith in a world of objects that are "already out there now." And there is an entirely different meaning to these terms insofar as the subject, led by questions, conceives the natures of data from an understanding of what it experiences, affirms the true from its grasp of the unconditioned, and apprehends being in the true as in a medium. Pre-philosophic knowledge is realistic in both senses, animal faith and genuine human knowing. But it cannot explicitly distinguish the two. Immanentism rejects uncritical realism, but without reaching a critical realism. Transcendental phenomenology, Lonergan says at this point – he became much more sympathetic at least to Husserl later – begins from uncritical realism, considers this naive reality to be a phenomenon, through its suspension of judgment as well as of subjective interest recognizes internal as well as external phenomena, rejects the uncritical tendency and orientation that reduces internal phenomena to external phenomena, and applauds a new "transcendental" orientation that reduces the external phenomena to the internal phenomena. But this merely effects an inversion of uncritical realism; for where before all was to be reduced to the object of uncritical realism, now all is to be reduced to the subject of the same realism, conceived of course in a more subtle fashion. Nor does one really reach the revelation of the human subject until one arrives at the true through the unconditioned and knows being in the true as in a medium. Now if the true and being, understood in this sense, are not attained, one can, of course, use the words "true" and "false," "being" and "existence," "the existent" and "the transcendent," "presence" and "participation," but one does not in that fashion really reach beyond the limits of some new type of immanentism.

We must, then, discuss the consciousness of a divine person as a reality that is made known through truth. Since "unconscious understanding" and "understanding unconsciously" have no meaning, and since the divine act of existence is the divine act of understanding, the divine act of existence is conscious and consciously is. Moreover, the divine processions, the divine subsistent relations, and whatever else is really said to be in God are also really identical with the divine act of existence, and so they too are equally conscious and consciously are. And so, if the real, subsistent, and really distinct divine relations are persons, they are conscious persons, and they are consciously distinct from one another.

Still, for Lonergan, the five elements that have entered into the history of the notion of person cohere with one another in such a way that, once the definition of Aquinas is posited, the other elements follow. Not all five items need to be established of Father, Son, and Holy Spirit before we are able to name them persons in the proper sense, for the verification of the definition suffices to attribute correctly to them the name "person." On the other hand, the elements that were arrived at later cannot be explicitly found in the earlier tradition. One would look in vain for Thomas's definition in Augustine. But that does not mean that the Catholic doctrine on the divine persons is simply the convenience of a common name that allows greater facility in discussing Father, Son, and Spirit simultaneously. Similarly, although the medieval theologians were not accustomed to disputes about consciousness, it is clear that neither Catholic theologians nor the Catholic faithful ever adored an unconscious God or unconscious divine persons, and so it pertains to the *sensus fidelium* that the divine persons are conscious. And if this is the case, then it is also incumbent on the theologian to seek to state clearly and distinctly what this consciousness is.

For Lonergan, Aquinas's definition of person, "subsistens distinctum in natura intellectuali," covers all of these issues, even though not all of them were made clear by the time Aquinas proposed his definition.[71] This is what I am questioning. That Aquinas's definition is open to the further developments is obvious. That it already includes them is not. At the time he wrote *The Ontological and Psychological Constitution of Christ,* to which he refers us at this point in the Trinitarian volume, authenticity for Lonergan took the form of what he calls a coherent intellectualism in cognitional theory. But such an intellectualism articulates only part of the constitution of an authentic human being, and to restrict authenticity to this dimension is to succumb to what John Dadosky and I, in distinct contexts and independently of each other, have called an intellectualist bias.[72] While Lonergan's treatment attempts to incorporate a number of the features that arose or were emphasized after Aquinas did his work, the framework is too narrow. And Lonergan came to see that this is the case. It could even be argued that he had come to this conclusion by the time of the 1964 text, which he just neglected to change in this section. The translator and editors of the Collected Works edition of *De constitutione Christi ontologica and psychologica* acknowledge that his talk of *ek-sistentia* is moving in the direction of an explicit acknowledgment of a fourth level of consciousness, and they indicate this by translating *ek-sistentia* as *Existenz.* But there is a development from the *Existenz* of *De constitutione Christi* to the *Existenz* of the 1964 lecture "*Existenz* and *Aggiornamento,*" and it has to do with the world that begins to be opened up as the fourth, existential level of consciousness takes on greater differentiation.[73] Moreover, Lonergan would go on from yet further development on the fourth level to speak of the movement from above as well as from below among the "levels" of consciousness, to acknowledge the contribution of psychic conversion, and to affirm a fifth level of consciousness, a distinct interpersonal level without which the appropriation of the dimension we call supernatural is not possible. These later moves would enable him truly to embrace the dimensions that were proposed regarding "person" subsequent to Aquinas's definition, to which Lonergan in 1956 gave a privileged status. They would also allow those coming after him to propose yet a fourth stage of meaning, the recognition of alterity made fully possible by the acknowledgment that what alone is normative is the transcendental structure of conscious intentionality. And that structure extends beyond the three strictly cognitional levels.

Moreover, in dialogue with Hans Urs von Balthasar, I am considering an explicitly theological notion of person, and again the Thomist definition that Lonergan privileges is too compact to embrace this notion in all its richness and detail, even when Balthasar's excesses are corrected with Lonergan's help.

I have nothing but complete admiration and acceptance of Lonergan's "notion of being," identified with the inquiring and critical drive of human intelligence and reason. I believe this is a major discovery in the history of Western metaphysics, one that renders Heidegger's attempt at the destruction of metaphysics not only premature but unnecessary. That is not the issue. The issue is around the *Existenz*, the subject, who is oriented to being, yes, but also, beyond what is intelligently grasped and reasonably affirmed, to value and indeed to an entire scale of values that sublates the orientation to being into a commitment to the human good in all its complexity and difficulty, a commitment awakened and sustained by the gift of God's love. Lonergan's 1956 correction of Heidegger's inauthentic *Sorge* with his own notion of *Existenz* is still limited to the pure and unrestricted desire to know. This is simply not enough. By the time of his 1959 lectures in the philosophy of education, his own meaning of *Sorge* has its "*fundamental and first appearance* in the pure desire to know that grounds the intellectual pattern of experience and sets the standards for one's morality."[74] With this I am in fundamental agreement. As the first chapter of *Theology and the Dialectics of History* makes clear, to begin one's delineation of the constitution of personal value with cognitional theory is sound procedure. The problem with the Lonergan of 1956 is that he had not yet moved beyond the horizon established by the first three levels of consciousness. The movement to a fourth level, the acknowledgment of psychic conversion, the significance of the affirmation of a movement from above downwards among the levels, and the repeated insistence in dialogue sessions at the Lonergan Workshop in the 1970s and early 1980s on a fifth level of consciousness have all yet to come. And move with him through these steps – and beyond – we must if we are truly to reap the fruits of his work and bring them to bear on contemporary exigences, including the demand for an adequate notion of the person.

In particular, I want to stress that the real objective of *Existenz*, the fuller correlative to the dynamism of the authentic subject, is not being but the integral scale of values. And because the scale of values is the social and cultural objectification of the relation between nature and grace, that correlative becomes for theology the heuristic structure of the reign of God. It is in that context that the identification of person with mission makes sense. The theological notion of person is "personal value" as functioning in the scale: "the person in his [or her] self-transcendence, as loving and being loved, as originator of values in [oneself] and in [one's] milieu, as an inspiration and invitation to others to do likewise."[75] The intending intention of being, of course, is essential to that dynamism, but it does not represent it completely. And the notion of person as a distinct subsistent in an intellectual nature is just not explicit enough to cover everything that is needed. This much is implied, I believe, when later, in the first chapter of *Method in Theology*, where Lonergan is outlining the basic pattern of operations, it is at the fourth level that "we emerge as persons."[76] In fact, the enrichment begins to take place in *The Triune God: Systematics* in the insistence in chapter 2, however brief, that the analogy for understanding divine procession is from the subject not as speculative nor as practical in some narrow sense, but as *existential, self-constituting autonomy*, and in the development in chapter 5 of the analogy of eternal and temporal subject in response to the question of how an existential notion of person can be acknowledged in God.[77] Not all of his students have followed his later development into new territory. Some may have found the movement to the fourth level difficult. Some may have found his acknowledgment of psychic conversion unacceptable. Some may have failed to grasp the significance of his affirmation of a movement from above downwards among the levels. And some have balked at his repeated insistence in dialogue sessions at the Lonergan Workshop on a fifth level of consciousness. I take my stand on the acknowledgment of all of these moves on Lonergan's part.

All of this leads me to suggest the quite simple reformulation of the definition of person: a person can be defined as a distinct subsistent in a *spiritual* nature. As "intelligible or intellectual emanations" was transposed in *Missions and Processions* to "autonomous spiritual processions," so "distinct subsistent in an intellectual nature" is transposed to "distinct subsistent in a spiritual nature."

And so we may repeat our thesis 80.

Thesis 80: *Lonergan's discussion of person in his Latin works on the Trinity and Christ must be sublated into a notion that takes more explicitly into account the developments subsequent to Aquinas's definition and to Aquinas's easy reliance on Boethius's definition as well as the developments in Lonergan's own thinking. As the cognitive levels of consciousness – experience, understanding, and judgment – are sublated by the fourth, existential level, and as these four are sublated by being in love in an unqualified fashion, so the objective of authentic subjectivity sublates being (the objective of the desire to know) into the full range of the scale of values, which is the objective that serves to define what is meant by "person." A person can be defined as a distinct subsistent in a spiritual nature. A human person, then, is a distinct subsistent potentially oriented to commitment to the integral scale of values, and an authentic human person is a distinct subsistent actually oriented to the same commitment. This definition, which is also open to what is meant by "personal value" in the scale of values, really does take into account the developments on the notion of person reached by the turn to*

> *the subject in modernity, by the turn to the other in postmodernity, and by*
> *the expansions of consciousness beyond cognitional levels in Lonergan's*
> *own work.*

Lonergan is too sanguine about being able to include those developments in the definition he prefers from Aquinas (even though, as we have indicated, Aquinas hardly emphasized this particular definition in the same way Lonergan does). The needed sublations are easy. We have been arguing for them almost since the start of this chapter. They have already been treated in our chapter on autonomous spiritual processions in *Processions and Missions*.

To thesis 80 we may now add a further thesis.

> **Thesis 81:** *The scale of values provides the heuristic structure of the reign of God. A human person can be defined theologically as a distinct subsistent oriented to the reign of God.*

5   Person and Mission in Balthasar

We are now ready to address in more detail Balthasar's connection of the notion of person with that of mission.

Balthasar's notion of person and its correlation with the notion of mission are based in his Christology, which is found in large part in the third volume of the second part of his trilogy, that is, in *Theo-Drama: Theological Dramatic Theory*, vol. 3: *Dramatis Personae: Persons in Christ*.[78] In the section entitled "The Acting Area," and in the context of kingdom and cross-resurrection as constituents of that area, Balthasar writes:

> … in the acting area Christ opens up as the fruit of his Resurrection, each individual is given a personal commission; he is entrusted both with something unique to do and with the freedom to do it. Bound up with this commission is his own, inalienable, personal name; here – and only here – role and person coincide. This personal commission … is actually constitutive of the person as such …[79]

After linking this statement with Ephesians 2.4–10, Balthasar goes on to write:

> Of course this does not mean that we are to trace a path already marked out for us, as if we were immature children – Paul speaks a great deal about the new Christian freedom given us in Christ – but it does mean that absolute freedom has "prepared" a personal path

for each one of us to follow freely, a path along which our freedom can realize itself. Here, once again, we have the mystery of the Holy Spirit whereby he gives us both things at once: a concrete plan of the future, in accordance with our own mission and hence with our own personality, and the inner free spontaneity to carry out, recall and follow this plan.[80]

The acting area for our emergence into such missional personhood "has been opened up in the three main articulations of Jesus' coming ('kingdom of God') and going ('Cross'-'Resurrection')."[81] Again:

> Since it [the acting area] is set in motion by the temporal, finite process and departure [*Vor-und Fort-Gehen*] of Jesus, it is a perduring event; and, in this perduring event, new players can continually act their parts, appearing onstage and leaving it, without their personal acting – and the entire play of world history – being condemned as an absurd and futile finitude. God has always been on his way to meet the world; the incarnate Son has always been in the process of returning to his Father. This means that the necessarily finite world drama takes place in the open realm of the Spirit, where men appear on the world stage and depart from it to be endowed with gifts and robbed of them … In this they are in harmony with the theodramatic meaning, which is ultimately trinitarian.[82]

Balthasar thus takes the notion of person one step beyond where we ended when we sublated Lonergan's interpretation of Aquinas's "subsistens distinctum in natura intellectuali" into "distinct subsistent in a spiritual nature" and, theologically, "distinct subsistent oriented to the reign of God." We have located authentic personhood explicitly within, and committed to, the realization of the integral scale of values in history – where "explicitly" means "cognizant of the identification of 'religious values' in that scale with the visible and invisible missions in history of the divine Word and the Holy Spirit." That definition applies, of course, only to the *Christian* person, who, through the explicit faith that is hers or his, is on mission from the Father through the Son and in the Holy Spirit to play her or his unique role, ever discerned anew in its concrete details, in contributing to the realization of God's reign in human affairs.

In the theology that I have been proposing to this point, however, authenticity in grace under God is also possible without that explicit Christian outer word. Grace and the universalist faith that is born of the gift of God's love are everywhere, at all times, and they always have been. Religious values are operative everywhere, at all times. Fidelity in response is also potentially everywhere, at all times. The *consciousness* of one caught up in

that "acting area" will be something we could call "mission consciousness."
But the *knowledge* that it is such may or may not be present. And it will be
present in direct proportion to one's explicit identification of the Trinitarian context in which all mission in fact occurs, whether we are aware of it or
not. These qualifications, I believe, must be added to Balthasar's account
from the beginning of our appropriation and transformation of the point
he is making. We need to sublate his account into a broader theological
notion of the presence of Trinitarian grace in the world.

That having been said, let us return to Balthasar's arguments. The first
task in substantiating his claims lies in the Christology that forms two
hundred-plus pages of his work *Dramatis Personae,* since it is primarily in
Jesus that the correlation between person and mission becomes clear. Jesus
possessed a sense of mission that was eschatological and universal. His mission was unique because the One sent, who he was, was equally unique. His
mission is caught in the tension between the present reality of the kingdom
and his looking ahead to a fuller reality that will inevitably come precisely
because of his fidelity to a mission with which his person is identified.

> Jesus' whole life and work exhibit both things simultaneously: he
> looks ahead to the reality that will come without fail, and he pos-
> sesses the peace of the man who unhurriedly performs his tasks
> each day that is granted him … He does not *merely* live with a view
> to that "hour" – "I have a baptism to be baptized with; and how I am
> constrained until it is accomplished!" (Lk 12:50) – but anticipates
> it, living constantly the immediacy of the Father's mission. He lives
> "proleptically" in both directions.
>
> There are thus two poles to the life and consciousness of Jesus:
> on the one hand, he expects the imminent arrival of the kingdom,
> but, on the other hand, he does so in the calm security of someone
> who lives entirely for his mission. And this life and this consciousness
> are heading toward death, that is, they are circumscribed by a finite
> duration. What is to come will implode into his life, of that he is cer-
> tain; but the precise time of this hour remains hidden. There is no
> contradiction between these two things. From Peter's confession on-
> ward, the Synoptic arrangement of the temporal framework (which
> does not contradict the Johannine in this matter) shows Jesus delib-
> erately walking toward this hour that awaits him in Jerusalem.[83]

Now it is at this point (after about fifty pages on problems of method)
that Balthasar takes a step that I don't think he was quite ready to take. If
we begin from mission, he says, we may construct "a portrayal of the person
of Christ that neither preempts the action undertaken by him nor falls back

into the kind of purely extrahistorical, static, 'essence' Christology that sees itself as a complete and rounded 'part one', smoothly unfolding into a soteriological 'part two.'"[84] Now it must be said that Lonergan's Christology, while it is anything but extrahistorical, static, or essentialist,[85] nonetheless does begin with an ontology of Christ and leads, through highly original and in my view permanently valid contributions on both the consciousness and knowledge of Christ, to a soteriology. I have proposed that we can *now* begin systematics with mission, and that proposal will eventually move beyond the impasse that Balthasar criticizes. But "eventually" means that the ontology, which one has accepted from figures in the tradition with whom one agrees, has first of all to be correct. This is as true in Christology as in Trinitarian theology. In the case of Christology, the positions on the consciousness and knowledge of Christ must flow from the ontological constitution of a divine person endowed with both a divine and a human nature. Because Balthasar's option to begin his Christology with Christ's consciousness/knowledge – and he does not adequately distinguish consciousness and knowledge – does not flow from such an ontology, what he has to say at this point is premature. Only when one has passed through that crucible of determining the actual and formal ontological constitutives of such a unique person can one successfully propose a position on that person's consciousness and knowledge. And at that point one will be forced to come to grips with the fact that if there are two natures, and two sets of operations, in that one person, as has been dogmatically defined, there must also be two consciousnesses in that same person. Furthermore, if one has indeed distinguished consciousness from knowledge, one will also have to attempt to understand how there can be both divine and human knowledge (as distinct from consciousness) in that one person. In my view, Balthasar has not negotiated the transition that would be required if he were going to begin his Christology successfully with mission as the basic concept expressing an understanding of Jesus. He begins prematurely the Christology of consciousness before fully coming to terms with the question of the ontological constitution of Christ.

My principal source of evidence for this statement is found in a long, complex footnote on pp. 228–30 of *Dramatis Personae*. I reviewed this material above,[86] where I indicated that in contrast Lonergan first provides unambiguous ontological statements that provide a foundation for both a distinction between person and mission even in Jesus and also an understanding of how there can be two consciousnesses in Jesus. To repeat: The secondary act of existence is the created consequent condition of the necessary procession of the Word being also a contingent mission of the Word. And, while Lonergan doesn't say it in so many words, it is precisely here that we can "flesh out" (literally) the distinction of the two consciousnesses: the divine consciousness is the eternal, uncreated, necessary consciousness of the one who proceeds as Son from the Father, and the human consciousness is the temporal and historical, created, contingent "mission consciousness" of the same Son sent as the man Jesus of Nazareth. Not only is "his being sent (*missio*) by the Father … a modality of his proceeding (*processio*) from the Father."[87] More emphatically, and in greater agreement with Aquinas, we must say that mission *is* procession, relation, person *joined to a created external term,* and that the mission is not understood theologically without understanding the created external term. In the case of the Incarnation, that created external term is the secondary act of existence that is the consequent condition of the truth of the proposition that the eternal Word of God *is* this man Jesus of Nazareth. Procession, as the Son's exercise of the *unicum esse* of God, is eternal and necessary. Mission, as the Son's historical task grounded in the created secondary act of existence that makes it true that the eternal Word of God *is* this man Jesus of Nazareth, is temporal and contingent. These are the central affirmations of our theses 77 and 78 above, pp. 100–101.

Thus I am not satisfied that Balthasar fulfils the conditions for identifying person and mission in Jesus. The resultant confusion, if I may call it that, is already clear, I think, in Balthasar's statement that in Jesus "we are presented with someone who never was, and never could have been anyone other than the One sent."[88] That statement, taken literally, makes the mission of the incarnate Word not contingent but necessary. What should be said is that the person that Jesus is, the second person of the Trinity, could never have been anyone other than *the One who proceeds as Word and Son from the Father.* That is necessary, not contingent. Jesus' *divine* consciousness is the one consciousness of the triune God exercised precisely as consciousness of the Word *eternally proceeding.* His *human* consciousness is the consciousness of one *sent,* where the sending, the mission, is identical with the eternal procession *contingently* joined to the created external term, the secondary act of existence, which is the created consequent condition of the procession being also a mission. That the divine decision behind the Incarnation is eternal does not make it necessary. The Father did not have to send the Son. Balthasar is correct when he writes that "Jesus experiences his human consciousness entirely in terms of mission,"[89] even if a more felicitous manner of expressing what he intends would be desirable. But for Balthasar, again, "we cannot ascribe a twofold consciousness to the Logos-made-man."[90] On Lonergan's reading, which I endorse, not only can we do this; we must. For Balthasar, this herald, in contrast to the prophets, is "sent" "… in such an absolute sense that his mission … coincides with his person, so that both together constitute God's exhaustive self-communication"; "… this is a 'role' that cannot be exchanged for any other role, since it is a 'mission' that has ultimately fused with the person and become identical with him."[91] If I am correct in claiming that dogmatically we must acknowledge not one but two consciousnesses in Christ and that the divine consciousness is that of one *proceeding* while the human consciousness is that of the same one *sent*, then, while there is complete continuity from one to the other,[92] we cannot say that his mission has "ultimately fused" with his person and become identical with him. I cannot put that claim together with what Chalcedon said of the two natures, which now we must say as well of the two consciousnesses: *not* confused, *not* changed. The procession would not be a mission were it not for the created consequent condition of the secondary act of existence of the assumed human nature. That the procession, itself necessary, is also a mission is entirely contingent. The consciousness of the one proceeding, which again is the necessary divine consciousness of the Word, must be distinct from, even though continuous with, the consciousness of the same one contingently sent, the human consciousness of the same one person, a created consciousness that is contingent upon divine freedom.

Lonergan's later formulation of the mystery of Christ puts the same point in another way: *the divine Word is the one subject of two subjectivities.* "The person of Christ is an identity that eternally is subject of divine consciousness and in time became subject of a human consciousness."[93] By "identity" is meant the Chalcedonian "one and the same," who now is called the subject, the single divine identity that is "at once subject of divine consciousness and also subject of a human consciousness."[94] By "consciousness" is meant the presence of the subject to himself as subject, not as object. "Though his identity was divine, still Jesus had a truly human subjectivity that grew in wisdom and age and grace before God and men (Luke 2:52) and that was similar to our own in all things save sin (DS 301). Nor is the timeless and unchanging subjectivity proper to the divine identity in conflict with the developing subjectivity of a human life. For as Chalcedon would put it, though the identity is without distinction or separation, *still the subjectivities are without modification or confusion* (DS 302)."[95] As for the human consciousness or subjectivity being that of one sent, Lonergan writes: "Moreover, the human subjectivity of Christ conforms to the divine ... [A]s the eternal Word is [proceeds as] the eternally true expression of the value that God as *agapē* is, so the Word as man by obedience unto death again expressed that value by revealing how much God loved the world (John 3.16)."[96] The person is identical with mission only insofar as that person is the divine subject of a distinct, created, contingent human consciousness. That qualification must be made, I believe, on Balthasar's undifferentiated identification of Jesus' person with his mission.

Thus we conclude this argument with another thesis.

Thesis 82: *Balthasar's correlation of person and mission needs to be qualified by a distinction that affects its Christological base. With Lonergan we affirm that the divine person of the incarnate Word is a subject of*

*two distinct consciousnesses. His divine consciousness is the conscious-
ness of the one who eternally proceeds as Son from the Father, Word from
the Speaker. His human consciousness, ontologically grounded in the
secondary act of existence that makes it true to affirm that the second
person of the Blessed Trinity is this man Jesus of Nazareth, is the mission
consciousness of the Eternal Word become flesh. The two consciousnesses
are continuous but also distinct. The first is eternal, uncreated, and
necessary. The second is temporal, created, and contingent. They are
united in the person of the eternal Word become flesh, who is the subject
of both a divine and a human consciousness. This will have implications for the mission of all who, explicitly linked to the visible missions of
Son and Spirit or consciously but not knowingly linked to their invisible
missions, have a divinely ordained role to play in establishing the reign
of God in human affairs. As persons, as personal value, they embrace a
mission that, while expressing their place in the whole scheme of things,
is not identical with their personhood. Their personhood is located in the
autonomous spiritual processions through which, when oriented to the
full range of the integral scale of values, they come to grasp, affirm, and
choose their divinely ordained missions. And these spiritual processions
are primarily identified in the effective history of the Trinitarian theology
that begins with Augustine, is transposed by Aquinas, becomes further
transposed by Lonergan, and, I hope, rejoins Augustine in my own attempt to create an analogy of memory, word, and love.*[97]

6

Transition to the Historical Jesus

1   Jesus' Human Consciousness and His Human Self-Understanding

We have just completed a chapter that attempts to interpret and develop in strictly systematic-theological terms Lonergan's thesis regarding the divine and human consciousnesses of Jesus. We are now going to move along another track, appealing to suggestions regarding sets of exegetical data that could provide some grasp of the concrete movement from the human mission *consciousness* of Jesus to his human *self-understanding.* How did he understand what he was sent to do? Such a movement can be retrieved only by serious exegetical and historical work. I am not equipped to do such work myself, and this is not the time or place for me to try to summarize all the work that exegetes have done on this issue. The most I can do here is point in a certain direction, namely, to what has been called the Third Quest for the Historical Jesus, and in particular to the work of the acknowledged pioneer of this movement, Ben F. Meyer. I will also indicate very briefly some of the ways in which N.T. Wright has appropriated Meyer's work and built upon it. But beyond that I cannot go in the present work.

The fifth chapter in this book marks a transition to an explicit consideration of the mission of the Word incarnate in Jesus of Nazareth. The systematic theology of that mission of the incarnate Word is by identity a soteriology: the mission of the incarnate Word has been articulated for two millennia as a mission to "save" us. We will, then, be pointing to the work of the exegetes proximately or remotely identified with the critical-realist thrust of Meyer to propose a position on the aims of Jesus, and will go on from there in the next volume to develop a contemporary soteriology that is both in continuity with those explicit aims and oriented to their transposition to the contemporary context. A further exegetical set of studies that will be brought into the volume on soteriology is found in the so-called dramatic theology of Raymund Schwager, where the emphases of René Girard come to the fore. But the incorporation of Schwager's work, both exegetical and systematic, will not enter into our discussion until the next volume.[1]

The principal emphasis of the previous chapter was to identify the human consciousness of the incarnate Word as "mission consciousness," and to begin to relate it to his divine "procession consciousness." The link is established in the identification made by Aquinas and accepted by von Balthasar and Lonergan – each in his own way but each complementing the other at least on this issue – that the divine missions *are* the divine processions joined to a created external term. It is the created external term that is the consequent condition for the procession to be a mission, that is, the created consequent condition of the truth of any contingent affirmation of a mission on the part of a divine person. Thus, the statement "The eternal divine Word, the second person of the Trinity, is incarnate in the man Jesus of Nazareth" is an instance of contingent predication, and contingent predication with regard to God is not possible without the designation of a created external term that is the consequent condition of the truth of the contingent predication.[2] The created external term in this case is what Thomas Aquinas called a "secondary *is*," a secondary act of existence, that pertains to the assumed humanity of Jesus and grounds a created relation of his human nature to the divine Word. Not only is it true that the eternal divine Word is incarnate in the man Jesus of Nazareth; it is also true that the eternal divine Word *is* the man Jesus of Nazareth. This "is" is the secondary "is" that is the created consequent condition of both propositions just cited being true. Moreover, in Lonergan's hypothesis concerning the missions, the secondary "is" of the Incarnation is a created communication of and participation in divine paternity. The eternal Word immanent in Trinitarian divine life does not speak but is spoken. The incarnate Word speaks, but he speaks only what he hears from the Father.

With the clarifications offered in the previous chapter regarding the transposition of *esse secundarium* into the ontological ground of the human mission consciousness of Jesus, we are ready, I hope, to link our systematic efforts much more explicitly to a set of exegetical and historical works found in the so-called "Third Quest for the Historical Jesus." As I have indicated, I will be very selective in performing this task. Distinctly representative of the relevant works, especially for our purposes, are the writings of Ben F. Meyer and N.T. Wright, each of whom has appropriated to a greater or lesser degree a critical realism that found its inspiration in Lonergan's cognitional theory as applied to the tasks of exegesis and history. In addition, James D.G. Dunn has initiated what Jonathan Bernier calls a Fourth Quest,[3] also grounded in Lonergan's critical realism. Dunn appeals to the memory of Jesus preserved in the earliest Christian communities as a source of what we can know about his intentions and objectives. My work here, however, is limited to the contributions made by Ben Meyer, with a very brief indication of some advances found in the work of N.T. Wright. I invite others to add what can be appropriated from other New Testament scholars, including Dunn.[4] I rely on Meyer and Wright for a clear but still preliminary delineation of what our soteriology will accept as the aims of Jesus, aims with which a systematic theology of redemption must establish and maintain continuity. And I rely on Peter Laughlin's appropriation of their work, where I find especially one affirmation that informs a thesis expressing the basic position of the present chapter.[5]

The divine Word was sent. The mission grounds, indeed creates, the term, the secondary act of existence, that is the created consequent condition of the truth of the affirmation that the eternal divine Word is this man Jesus of Nazareth. But he was sent precisely to announce and inaugurate what he called the kingdom or reign of God, and that announcement and inauguration occurred within the historical circumstances of first-century, second-Temple Judaism. His announcement and inauguration amount to the proclamation that the promises of God to Abraham have been fulfilled, precisely in the figure of Jesus, in his life, ministry, death, and resurrection, and in the appropriation of that fulfilment by a new community informed explicitly by the new covenant sealed in his blood. Even the idea of sealing a covenant with sacrificial blood cannot be understood except against the backdrop of Jesus' relation with Judaism.

The fulfilment of the Abrahamic promises was very different, however, from what his contemporaries, even his own disciples, and indeed much of the Jewish tradition that stands behind them, expected.

> First-century Jews looked forward to a public event, a great act of liberation for Israel, in and through which their god would reveal to all the world that he was not just a local, tribal deity, but the creator and sovereign of all. YHWH would reveal his salvation for Israel in the eyes of all the nations; the ends of the earth would see that he had vindicated his people. The early Christians, not least in the writings that came to be called the New Testament, looked back to an event in and through which, they claimed, Israel's god had done exactly that. On this basis, the New Testament, emerging from within this strange would-be "people of god," told the story of that people as a story rooted in Israel's past, and designed to continue into the world's future. It repeated the Jewish claim: this story concerns not just a god but God. It revised the Jewish evidence: the claim is made good, not in national liberation but in the events concerning Jesus.[6]

The making good of the claim puts into operation a new community, one rooted in the fulfilment of the Abrahamic promise borne for centuries by the people of Israel, but now stretching far beyond those narrow national boundaries, a community that Paul refers to as "the Israel of God" (Galatians 6.16), which is part of the fulfilment of the statement in the so-called second Servant song in Deutero-Isaiah: "It is too light a thing that you should be my servant to raise up the tribes of Jacob and to restore the survivors of Israel; I will give you as a light to the nations, that my salvation may reach to the end of the earth" (Isaiah 49.6).

The relation between the reign of God and that salvation provides us with our next thesis.

> **Thesis 83:** *Salvation, the core focus of soteriology, is precisely the reign of God that Jesus announced and inaugurated, the explicit and revealed presence and operation of the God of grace in human history as mediating a participation in and communication of divine life that will extend into a new creation. At its heart is the message of forgiveness, reconciliation, divine compassion and mercy, forgiveness even of those responsible for the crucifixion of the bearer of the good news.*

And to be perfectly clear, we add:

> **Thesis 84:** *The community of the church is not the kingdom of God. Its mission is to catalyze the kingdom of God in human affairs, principally by embodying the message of forgiveness in word and deed. Nulla salus extra regnum Dei, there is no salvation outside the reign of God, for salvation and the reign of God are coterminous. But the reign of God extends far beyond the church.*

Already then, we have moved from a consideration of Jesus' human consciousness to concern with his human self-understanding. The movement from consciousness, self-presence, to self-understanding is difficult for any of us to unravel. Meyer was a careful student of Lonergan's work, and so I dare say that he would, if pressed, have acknowledged that Jesus' mission *consciousness* is one thing, while his human *self-understanding* in terms of mission is a quite distinct psychological reality. But there is an important paragraph in *The Aims of Jesus* in which he mentions both consciousness and self-understanding in a way that does not distinguish them but conflates them. The challenge that Jesus presented to Israel was, Meyer writes, "rooted in a consciousness of mission. It was a unique consciousness, for he did not understand himself to have happened onto the scene of Israel at a turning point fixed independently of him. Moment (*kairos*) and message (*kerygma*) converged by divine design." He conceived himself "to function as fulfiller."[7]

I propose that Meyer is here referring not to Jesus' human consciousness but to his human self-understanding, his human *knowledge* of himself and of his mission, built on but not identical with his mission *consciousness*. Consciousness is not conception. Conception – "he conceived himself" – is a particular conscious act that proceeds from another particular conscious act, the act of understanding or insight. Conception of self emerges from self-understanding. The human Jesus' self-understanding and his conception of who he was were rooted in a mission consciousness that, precisely as consciousness and not as self-knowledge, was his from the beginning, even before he knew and could express in human language just what it meant.

Recall that in thesis 78 we affirmed: "The divine consciousness of Jesus is the consciousness precisely of the One who proceeds eternally as Son and Word from the Father, while his human consciousness is the consciousness of the One who has been sent in time as Son and Word made flesh." The divine consciousness of the incarnate Word, then, would be the consciousness "on the side of the subject that is the Son in being consciously generated by the Father" as well as "on the side of the subject that is the Son who with the Father consciously spirates the Spirit." His divine consciousness must include an awareness of the Father and of the Holy Spirit, since he *is* a subsistent relation to the Father and the Holy Spirit. *He cannot be present to himself in any other way than precisely as the relation that he is, and those to whom he is related in his very being, the Father and the Holy Spirit, must enter into his own self-presence.* The incarnate Word is present to himself through divine consciousness in the same unchanging way, *conscious* as well of the Father from whom he proceeds and of the Holy Spirit whom, together with the Father, he spirates. He *must* be conscious of the Father and the Holy Spirit in being conscious of himself through divine consciousness, for he *is* relation to the Father and the Holy Spirit.[8]

His human consciousness, I have argued, is ontologically grounded in the secondary act of existence that makes it true to affirm that the second person of the Blessed Trinity *is* this man Jesus of Nazareth. But this human consciousness is the mission consciousness of the Eternal Word become flesh. As his divine consciousness is the consciousness on the side of the subject that is the Son consciously proceeding from the Father, so his human consciousness is *the consciousness on the side of the subject that is the Son being consciously sent by the Father*, or perhaps at first simply *being consciously "from."* It is grounded in the "is" expressed in the affirmation that the second person of the Trinity *is* Jesus of Nazareth, an "is" that Aquinas and then Lonergan express in ontological terms as his *secondary* act of existence. The mission *is* the procession joined to the created external term, the secondary *is*. Procession consciousness becomes mission consciousness through the secondary act of existence that makes it true to affirm that the second person of the Trinity is this man Jesus of Nazareth; the secondary act of existence names the "is" in this doctrinal claim. If, as divinely proceeding, the Son is conscious of proceeding from the Father, then, as sent, he must be *conscious* of being sent by the Father; that is, more precisely, his awareness must be marked by that "being from," even before he understands, conceives, and affirms, that is, *knows*, that this is the case. It is not stretching the exegetical data too much to suggest that this knowledge emerges clearly at the time of his baptism and his retreat into the desert. His mission consciousness is consciousness on the side of the divine subject of his human consciousness, who *exists* as Jesus of Nazareth; it is not knowledge. It is consciousness in a manner analogous to that in which the divine consciousness "on the side of the subject that is the Son in being consciously generated by the Father" is consciousness: not knowledge *that*, but consciousness *of* self precisely in relation. His divine consciousness is procession consciousness, and his human consciousness is mission consciousness, because mission *is* procession joined to a created external term. If his mission is the divine procession of the Son from the Father joined to the created external term of the secondary act of existence that makes it true to say that the eternal Son of the Father *is* this man Jesus of Nazareth, then the human mission consciousness has a relational character analogous to the Son's instantiation of the one divine consciousness common to the three divine persons.[9]

I have approached the work of Meyer and some advances made by Wright in seeking for help in understanding the movement *from* the mission consciousness *to* the precise and context-influenced self-understanding that we are beginning to explore. How did Jesus come to *understand and articulate* the mission that already and from the beginning set the tonal quality of his human self-presence, with all that this entailed in terms of his relation to "Abba"? And especially, how did he understand his death? Meyer's work in *The Aims of Jesus* and Wright's work in *Jesus and the Victory of God* are the products of biblical exegetes, historians, scholars, attempting not to understand systematic-theological positions on the consciousness and knowledge of Jesus, but to articulate how the historical Jesus of Nazareth concretely understood and conceived his mission. I am looking to their work for help in understanding and expressing the concrete transition from his mission consciousness to his self-understanding, not in its formal structures, which are what we have been concerned with to this point, but in its concrete happening.[10]

While we will attempt to follow Meyer and Wright – the latter very briefly – as they unpack that self-understanding, only to a point can we repeat the intricate details to be found in their work, and only to a point can we adjudicate the relatively incidental disagreements with Meyer that occasionally mark the work of Wright. I will end this chapter with a brief summation of conclusions that can be drawn from their work regarding the intentions of Jesus as he went to his death. That summation will be filled out in what follows in the next chapter, which is almost exclusively devoted to Meyer. But even the summation itself can yield a new beginning for soteriology, connecting the message of salvation with the mission and aims of Jesus in concrete historical circumstances and simultaneously overcoming centuries of misplaced or at least unfounded emphases in this crucial doctrine of the faith.

2   Faith, Theology, and History

We should address first, however, a problem that Meyer and Wright have begun to help us solve, namely, the divorce of theological meaning from what was going forward in the history involving Jesus of Nazareth.

> … orthodoxy, as represented by much popular preaching and writing, has had no clear idea of the purpose of Jesus' ministry. For many conservative theologians it would have been sufficient if Jesus had been born of a virgin (at any time in human history, and perhaps from any race), lived a sinless life, died a sacrificial death, and risen again three days later … The fact that, in the midst of these events Jesus actually said and did certain things, which included giving wonderful moral teaching and annoying some of his contemporaries, functions within this sort of orthodox scheme merely as a convenience … If the main purpose of Jesus' ministry was to die on the cross, as the outworking of an abstracted atonement-theology, it starts to look as though he simply took on the establishment in order to get himself crucified, so that the abstract sacrificial theology could be put into effect. This makes both ministry and death look like sheer contrivance.[11]

Once we grasp that the gospels *do* provide data that enable us to define the self-understanding and the aims of Jesus in the concrete circumstances of first-century second-Temple Judaism, and that these data are theologically significant since they indicate precisely what his mission was and why he was killed, radical nuances are introduced that will affect the tenor of the whole of systematic soteriology, and from there most of the rest of systematic theology. Meyer and Wright help us acknowledge that the kerygmatic character of New Testament faith formulations does not disqualify their historical character, nor does the disengagement of that historical character lessen their theological impact. *Early Christian faith formulations intended past events as the very content of the faith they expressed.* They were historical affirmations *precisely in and as formulations of the faith of the early church.* That faith is precisely the affirmation of something that *happened*, the affirmation of theological meaning in concrete historical events. This is not unconnected with the emphases I raised above, especially in chapter 3, on the locus of the sacred *in human history*.

The movement into soteriology normally begins with a question such as, What, concretely, does it mean to say, "Jesus died for our sins?" Or more broadly, just what *is* salvation, and how is it related to the death of Jesus, precisely as that death follows upon his life and precedes his resurrection? I want to address these questions as a doctrinal and systematic theologian, and so as someone who is engaged in what Lonergan's *Method in Theology* would call theology's second phase, the phase where theologians stand on their own two feet and say, not what others have said, as is the case when one is working in interpretation and history, but (1) what they themselves hold to be true and (2) how they understand what they hold to be true. However, for systematicians to fulfil this task, they must be prepared to negotiate in a responsible fashion the process from the data of the sources to the contemporary effort to state Christian constitutive meaning in a systematic fashion. The first of the questions just mentioned, "What, concretely, does it mean to say that Jesus died for our sins?" *cannot be answered in any meaningful way apart from at least some minimal understanding of the Jewish observances regarding temple sacrifices and the removal of sin and a more robust understanding of the intention of Jesus radically to shift the locus and meaning of sacrifice, sin, atonement, and expiation: to shift the locus from the temple to human history, and to shift the meaning from cult to human relations.* "Truly I tell you, just as you did it to one of the least of these who are members of my family, you did it to me" (Matthew 25.40). *That shift of focus and meaning from the temple to himself and from ritual sacrifice to self-sacrificing love in history is what led to his death.* He reinterpreted the entire meaning of the Jewish Temple sacrifices, so that mercy, forgiveness, and table fellowship with the outcast become the embodiment of the reign of God and the clear mark of the return of Yahweh to Zion. This *is* the new covenant, and the expiatory sacrifice that mediates its arrival was not performed in a building but in the concrete historical encounters with the political and religious leaders of his day and with the poor and lowly who became his followers and spread his message and word to the ends of the earth. Still, the point remains that even the language of "expiatory sacrifice" cannot be understood except against the backdrop of his radical reinterpretation of the entire Jewish liturgical tradition. The reign of God occurs in human history, not inside a building. It occurs in self-sacrificing love in human relations, not in the sacrifice of animals.

Eventually, our contribution to a contemporary systematic soteriology in the next volume will include an affirmation of the significance of the scale of values. But we must first say something about the starting point in the data found in the biblical sources. What did it mean when biblical authors affirmed that Jesus died for our sins? What is the connection between that biblical affirmation and *Jesus' own aims and intentions?*

I begin, then, with a proposal offered by Peter Laughlin in *Jesus and the Cross.* Laughlin's thesis may be expressed in two statements.

First, if we are going to understand what is meant by the nearly universal Christian doctrinal affirmation that Jesus died for our sins – 1 Corinthians 15.3, probably one of the earliest written statements of the original Christian message – the first step beyond assenting to this affirmation must lie in an attempt to state *how* his death functions to "save" us from our sins. "How can this be true?" and "What does this mean?" are the constant questions of the systematic theologian, especially when "this" refers to a statement that can legitimately be viewed as a doctrinal affirmation expressing the mystery that functions as the constitutive meaning of the community of the church. And perhaps no other statement fulfils that description more than "Jesus died for our sins."

Second, in responding to the questions "How can this be true?" or "What does this mean?" there is incumbent upon us a commitment to "*demonstrate a degree of continuity*" with *the meaning that Jesus himself understood his death to have.*[12] This mandate enables us to state another thesis, taken directly from Laughlin's recommendation.

> **Thesis 85:** *Contemporary soteriologies will inevitably and correctly attempt to seek the redemptive meaning of Jesus' passion, death, and resurrection in categories appropriate to the situations in which these theologies are developed. Our efforts in this direction will be mediated by work on the scale of values. Still, the fundamental criterion for the validity of a soteriology is not its relevance to contemporary issues but its ability to demonstrate a degree of continuity with the meaning that Jesus understood these events to have, that is, with his aims and objectives as his pursuit of them led him to the cross.*

This means, of course, that every legitimate soteriology must also be prepared to take a stand on precisely what that meaning is that Jesus understood his death to have. And for this we will attempt to synthesize the results of critical-realist exegesis and history as these bear on the question of Jesus' understanding of his mission. In this way, we are moving from the position on the consciousness of Jesus presented in the previous chapter to a position on his human self-understanding, his human knowledge of who he was and what he was to do. In order to do this, we must not only keep in mind such systematic-theological doctrines about Jesus' human knowledge as that proposed by Lonergan,[13] but also rely on the fruits of critical-realist biblical exegesis. Perhaps there is no issue more appropriate for integrating the hermeneutical/historical and the doctrinal/systematic phases of theology than the issue of the consciousness and knowledge of Jesus of Nazareth.

This intended convergence is really not a reconciliation, because exegesis and doctrinal/systematic theology have hardly ever really been joined in any truly methodological way as parts of a common enterprise. They have in general not been regarded as moments in a collaborative process that moves explicitly and methodically from the data of exegesis and historical research to contemporary systematic theology and to the subsequent communication of the meaning of Christian faith to the many cultures of humankind. True, manual theologies started the exposition of many of their theses with biblical texts, then moved to opinions expressed in the course of history, especially those of "adversaries," and concluded with some kind of attempt at systematic understanding of a doctrine. But the biblical texts rarely received any methodical exegesis, and the appeal to opinions expressed in history was in no way to be thought of as a critical history of what was really going forward. The two phases never were regarded as moments in a collaborative process that moves from the data provided by research through methodical exegesis and critical-historical reconstruction to contemporary systematic theology and to the subsequent communication of the meaning of Christian faith to the many cultures of humankind; or if they were so regarded, it was in an uncontrolled, merely random fashion.

The scholarly differentiation, and so what we have come to call historical mindedness,[14] emerged as a cultural force during the nineteenth century. But this emergence occurred before anything along the lines of a move to interiority as control of meaning had been proposed. With that proposal, there has been made possible an explicit appropriation of the schemes of recurrence of cognitional operations. The proposal was offered initially, in Lonergan's book *Insight*, in the context of modern science. But the emergence of historical mindedness is responsible for inspiring Lonergan to develop his cognitional theory beyond what is found in *Insight*, especially by investigating the realm of historical knowledge. *Method in Theology* has made possible the appropriation of a critical-realist epistemology of exegesis and history.

The doctrinal/systematic side of the divide is not without responsibility for the alienation within theology that, I am proposing, can now slowly be transcended. While serious scholarly work was going forward without an adequate cognitional theory to guide it, the late phases in what Lonergan called the second stage of meaning, where meaning is controlled by theory and theory is governed by logic, were active in the culture of much twentieth-century Catholic systematic theology, including, as is evident from Lonergan's Latin texts, the theology that he had to write and teach at the Gregorian University in Rome. Given the simultaneous functioning of serious scholarly work that was not guided by a critical-realist cognitional theory, on the one hand, and an outdated Scholastic systematic theology, on the other, we have the situation that Lonergan describes when he writes,

"Scholarship [built] an impenetrable wall between systematic theology and its historical religious sources."[15] But, he continues, "this development invites philosophy and theology to migrate from a basis in theory to a basis in interiority. In virtue of that migration, theology can work out a method that both grounds and criticizes critical history, interpretation, and research." That is to say, the method that interiorly differentiated consciousness makes possible grounds and criticizes the very scholarship that, when left ungrounded and uncriticized, built the impenetrable wall. But it also prepares the way for the grounding in interiority of the categories of systematic theological thought – an essential step in the integration of the entire discipline of theology, and especially in the convergence of historical research with systematic thought. Ultimately, the method allows functional specialization, which is the core of the method itself, to redraw the map of theology in its entirety. Perhaps no task was more urgent for Lonergan when he went to work on developing the method that in February of 1965 took the form of functional specialization. Critical-realist exegesis and history, combined with a systematic theology grounded in interiorly and religiously differentiated consciousness, are part of the set of dynamics that make possible a collaboratively and cumulatively organized process from data to results in theology as a collaborative discipline.

If Lonergan speaks of an impenetrable wall, Laughlin proposes a different image of the same estrangement of exegesis from systematic thought:

> Theology and historical Jesus studies could be compared to estranged cousins who through some strange turn of events happen to arrive at the same family party [with each one not knowing] that the other was going to be there. [Once they see] each other across the room, much effort is then expended on both sides ensuring that a sufficient number of other guests remain between them so as to prevent a direct confrontation. For their part, theologians tend to decry the various quests for the historical Jesus as misplaced adventures into history that result in nothing but irrelevancies for faith. On the other hand, historical Jesus scholars are quite critical of the theologian's practice of playing ostrich – willfully hiding their head in the sand, hoping that the flurry of historical activity around them will go away without disturbing their carefully laid and systematized nest.[16]

In Laughlin's description, it may be noted, the systematic theologians are at least as responsible for the fragmentation of theological knowledge as is the epistemology of many exegetes.

Functional specialization has slowly been tearing down the wall, if I may return to Lonergan's image, or filling the room with guests who will mediate a meeting, to use Laughlin's portrayal of the situation. Ever so gradually, a theology is communally being constructed that displays a cumulative process from data, that is, from historical religious sources and especially from biblical sources, to results, to a renewed systematic theology and to communications that are rooted in sound exegesis and history, in transposed doctrinal statements, in coherent systematic understanding, and in responsible discernment of the signs of the time. Or again, functional specialization has seen to it that among the guests positioned between systematic theologians and historical Jesus scholars are people well versed in dialectic, in horizon analysis based on the appropriation of interiority, in the derivation of theological categories, and in the contemporary formulation of theological doctrines: that is to say, in what in my slight but not insignificant departure from Lonergan's listing of functional specialties would be the fourth (dialectic), fifth (horizons), sixth (categories), and seventh (doctrines) specialties, out of nine.[17] These guests are well trained to mediate a homecoming of exegetes and historians to a long theological tradition and of systematicians to the ultimate source of all they do, the biblical word of God, as they start to engage in the massive work of transposing permanent achievements, including those of "medieval theory," from the second stage of meaning into a systematic theology truly written at the level of our time. These guests are equipped to introduce historical Jesus studies to systematic theology, and systematic theology to the renewed quest for the historical Jesus that is being carried on under the guidance of the critical realism that is the first fruit of the movement into the third stage of meaning. They are equipped to make possible the communal process from data to results that a functionally specialized theology *is*.

All of this sounds very wonderful, of course, but we must admit that we are in a very early phase, almost an initial phase, in developing the kind of theology that functional specialization makes possible. The wall that modern scholarship has built between sources and system was impenetrable until a cognitional theory was proposed that could ground and criticize critical history, interpretation, and research, that is to say, until exegetes, historians, and scholars became, at least functionally, critical realists, *and* until systematicians started to take seriously Lonergan's prescriptions for transposition from medieval theory to contemporary interiority.[18] To date, only a few exegetes, historians, scholars, and even systematicians have been influenced, directly or indirectly, by such a cognitional theory. But to the extent they have, they have migrated (some more than others) to a basis in interiority, and in so doing have begun either, as exegetes, to recover the historical religious sources in a manner that allows a cumulative process from data to results to go forward or, as systematic theologians, to process all categories through a transpositional movement based in interiorly and religiously differentiated consciousness. They have begun to tear down the wall.[19]

Thus, Wright wants to link concern for rigorous historical construction with a new integration of history and theology that will do justice to both. What Wright calls the third quest for the historical Jesus, of which he is arguably the most prolific and influential proponent to date, "has produced tools that enable us to attempt this task with high hopes."[20] In his view we must take the historical questions and challenges on board, *expecting to find theological meaning in historical events*. We cannot retreat into a private world of "faith" which history cannot touch. The third quest is the basic starting point of his book *Jesus and the Victory of God*. It highlights first-century second-Temple Jewish eschatology, correctly understood, as the key to understanding Jesus, his mindset, his aims, his intentions. Wright insists that we can attain a real advance in our understanding of Jesus within his historical context, and thus raise in new ways the vital questions of continuity and discontinuity between Jesus of Nazareth and Christian faith, and between the agenda of Jesus of Nazareth and the contemporary task of the church. *Pace* Bultmann, "we can know quite a lot about Jesus." What we can know is extremely important to the whole of Christian theology. "What we know, with the kind of 'knowledge' proper to all historical inquiry, may turn out to generate theological and practical significance far in excess of, and perhaps quite different from, anything that recent scholarship, and recent Christianity, has imagined or wanted ... Authentic Christianity ... has nothing to fear from history," for it is rooted in it.[21]

But Wright would also admit that, at least for him, the first dominant figure in this movement was the late Ben F. Meyer. Pages 76–110 in *The Aims of Jesus*, that is, the two chapters entitled "Jesus and Critical History" and "History and Faith," are the foundation of much that came later, not only in that book but also in a renewed quest for the historical Jesus. Wright joins Meyer, adds to his accomplishments, and, where he judges it to be necessary, carefully and respectfully suggests developments on them. He proposes as well what in effect is a needed explicitation of one component in Lonergan's cognitional theory, by drawing attention to the specific kind of knowledge contained in and expressed through symbols, stories, and praxis, through what Lonergan calls the carriers of *elemental meaning* or pre-conceptual communication, as well as through the questions and answers so central to Lonergan's work.[22] The initial revelation especially of *redemptive* significance is, I dare say, always conveyed at this pre-conceptual or elemental level, and conceptualization of that elemental meaning is always a complicated affair – never more complicated than the movement from the death of Jesus as a political prisoner to the affirmation that "he died for me."

The difficulty of articulating in conceptual terms the same meaning that was expressed in symbol, story, and praxis is analogous to the difficulty that Lonergan expresses when he speaks of moving from ineffable to effable knowledge. It also has gone through a series of transpositions from one context to another. The precise naming of those transpositions is the task of historical scholarship guided by interiority analysis, but perhaps we may suggest that the first transposition was suggested by Jesus himself at the very end of his life, including during the Last Supper: a transposition from the political circumstances of his death to the grounds of Pauline soteriology. Paul himself suggests precisely this in 1 Corinthians 11.23–26. We may also claim that another transposition (I won't say "the second one" for there may have been several in between) occurred in moving from Paul's "justification" to Thomas Aquinas's *gratia gratum faciens*, "sanctifying grace"; and that yet another was offered in Lonergan's movement from "sanctifying grace" to "the dynamic state of being in love with God."

To be sure, we must also acknowledge that Meyer had already anticipated Wright's advances in regard to elemental meaning in general, at least in his claim, very important to his book *The Aims of Jesus*, that prophetic symbols intend what is identical with what God, for whom the prophet speaks, intends, *even if this may enter the prophet's own horizon only partially and imperfectly.* Did even Jesus have determinate "literal" human knowledge of what God intended by the symbolic scheme of things which he was commissioned to announce and in fact to incarnate? His formulable, "effable" knowledge of the historical matters conveyed through his symbolic expressions grew in several ways, as the result of two distinct processes: acquired human knowledge resulting from his own human experience, human understanding, and human judgment yielding a reasonable affirmation of an understanding of his situation, and the insights that were revelatory actual graces communicated to him in prayer and reflection. But what Meyer calls his prophetic knowledge remained limited knowledge. It was distinct in kind from so-called "empirical" knowledge. History understood in hindsight within the perspective of faith does what the prophet cannot do as he or she enunciates the symbols. The work of the historian deciphers prophetic symbols, and translates images into events, schematic sequences into actual sequences, and symbolic time into real time.[23] Thus, to use an example proposed by Meyer, for the eye of faith the visionary imagery of Jesus about the many coming from east and west to recline with Abraham, Isaac, and Jacob in the reign of God is inchoately transposed into time, place, and action in terms of the world mission of the church, which in turn is constrained by the connection with Jesus' symbolic discourse to remain faithful to what really constitutes God's reign. Again, Wright's crucial insistence that the language of Mark 13 and parallel passages does not refer to the end of the space-time universe but to the destruction of the temple and of Jerusalem makes the kind of sense that only a historian can make of the symbolic language of Jesus in these texts. The prophet knows the symbols and attains only a gradually developing understanding of at least part of what they symbolize.[24] As Jesus admitted, even the Son did not know the exact time when these things (the destruction of Jerusalem and the temple) would take place (Mark 13.32). He knew *that* they would take place, not *when*.

Thus, where the systematician Lonergan will write that Jesus had human knowledge of everything that pertained to his mission, the critical-realist exegete will say, Yes, he did, but at first it was prophetic, symbolic knowledge that had yet to be translated into the particularities of history. In systematic-theological terms, we may say that it was translated for him to an extent by revelation, that is, by divinely given insights that were actual graces disclosing step by step what was to be done, what was to be said, how to do and say it, and what would happen as a result.[25] And for us it is further translated into an understanding of the actual historical events that we can know *because they have already occurred.* Wright has expanded what Meyer thus writes about prophetic knowledge into the specific kind of knowledge contained in and expressed through the symbols, stories, and praxis employed in biblical literature.

I am trying, then, to disengage from the work of Meyer and Wright what we may say with respect to the limited issue of Jesus' *understanding* of what his mission entailed, and especially with respect to his attitude regarding his own impending death. Wright claims that such a task is doable and that it is of the utmost theological significance.[26]

In his foreword to Laughlin's *Jesus and the Cross*, Neil Ormerod recalls how Meyer's book *The Aims of Jesus* stood out as something very unusual when it appeared. It was a serious, scholarly, patient, and measured approach to a renewed quest for the historical Jesus. What perhaps made it most unusual was that it was probably the first serious attempt on the part of a biblical scholar to display Lonergan's method in interpretation and history. This may be what accounted for its other unusual characteristics.[27] In effect, it began a movement. Ormerod draws attention to the implications of the title of Meyer's book: Jesus had intentions, aims, a purpose to his actions. Central to Meyer's work was the uncovering of those aims. "Only then would we understand the nature of his mission and its relationship to the coming Kingdom of God."[28]

Laughlin focuses the issue of Jesus' aims around Jesus' self-understanding as he went to his death. He puts the problem that Meyer and Wright have begun to help us answer: What relationship, if any, exists between our understanding of Jesus' death as redemptive and the meaning Jesus himself gives to his death? The history of Christian theology is littered with answers to the meaning of Jesus' death as redemptive, but what is surprising is how little attention has been given to the meaning that Jesus gave to this event. "While all Christians agree that Jesus' death and resurrection have saving significance, we are hardly so clear as to how or why this is the case. That it might have something to do with the meaning Jesus himself gave to his death is rarely if ever pursued."[29] If we can understand how Jesus understood his death, then that is where a contemporary soteriology must begin. In fact, if we cannot understand the meaning he gave to his death, then it must be asked if we have any reason at all to call his death redemptive.

I am going to take a slightly different approach to the question, however, from the one taken by Laughlin. For Laughlin, the first step is "to unpick the knotted skein of questions in relation to necessity and contingency, of God's relationship to the created order and God's permissive will in relation to the problem of evil." If that can be done, it "frees Laughlin from the commonly expressed concern that Christian theologies of the death of Jesus somehow turn God into a divine child-abuser, needing the death of Jesus to appease his anger at human sinfulness."[30] And the second step is the question of the relationship between history and theological meaning. "Should there be any connection at all between the faith proclaimed by the church (theological meaning) and the historical events constituted by the meaning and value of Jesus' life and death?"[31] In my view, the historical question must be faced first. There is no point to the other question if there is no satisfactory answer to the question of the relation of faith and history. We will take up the further question of the redemptive significance of Jesus' death in our third volume, partly by studying, developing, and critiquing Lonergan's contributions to soteriology. These are contributions in which Laughlin's first step is adequately and fully taken. But the movement begun by Meyer's call for a critical-realist approach to exegesis is the first source of soteriological meaning that we will investigate: the meaning of Jesus himself.

The disastrous split between theological meaning and historical research

> … is nowhere more evident than in the understanding of what happened when Jesus hung on the cross. Theologians have tended to systematize the cross event into an overarching salvific narrative which has no need for, or any sense of, the historic particulars; whereas the majority of historical Jesus scholarship understands the cross to have no real meaning at all; it is simply what happens when one goes up against the established might of Rome. For the former, the perilous task of peeling back the layers of history to try and discover the "real Jesus" yields nothing of the truth and can be safely ignored. For the latter, theological interpretations of Jesus' death are merely later accretions of the faith community which are stitched together by devoted followers in the hope of making sense of what happened to their dearly beloved, and recently departed, leader.[32]

In Wright's words, "Generations of gospel readers in search of atonement-theology, or at least atonement-homiletics, *ignored the actual story the evangelists were telling, with all its rough political edges, in favor of the theological scheme the story was deemed to be inculcating, or at least illustrating.*"[33] More precisely, "ever since the early church reflected upon what happened on the cross, Christians have proclaimed a consistent message: 'Christ died for our sins' (1 Cor 15.3). But the question of how Christ's death functions to 'save' us from our sins remains. What is it ... that makes the atonement 'work'?"[34] Meyer and Wright beckon us to retrieve the aims of Jesus himself as we attempt to answer this question.

Wright's genealogy of the building of the wall between historical scholarship and theology begins with the Reformation. "... it may be questioned whether [the reformers] ever found a satisfactory way of making the literal sense of the *Gospels* yield worthwhile theological results."[35] The gospels function more as "repositories" of the same "timeless truth" that can be found more clearly in the epistles. They are not "stories which were there for their own sake, but ... collections of sayings of Jesus which then became, as it were, mini-epistles; or of events which showed the clash between false religion ... and the true one offered by Jesus."[36] The death and resurrection of Jesus are together an event to be understood "not as the execution of an awkward figure who refused to stop rocking the first-century Jewish or Roman boat, but as the saving divine act whereby the sins of the world were dealt with once and for all," a divine act that "did not have very much to do with what went before ... The reformers had very thorough answers to the question: 'Why did Jesus die?' They did not have nearly such good answers to the question: 'Why did Jesus live?'"[37] Some reformers intended a break with history in founding new churches in supposed continuity with Christ but decided discontinuity with the medieval church. But their work sparked another break with history, one at the very heart of the faith. "Continuity with Christ meant sitting loose to the actuality of Jesus, to his Jewishness, to his own aims and objectives."[38] Nor have Catholics fared better.

> Within post-Reformation circles, both Catholic and Protestant, there has been a general use of the Gospels as sourcebooks for ethics and doctrine, for edifying tales or ... allegory ... Jesus was the divine Christ who redeemed the world and whose derivative authority, whether through pope or preacher, was exercised to the supposed benefit of [the] world. The icon was in place, and nobody asked whether the Christ it portrayed – and in whose name so much good and ill was done – was at all like the Jesus whom it claimed to represent.[39]

Wright offers us in at least two places a nice history of the Quest and of the New Quest for the historical Jesus[40] and then asks us to consider the merits of his own proposal of a "Third Quest." It is with some of the fruits of the so-called Third Quest that we will attempt to find an answer to our question: What relationship exists between our understanding of Jesus' death as redemptive and the meaning Jesus himself gives to his death?

Laughlin emphasizes that even in the New Testament there is "not a reduction of the power of the cross to a single understanding but a number of metaphors and images that collectively weave a tapestry of meaning": the death of the Paschal lamb (1 Corinthians 5.7), the inauguration of a new covenant (Hebrews 8.8, 9.15), the paid ransom price (Mark 10.45), a sin offering (Romans 8.3), and an example to follow (1 Peter 2.21).[41] What we are attempting to do may be understood as an effort to find a way to bring together what is symbolized in these various expressions. "The fact that these multiple reflections exist is perhaps why the Nicene Creed simply stated without any elaboration that Christ died 'for us and for our salvation.' But that does not prevent us from attempting to find some systematic framework that will integrate things. It seems that the early church quickly recognized that the meaning of the cross readily transcended any one interpretation,"[42] but what happened as well is that theories of atonement were left to describe for themselves how it is that the cross functions *for us.* No connection was drawn in a convincing way between the biblical images, which were left unintegrated, and the fancies of the theories of atonement. Diverse motifs emerged as differing cultures and contexts appropriated the cross event anew. "… changing cultures and contexts demand new articulations" if "the saving significance of the cross can continue to be meaningfully appropriated."[43] Such reflections are temporal and often only temporarily relevant, but because of the universal significance of the cross it is tempting to elevate our favorite motifs above cultural considerations and declare them to be equivalently universal. Laughlin says this is perhaps what Bernard of Clairvaux did in defending Anselm against Abelard.[44] Can we honestly think Jesus would see himself and his aims and intentions in Anselm's satisfaction theory, to say nothing of the gross misinterpretations Anselm has received? I doubt it. But, however that may be, "… it is *people* who are saved – not theological expressions."[45]

Still, while Christ's death remains *pro nobis,* the challenges facing our own communities do have to be considered as we try to understand how the death of Christ functions "for us," in the here and now. And in the light of that tension, Laughlin asks, Are there any limits, and if so where are they to be found? His answer is one with which I agree and have transferred to a thesis in this chapter: "a faithful atonement motif will demonstrate a degree of continuity *with the meaning that Jesus of Nazareth constituted for his death.*"[46] While I would use another word than "constituted" here, the point Laughlin is making is essential. We must treat the historical intention of Jesus with the utmost theological respect. Jesus' self-understanding has played very little part in Christian interpretations of the cross. We find "systematizations of a universal soteriology rather than direct historical questions as to what Jesus thought his death would accomplish."[47] Our stories of salvation have to do "not ... with a first-century Galilean Jew in conflict with the religious authorities of his day, but with God's holy nature and the satisfaction of its just demands, the enslavement of all humankind to Satan, sin, death and evil and our subsequent liberation, or the creation of a 'new humanity' embracing all who follow Christ's teachings and example or participate in his death and resurrection."[48] "... if God really did become flesh as the New Testament proclaims then we cannot abstract the eternal meaning of the cross from its historical actuality."[49]

> Jesus' intention for his death ... should be investigated in the first instance for what it might contribute to a theology of the atonement. This is not to say that our atonement motifs must be limited to what we know of Jesus' self-intention, but it *is* to say that our motifs should not be articulated [in abstraction from that intention]. Faith in the preached Christ cannot be allowed to float free from the Jesus of history. Without such an anchor, Christology itself pays the ultimate price.[50]

Hans-Georg Gadamer has called attention to the hermeneutical significance of application to contemporary situations, and as well to the effective history, the *Wirkungsgeschichte*, that successive applications will exercise in the expansion of a tradition. Neither Laughlin nor I are attempting to deny these facets as they influence the development of soteriology. I will be making my own applications in the next volume, drawing very much on the contributions to soteriology of René Girard and of Bernard Lonergan, and moving these contributions into my own exposition of the scale of values. But what both Laughlin and I would want to insist on is that applications and their effective histories must be in continuity with Jesus' self-understanding. In fact, *part of the effective history of Jesus' own self-understanding enters into the New Testament expressions of soteriological meaning*. The first historical issue has to do with how much these expressions tie back to Jesus himself. And here Laughlin writes, "What I have yet to discover is a theological work that attempts to seriously integrate the results of historical Jesus research into its own atonement discussion."[51] Again,

> Either Jesus' intention is considered completely irrelevant, or it is portrayed as reflecting the atonement motif in question [in various theologians' proposals] and thus changes dramatically from one discussion to the next ... whatever it was that Jesus intended his death to achieve has very little bearing on the discussion at hand ... should this be the case? ... recent work on the historical Jesus does have a

significant contribution to make to an understanding of the cross, and this contribution should be incorporated as far as possible into our presentations of the atonement.[52]

This is what Laughlin attempts to do in his book, and it is what we will attempt to do inchoately in the next chapter, drawing extensively on Meyer and briefly on Wright, and more fully in the third volume, where I will speak once again in direct discourse.

The problem that Laughlin takes up first, and that we will postpone until after we have treated the relation of faith and history, should at least be signalled at this point. It is a twofold problem: how can divine meaning be created for contingent events, and how can salvific meaning be derived from violence and suffering? Laughlin's argument and our own (both relying on Lonergan) is that God can create meaning out of the cross event without requiring that the evil in that event be divinely caused. If that is the case, then the historical intention of Jesus should have a role in faith's understanding of salvation, without fear that it will be understood to justify acts of oppression and abuse.

It is generally assumed that Jesus knew his death would have universal atoning significance, but rarely is anything said as to *why* such an understanding would make sense for him within his Palestinian first-century context. The cross's saving significance is found not in Jesus' intention per se but in some overarching salvific narrative that is presumed to be God's account of what happened and why. Jesus' life is merely the prerequisite for his all-important and all-conquering death. As Wright says, if all we knew about Jesus' life came from the traditional atonement motifs, it could readily be assumed that Jesus' ministry was simply designed to bring him up against the establishment so that he could get himself crucified.

Thus, texts such as Mark 10.45 and the Last Supper accounts (both narrating events that happened within days of each other) are usually read in theological contexts that have nothing to do with their first-century setting. As Anselm did not think of making any serious attempt to demonstrate that the historical Jesus believed his death would restore God's honor, so there is a danger as we develop contemporary soteriological motifs that we would also ignore the historical particulars of Jesus' death, and especially his Jewish expectations and the eschatological context of the first century, in favor of some coherent contemporary contextualization. When interest in what actually happened is subordinate to how we can incorporate the cross into some contemporary salvific model, the effect is to de-historicize the cross, so that Jesus' intention as he went to his death has no part to play in theological interpretations.[53] The impenetrable wall is simply taken for granted. If we begin with an ahistorical interpretation, it is doubtful that an appropriation of the life and ministry of Jesus will yield anything other than our own soteriological conception. The focus is not on getting right the narrative of the past events, but on somehow making the cross fit into a coherent narrative for the present. The operative assumption is that there is no normative Christian way of proclaiming salvation. We must allow the contemporary context *alone* to dictate the theological appropriation of the Christian hope. A divine soteriological narrative is woven together in a manner predefined along the lines of a contemporary context. It may even be the case that the divine soteriological narrative can be redefined to exclude the cross. Then the narrative is limited to some present contextual need. That is to allow the contemporary context to dictate to theology what should and should not be included in telling the salvific story.

Over against these tendencies, Laughlin, and behind him Meyer and Wright and others, are insisting that we need to get to the aims and intentions of Jesus. We need to face the question of what narrative he found himself in as he went to his death on the cross. What is the meaning he gave to his life, ministry, and death? Contemporary soteriologies must be equipped to demonstrate continuity with that meaning.

3   Concluding Theses

We conclude the present chapter by stating several theses that sum up where we have arrived and anticipate where we are going.

> **Thesis 86:** *Redemption occurs, in part, in and with respect to concrete historical events, as the inbreaking of the reign of God in history.*

Countless references can be found in Lonergan's works to substantiate this claim and indicate what it means. Here we present just four.

> … a religion that promotes self-transcendence to the point, not merely of justice, but of self-sacrificing love, will have *a redemptive role in human society* inasmuch as such love can undo the mischief of decline and restore the cumulative process of progress.[54]

Again,

> As human authenticity promotes progress and human unauthenticity generates decline, so Christian authenticity – which is a love of others that does not shrink from self-sacrifice and suffering – is the sovereign means for *overcoming evil. Christians bring about the kingdom of God in the world* not only by doing good but also by overcoming evil

with good (Romans 12.21). Not only is there the progress of mankind but also there is development and progress within Christianity itself; and as there is development, so too there is decline; and as there is decline, there also is the problem of undoing it, of overcoming evil with good not only in the world but also in the church.[55]

Again,

> The church is a redemptive process. The Christian message, incarnate in Christ scourged and crucified, dead and risen, tells not only of God's love, but also of man's sin. Sin is alienation from man's authentic being, which is self-transcendence, and sin justifies itself by ideology. As alienation and ideology are destructive of community, so the self-sacrificing love that is Christian charity reconciles alienated man to his true being, and *undoes the mischief initiated by alienation and consolidated by ideology.*[56]

Finally,

> … the fundamental theorem [in the becoming of us and of Christ] is transforming evil into good, absorbing the evil of the world by putting up with it, not perpetuating it as rigid justice would demand. And that putting up with it acts as a blotter, *transforms the situation, and creates the situation in which good flourishes.*[57]

In other words, redemption is something one dimension of which occurs within history,[58] as a result of what a metaphysical theology would call the formal effects of habitual and actual grace as these lead to lives conformed to the law of the cross. Those formal effects come together in the theology presented here under the category of "social grace," and that category is presented as a contemporary transposition of the biblical notion of the reign of God. The integral scale of values will be appealed to as naming the constitution of both social grace and the reign of God in history. As we have seen, the scale of values is the key to the notion of social grace, which itself is a contemporary transposition of at least part of what is meant by "the reign of God."[59]

I have used the category "social grace" to refer to the formal effects of actual and habitual grace in the dynamic functioning of the scale of values. Chapter 2 of the first volume in this work, *Missions and Processions*, is devoted to exposing the Trinitarian structure of habitual grace as a participation in, and communication and imitation of, divine active spiration, of the Father and the Son together as they spirate the Holy Spirit. Chapter 3 of this volume, "Actual Grace and the Elevation of the Secular," establishes the relation of actual grace to habitual grace. For habitual grace is conveyed in two ways: by sacramental baptism, yes, but also, and probably far more frequently in the course of history, as the outcome of at least some instances of what would become known after Aquinas as actual grace, operative and cooperative. This dynamic may be expressed in brief fashion in another thesis.

> **Thesis 87:** *The invisible missions of Word and Holy Spirit are initially, and respectively, the actual grace of divinely given insights into the reign of God in concrete circumstances of human life and divinely prompted elevations of horizon to the ends dictated by supernatural charity. As the operative grace of these gifts becomes the cooperative grace that enables human assent, the justifying gift of God's love, a created participation in and communication and imitation of divine active spiration, starts into movement what* in Missions and Processions *I called the immanent constitution of life in God, the indwelling of the three divine persons, that is, habitual grace.*

The connection with the scale of values can be expressed in a further thesis.

> **Thesis 88:** *This immanent constitution is the structure of the realm of religious values in the scale of values, in the form of elevated* memoria, *from which there proceed faith, charity, and hope.*

Elevated *memory* is an analogue for the Father; *faith,* the knowledge born of the gift of love, is an analogue for the Son; *charity* is an analogue for the Holy Spirit; and *hope* is the disposition that keeps the person who is endowed with faith and charity, and so sharing in the life of the Son and the Holy Spirit, ever headed toward the eschatological "vision" of the Father. As we have seen, such "religious values" are the condition of the possibility of sustained personal integrity (personal value); persons of integrity represent the condition of possibility of genuine meanings and values informing ways of living (cultural values); the pursuit of such cultural values is a constitutive dimension in the establishment of social structures and intersubjective habits (social values) that would increase the probability of a more equitable distribution of vital values to the human community (vital values). The integral functioning of the scale of values thus represents a set of formal effects of the gift of God's grace (religious values). It constitutes in effect at least a heuristic anticipation of what the reign of God in human affairs would be.

Another thesis anticipates what we will labor to establish.

Thesis 89: *Redemption as end in this life and in the life to come is the reign of God, mediated by the suffering, death, and resurrection of the incarnate Word. These events are themselves redemptive mediation. They are also a revelatory event displaying a universal pattern through which the reign of God is advanced, a pattern of returning good for evil and so transforming the evil into a greater good. The greater good is the new community, which continues in this life to mediate the reign of God through the suffering that returns good for evil, and which will enjoy forever in the new creation the most intimate realization possible of God's victory.*

And finally, as promised, we offer a brief summary statement of the conclusions that can be drawn regarding the self-understanding of Jesus as he went to his death:

Thesis 90: *In the process of moving from mission consciousness to self-understanding in the context of mission, Jesus wrought radical changes on, and then integrated, the familiar Jewish conceptions of sin, sacrifice, and expiation, and the familiar Jewish figures of Messiah, Son of Man, and Servant of Yahweh. The radical changes had to do with the growing realization that redemptive and expiatory suffering in the concrete historical details of his own life, and as mediating a new covenant, would be a principal characteristic of who he was. All of these conceptions were Jewish, human categories, processed and brought together through his developing human self-knowledge. Jesus came to adjudicate them in the light of a further, divine knowledge of his equality with God, which over time became also part of his human self-understanding and was manifest in his doing what his compatriots knew only God could do. All of these developments came to pass as Jesus discovered his mission in the concrete historical circumstances and details of first-century second-Temple Palestinian Judaism. The basic pattern of what redemption actually means is embodied in his negotiation of those historical details and circumstances.*

7

Ben F. Meyer, *The Aims of Jesus*, and the Third Quest for the Historical Jesus

1   Two Affirmations

We begin our exposition of Ben Meyer's contribution with two affirmations.

First, Meyer insists that the gospels *do* provide data that enable us to define the self-understanding, the aims, of Jesus. The kerygmatic character of New Testament faith formulations does not disqualify those formulations from being historical. Early Christian faith formulation *did* intend past events. It made historical affirmations as faith statements. Faith and history are not opposed. Faith is precisely the affirmation of something that *happened.*[1]

Second, for Meyer, "the resurrection is the key to all Christian witness to Jesus."[2] It is the key to the transformation of Jesus' disciples into a religious body presenting itself to Israel as the seed of messianic restoration. This simple affirmation was later filled out and developed in enormous detail by Wright's massive book *The Resurrection of the Son of God.* The resurrection can take this role in New Testament writings because and only because, as Wright says with a clarity that we can only wish earlier exegetes had been able to achieve, it really happened.[3]

2   Paul and Acts

Numerous expressions of primitive, pre-gospel christological faith are accessible to us, mainly in Paul and Acts. But these two sources differ, says Meyer, in that (1) very early on, Paul asserts the traditional, handed-on character of given faith formulae, some of which are traced back to Jesus himself, and some of which are formulae that (2) contain an explicit affirmation of the expiatory value of Jesus' death, seemingly with Jesus' own authority (e.g., 1 Corinthians 11.23–24, 15.3–5), while the relevant speeches in Acts (1) reveal no explanation of the transmission of the discourses and so are difficult to locate in terms of their relative antiquity, and (2) contain no reference to expiation.[4] The Pauline material, then, promises to deliver more to meet our current question than does the material in Acts.

With respect to Paul, Meyer concentrates on 1 Corinthians 15.3–5, Romans 4.25, and Romans 8.34: "For I handed on to you as of first importance what I in turn had received: that Christ died for our sins in accordance with the scriptures, and that he was buried, and that he was raised on the third day in accordance with the scriptures, and that he appeared to Cephas, then to the twelve" (1 Corinthians 15.3–5). "… who was delivered up for our transgressions and raised for our acquittal" (Romans 4.25). "… who died, but more, was raised, who is at the right hand of God, who makes intercession for us" (Romans 8.34).[5] Meyer asserts of these passages that their "primary thematic accent is 'he died for our sins' and 'he was raised on the third day.'"[6] *Expiatory death* – for our sins, for our trespasses, for our justification – "*finds conscious expression" as an articulation of the meaning of historical events*[7] – he died and was raised on the third day. *Historical events have theological significance, and sometimes that significance is both expiatory and redemptive.*

An early statement of Meyer's position on the aims of Jesus is helpful in organizing the key materials, for Meyer seems not to have departed much from this early position. Jesus "incorporated his death into his mission by intending it as *covenant sacrifice* and *expiatory offering*,"[8] but precisely as he had appropriated these themes from his own Jewish tradition, made them his own, and transformed them in accord with his own identity and mission. The first, covenant sacrifice, he understood in accord with the promise of the new covenant in Jeremiah 31.31–34, but against the Jewish background of the relation of blood to the sealing of a covenant. He implied in his Eucharistic words that the goal of his mission was "the eschatological restoration of the people of God, correlative to the advance presence of the *reign of God.*"[9] This restoration is precisely the meaning of the new covenant in his blood. With the second theme, expiatory offering, he took "the Isaian Servant as a 'type' to be realized: expiation on behalf of Israel and the peoples."[10] This second dimension "penetrated, broadened, and deepened the first," the covenant sacrifice in his blood. "In life and death Jesus was bent on a mission of reconciliation 'for the life of the world' (John 6:51d)."[11] To use the words of the title of a book by Michael J. Gorman, the expiatory death of the Messiah was, *in the very self-understanding of the Messiah,* the mediation of the birth of the new covenant.[12] This, we will see, is precisely the intelligibility contained in what Bernard Lonergan has called "the just and mysterious law of the cross": *expiatory suffering mediates redemption for those affected by the disorder that led to the suffering itself.* This is a law that is simultaneously revealed and implemented in the death and resurrection of Jesus. The revelation *is* the implementation, and vice versa.

Meyer insists that the scriptural background appealed to in the Pauline expression in 1 Corinthians 15.3 ("in accordance with the scriptures," "for our sins") has to do with "the suffering and glorified Servant" in the Deutero-Isaian sense. "For our sins" derives its very wording from Isaiah 53.5, and so "in accordance with the scriptures" can readily be taken to refer to Deutero-Isaiah on the Servant.[13] The distinctive intention of primitive Christianity's defining confession as reported by Paul is salvation through the paschal mysteries of Jesus, which occurred on the pattern of the Servant displayed in the fourth of Isaiah's so-called Servant Songs. *How* this is redemptive, *how* it is "for us," remains to be seen, but *that* it is affirmed to be redemptive and for us is clear. And it is not only redemptive but also in some sense expiatory, "*for* you," where expiation entails healing the situation affecting all by willingly taking upon oneself the effects of the basic sin that led to the situation itself. Recall Lonergan's image: "… the fundamental theorem is transforming evil into good, absorbing the evil of the world by putting up with it, not perpetuating it as rigid justice would demand. And that putting up with it acts as a blotter, transforms the situation, and creates the situation in which good flourishes."[14] This is the precise locus of the sacred in history, as we argued above in chapter 3.

1 Corinthians 11.23–25 cites a liturgical formula that affirms in faith and interprets the Last Supper, passion, and death: Jesus himself explicitly offers his life "for you." "For I received from the Lord what I also delivered to you: that the Lord Jesus on the night he was betrayed took bread, and having spoken a blessing, broke it and said, 'This is my body which is for you. Do this in remembrance of me.' In the same way also the cup after supper, saying, 'This cup is the new covenant in my blood. Do this, as often as you drink it, in remembrance of me.'" The words "I received from the Lord" indicate that *the origin of the interpretation in terms of the Deutero-Isaian Servant is Jesus himself.*[15] So too, for that matter, is the origin of the interpretation in terms of the mediation of the new covenant in the blood of Jesus. It is Jesus who evokes the prophetic themes of the Servant (Isaiah 53) and the new covenant (Jeremiah 31.31), and who "expresses the intent to make his death an expiation … and a covenant sacrifice …"[16] As we can see, the themes announced in the early article remain central in *The Aims of Jesus*.

In terms of the themes raised in the previous chapter, let us note once again that these are texts whose faith affirmations or kerygmatic messages bear on past historical events. Christian faith is a faith that "intends and interprets events: present meaning hinges on past happening … precisely as the object of the proclaiming and confessing: Christ died for our sins."[17] The original doctrinal expressions are faith affirmations concerned to express the meaning of historical events.

Again, in Philippians 2.6–11, where attention is focused on Jesus in relation to God, on his obedience and dazzling exaltation,[18] "[t]he pivotal 'therefore' ['Therefore God also highly exalted him …'] derives from Isaiah 53 ['Therefore

I will allot him a portion with the great …'], which is likewise a literary source of the general scheme 'obedient lowliness/exalted lordship.'"[19] But Philippians adds a unique emphasis, with its motifs of pre-existence and incarnation. "… the inescapable motifs of pre-existence and incarnation and the terms in which the divinity of Christ is described create the impression of a lyric flowering from the soil of speculation."[20] The text discloses perhaps the church's first speculative or contemplative Christology, probably from a milieu of Jewish-Hellenistic Christians – perhaps, says Meyer, in Antioch. The most distinctive testimony of this text is its affirmation of incarnation, which is assimilated to the humiliation theme. The humiliation of the Servant has two phases: first incarnation, and then obedience unto death.[21]

In Acts, on the other hand, we have evidence of a primitive kerygma, in which "[t]he resurrection, immediately interpreted as messianic event, is understood as the divine *vindication* of Jesus."[22] Again, the proclamation was related from the outset to history: the resurrection formed the climax to a set of historical events. Importance is again accorded the theme of the Isaian Servant's passion and glorification, and yet here there is no reference to the motif of expiation.[23]

Meyer does not indicate here whether he regards the kerygmatic tradition reported in the speeches in Acts as prior, precisely as a tradition, to that found in the Pauline texts to which he refers, but it is likely that he does. If the tradition *is* prior, however, then the motif of expiation arose a bit later than the Pentecost preaching – not much later, of course, since the Pauline texts reflect very early, "definably pre-Pauline confessions of faith."[24] However this is to be interpreted, Meyer's analysis places the Isaian Servant of God at the heart of the early kerygmatic statements about the historical events surrounding the death and resurrection of Jesus, and in fact *traces that interpretation back to Jesus himself.* The pattern of passion and vindicating glorification may have registered first in the understanding of the community, but the expiation component followed quickly, as did the incarnation component found in the passage from Philippians, as the community assembled, with the help of its own collective memory, an understanding of what really happened in the death and resurrection of Jesus, and of who he really was. Both Jesus' equality with God and the expiatory significance of his death and resurrection were the objects of very early Christian faith.

3   Gospel Literature

Meyer finds fundamental continuity, "a generic homogeneity,"[25] between these earliest faith formulations and later gospel literature. The rise of the gospel traditions was a natural outgrowth of Easter faith. "Because the resurrection was seen as vindication, it was by that very fact related to the historic drama of Jesus' mission and rejection."[26] Meyer proposes a sketch of how the gospel tradition developed in successive phases,[27] only to conclude that the gospels do intend the past and so do supply data on Jesus.[28] Their central intent is the nourishment of faith, but past events are not only relevant to revelation and response; they constitute, precisely as the events they are, the meaning of what is revealed.[29]

Meyer's study of the gospels focuses on three sets of data: traditions relating to John the Baptist, public traditions on Jesus, and so-called "esoteric" traditions on Jesus. It is principally in the last of these that the central themes of covenant sacrifice and expiatory self-offering are stressed. But the three are intimately related to one another. There is *a clear progression from lesser to greater differentiation and specificity* as we move from the conclusions on Jesus and John the Baptist through the conclusions on the reign of God in the public traditions to the conclusions on the remnant symbolized by the new temple in the esoteric traditions. "The three sets of conclusions converge, but in their convergence *the second set sublates and interprets the first, [and] the third sublates and interprets the second.*"[30] We will see what this reference to "sublation" means when we treat the second and third sets.

3.1 John the Baptist

Meyer begins his study of the gospels with traditions relating to John. John began his ministry no earlier than the autumn of AD 27 and no later than midsummer of 29.[31] The Baptist's career was a "call to decision" which implied "the assembling by baptism of an open remnant: the Israel of the converted, soon to be purified by Spirit and fire." John's ministry marks for Meyer the return to Israel of prophecy (and to prophecy of Israel)[32] and thus functions as an eschatological symbol, where "eschatology" refers to a decisive break and new beginning. John's baptism was "designed to symbolize and seal the conversion of Israel in the face of approaching judgment."[33] A supremely critical moment for Israel was impending. "... *the standing religious resources, e.g., cultic means of expiation, could not meet [the] imperatives [regarding the conversion and washing of the whole nation].*"[34] Only repentance and baptism could. The themes of the transcendence of evil and the forgiveness of sins are thus central from the beginning, and both of these in relation to *the inadequacy of the temple sacrifices.* John himself discloses "a scheme of salvation in two phases: the water baptism of John and the 'mightier one's' baptism in 'the holy Spirit and fire.'"[35] The clear points are two: "(1) John's own mission was wholly relative to that of the coming judge (2) whose messianic epiphany was imminent."[36] And Jesus' ratification of John's ministry indicates a fundamental agreement with the critique of such "standing religious resources" as the temple sacrifices.

John's baptism of Jesus marked the beginning of Jesus' public religious "career." The baptism and temptation narratives begin to answer the questions that were asked about him from early on: "Who is this Jesus and what is he about?" These narratives depict him as the "Spirit-filled Servant of God and obedient Messiah."[37]

After his time in the desert, Jesus remained in Judea until John's arrest (Mark 1.14, Matthew 4.12). Thus, his public career had two phases: (1) working as baptizer or organizer of baptizers in alliance with John in Judea, which we know a bit more about from the Fourth Gospel, and (2) the ministry in Galilee after the arrest of John, followed by the journey to Jerusalem that takes up so much of Luke's gospel.

In the first phase, Jesus, like John and in alliance with him, preached repentance and baptism. This very fact stamps his own horizon as eschatological in the sense already indicated. It manifests his participation in John's aim to reconstitute Israel in view of the impending judgment. He joined John in calling the powerful and righteous to repentance, and thus already began to sow the seed of conflict between himself and the religious elite of Israel. Jesus refined and extended John's fundamental religious stance. "To the representatives of Torah piety, repentance was supremely difficult for professional sinners such as publicans. John's ministry showed the opposite ... Repentance in the Baptist's sense, with its renunciation of all claims on God, proved supremely difficult to the professionally holy."[38] Moreover, "[a]s the Baptist's career evidences a prophetic self-understanding ... so do the beginnings of the career of Jesus. Both his embarking on a ministry within the cadre of the Baptist's call to Israel and, even more, his withdrawal to Galilee on the signal of the Baptist's arrest only to inaugurate a new proclamation and ministry of his own, point to an eschatological and prophetic self-understanding,"[39] where "eschatological" has the meaning of conversion in the face of impending judgment.

Thus, Meyer's first formulation of a hypothesis on Jesus' own aims states that he understood his role "in terms of the age-old scriptural promise of the restoration of Israel; and ... he understood this restoration not as a divine act exclusively reserved for post-historical realization ... but as called for now and already begun! Its beginning was effected by 'the baptism of John'. As an ally of John, Jesus had already plunged into the prophetic and eschatological task he took to be his destiny."[40]

3.2 Jesus' Public Actions and Words

Meyer regards as "[o]f the most fundamental importance" a "distinction between gospel texts presenting Jesus' proclamation, teaching, and actions before the public and those ... that present acts and words reserved exclusively to his disciples."[41] And he divides the discussion of Jesus' public actions and words into two principal sections: (1) the proclamation of the reign of God and (2) public actions. Among the latter he lists the call and sending of the disciples, miraculous signs of salvation, table fellowship with sinners, public debates and public formulations of his mission, and his entry into Jerusalem and the cleansing of the temple.[42]

This period sublates the involvement with John in that Jesus affirmed John's scheme of meaning by entering into it as an ally and by qualifying John as "more than a prophet" and his baptism as "from heaven."[43] But his own mission as herald of the reign of God

> ... included exorcisms and cures as well as proclamation and teaching, and these elements were (so to speak) doubled by a circle of disciples instituted to share in the same eschatological tasks ... The reign of God was the focal point. Proclamation and teaching centered on it; cures and exorcisms were signs of it ... the reign of God as imminent meant the imminent restoration of Israel, and the reign of God as already overtaking Israel in Jesus' words and acts meant that Israel was already in process of being restored. His teaching was Torah appropriate to restored Israel and requisite to perfect restoration. His wonder-working signified the restoration of Israel and effected it by restoring the afflicted to their heritage as children of Abraham. The appeal to "the sinners" likewise belonged to this context. Offering forgiveness and eliciting conversion, it was designed to restore the outcasts to Israel. This is confirmed by Jesus' repeated efforts to reconcile the righteous to this move toward socio-religious integration ... Its distinctive notes are, first, the gratuity and present actuality of Israel's restoration and, second, the choice of its privileged beneficiaries: the simple, the afflicted, and the outcast ... "eschatological restoration" correlates the whole of Jesus' post-Johannite public ministry with his earliest activity as an ally of John and with his career-long affirmation of John's eschatological role.[44]

3.2.1 Proclamation of the Reign of God

Jesus ceased his involvement in a baptismal ministry because he "saw the arrest of John as closing an initial, limited, distinct phase in the scheme of divinely willed fulfilment events ... Jesus understood his own new career of proclamation, teaching, and healing as constituting another distinct phase in the eschatological scenario." In this new phase "the reign of God" assumed priority over "the wrath to come."[45]

"The reign of God" signifies "God's final and climactic saving act ... the restoration of Israel and the concomitant salvation of the nations."[46] The key to the difference from the previous accent on judgment is the motif "free gift": thus "gospel," "news of salvation," the phrase "Happy are ...," and so on. Why are the poor, the mourners, and the hungry happy? Because God is good – period. The beneficiaries of the eschatological blessings are "the literally poor, the literally mourning, the literally hungry."[47] These are "*those whom God has chosen* as beneficiaries of his saving intervention ... The hour of great reversals has broken out! ... The theme 'salvation as pure gift' runs through the whole of Jesus' public proclamation."[48] It was established especially by his style of action, and even more particularly by "his initiative toward and table fellowship with the irreligious," which marked "a decisive break with the tradition of Torah piety."[49]

Salvation, then, is equivalent to the reign of God. What, then, is the reign of God? For Jesus "the reign of God" was "the triumphant consummation of God's lordship over man and events."[50] The term was eschatological, and the eschatology was climactic ("standing implicitly in a positive relation to God's lordship over history"),[51] and definitive ("signifying the end of time and the inauguration of the age to come").[52] It is free gift, not achieved or developed or controlled or disposed of by human beings. It is already operative in Israel. It "has already come upon you."[53]

The explosive combination of gratuity and present realization had a power that is "attested to by the diversity and vehemence of the responses it evoked."[54] "[T]he heirs of the reign of God were the poor without qualification – not the deserving poor. They deserved nothing, yet salvation was theirs. Their virtue was merely to reveal God's goodness."[55] Jesus "reversed ... the exclusion of the sinners from Israel."[56] If the reign of God was a gift, "the core of repentance was acceptance of it *as* a gift. To repent ... was to become a child. Repentance did not prompt God's mercy but attested it. It was joy and thanks as well as tears, remorse, resolution. It did not bring the reign of God near. Rather, the drawing near of the reign of God was the presupposition of ... repentance."[57] Accepting the reign of God means renouncing all claims on God. This is hard for the pious, the upright, the holy. Repentance is accepting the gift and expressing thanks for it. Jesus' preaching of the reign of God is nothing short of "a phenomenon new in the history of religions ... 'the joy of repentance' ... 'Gratuity' and 'present realization' – the electrifying immediacy of 'free' and 'now' – are probably the most distinctive accents in Jesus' message."[58]

But there must not be overlooked "the tie between the reign of God and the restoration of Israel."[59] "Three motifs from Isa. 52.7–9, namely, the herald of salvation ... the reign of God ... and the restoration of Israel ... make up a thematic constellation variously in evidence from the time of the exile on."[60] When Wright will later emphasize, as he does constantly, that a defining characteristic of the ethos of Palestinian Judaism in Jesus' time was the sense that the exile was not really yet over, that the God of Israel had yet to return to Zion, it is this constellation to which he is referring: the end of the exile had not yet come, but with the proclamation of Jesus it has arrived on the scene. "Scholarship ought never to have lost sight of this basic correlation," Meyer writes. "In the biblical perspective salvation was always and everywhere understood as destined precisely for Israel. 'Salvation' and 'Israel' were utterly inseparable ... Where the salvation of the nations was promised or announced, this was conceived as an assimilation to saved Israel."[61] The proclamation initiated what was being proclaimed, the dawning salvation of Israel and, through Israel, the renewal of the world. In this sense, we may claim that *the original meaning of "salvation" had to do with the forgiveness of sins and the return of* YHWH *to Zion that would signal the restoration of Israel,* which itself would mediate salvation to the nations.[62] Only with the origin of a distinct Christian community did this meaning of both salvation and the reign of God expand.

All of this means for Meyer that "Jesus must have conceived goals bearing on the life of Israel as such; and he must have conceived them as belonging to a divine scheme of fulfilment events. In a word, he must have conceived his work as *an eschatological vocation.*"[63] And he conceived *himself* as central to the divine scheme. The phrase "the reign of God" was "charged with his own religious intentionality: his existential understanding of God (i.e., of how he himself related to God) and his understanding of God's will for the world and activity in it at this moment."[64] It reveals a "prophetic claim to insight into God's good pleasure ... his will to lavish the blessings of the eschaton on the poor, the mourners, the hungry. 'The reign of God' signifies 'God' and signifies God *precisely as Jesus knows him.*"[65]

The vital context of Jesus' personal aims was constituted by his understanding of God and God's will, and of Israel and Israel's destiny. God's will and Israel's destiny were one and the same, and "the reign of God" has immediate reference to Israel. "At Yahweh's reign ... the ends of the earth would see salvation ... and Gentiles would sing the Lord a new song of praise,"[66] but God would reign on the holy mountain and for Jerusalem. "His reign would be his return to Zion."[67] "The reign of God is near" means "God is near, at the door, already here."[68] The point was salvation, the banquet with God. It was to be a banquet for all, and so his imagery contains universal renewal. But the "restoration of humankind would hinge on the historically rooted restoration of Israel. And Israel's restoration would not be realized without a willed act of acceptance." All his words and actions were relative to the reign of God thus understood by him.[69]

Examining Jesus' teaching, its burden, its center of gravity, its express and unexpressed presuppositions, will help us grasp how concretely he understood his mission. His words and actions, the whole of his career, were consciously and all-pervasively relative to the reign of God and its proclamation. Proclamation determined his teaching. His proclamation of the reign meant both salvation and ruin. But there was a unique and original perspective. The proclamation of the reign of God was coupled with the call for conversion, where conversion meant the repentance that consisted simply in the acceptance of salvation as a gift. This acceptance of salvation as a gift involved an ethical commitment. This was not a natural ethic, nor a scribal ethic, but an eschatological ethic. His eschatology was not exclusively futurist, but already in process of realization, as a restoration of the ideal order of things. Eschatology closes the gap, restores the ideal. "Eschatology" here refers to the new beginning of the nation. This beginning was already in process of realization. Torah for a graced and restored Israel is being proclaimed. The Torah in its provisional aspects is finished. The code of an eschatological Torah implies gift, and joy attests to the gift. The consummation has begun. The present public career of Jesus is the fulfilled condition of the restoration, which is ultimately addressed to the restored Israel coming into being in response to his call.[70]

Jesus' authority thus transcends the Mosaic economy, correcting and perfecting it. The Torah is revised. "The whole scribal system, its rationale and its prestige, was suddenly and totally passé."[71] His ethics is "an ethics of realized eschatology," for "a community of the transformed."[72] It remains a prescriptive ethic, but the prescription is one of boundless love, a love that leaves all earthly security and clings to God's word alone. "The Torah would be thereby surpassed, but only in its own direction."[73] No longer would it involve confidence in the system. The antithetical form, "You have heard … But I say to you," derives from Jesus himself. God's reign transforms the person who accepts it, so that one is enabled to fulfil the eschatological Torah. There is occurring in his preaching a trans-valuation of values: from wealth to selling one's possessions and giving alms, from the desire to be first to insisting on being last, "the radical devaluation of religious prestige." His teaching had no other point than to realize the Torah's inmost spirit of self-forgetfulness in its full purity, the supreme form of the Torah. This was the controlling center of gravity for his teaching.[74]

The climactic response without limits goes beyond the decalogue but not by contradicting or nullifying it. Jesus understood allegiance to the decalogue as a seedbed of discipleship. He engaged in polemic against the self-deception that met moral demands with ritual observances. He differentiated the command of God and the tradition of men. He appealed to the religious good sense that relativized the scribal legalisms. Eschatological consummation crosses the grain of ritual tradition and violates religious sensibilities. There is a new presupposition and source, the coming of the reign of God. The great commandment itself had a new orientation, a new compass point: "the reign of God, impending and already effective, with its own economy of demands and dynamisms." The abiding validity of the great commandment lay in "the open-endedness of boundless love." The reign of God takes over the covenantal role of the exodus, and his own code of discipleship brings Sinai to completion.[75]

So "[t]he unique and original perspective of Jesus' teaching, the context in which all the particulars of that teaching fall into place, was 'Torah for a graced and restored Israel.' It was Torah transformed by reference to the new and public revelation" in his proclamation and teaching.[76] And this *is* revelation, not interpretation. "He was the unique revealer of the full final measure of God's will," and he understood himself to be precisely that.[77]

Thus we have an answer to the question, Is there a single thematic perspective that holds together all the prescriptive particulars of his eschatological ethics? The single thematic perspective of his teaching was *himself*! It was his relation to God, to "Abba," that made him God's only possible and absolutely reliable revealer. He presented his teaching as the definitive revelation of God's will for Israel. This revelation discredited the tradition of the scribes but it fulfilled the Torah. His purposes fitted into an interlocking scheme of divine and human acts. Jesus' world of meaning was eschatological, and in his own view he belonged to the center of the eschaton as its revealer.[78]

3.2.2 Public Actions

This review of Jesus' public teaching is filled out by studying his public actions with an eye to the questions, With what meanings did Jesus charge them, and on what do these meanings converge?[79]

First, there is the call and sending of the disciples. Discipleship arose through his call, which was peremptory, intolerant of delay, demanding full-time commitment, in the context of the reign of God and its demands.[80] The reality of "the twelve" was symbolic of Israel restored, as was their composition of radically disparate elements: Galilean, Judaean, religious and irreligious, Johannite and Zealot.[81] Sending them out gives them a share in the coming-to-be of the future, and a sense that the "fate of the nation would hinge on its response to their message ... [I]t is impossible to define the aims of Jesus plausibly without reference to a mission or task, central and urgent, set by the imminence of God's eschatological reign, bearing on the whole nation of Israel, and pressing Israel to a decision of faith or unfaith."[82]

Second, there are miraculous signs of salvation. Again, they reveal the dawning of God's reign. This is especially the case with exorcisms, which are signs of the eschaton, of God's imminent triumph over all evil. Satan is coming to an end. In fact, Jesus has defeated Satan already, in the desert. As he combines his proclamation with exorcisms and cures, he commissions the twelve to do likewise. Proclamation, cures, and exorcisms were for a time strictly reserved for the lost sheep of the house of Israel. The exceptions manifest the faith that he finds elsewhere and wants to find in Israel. He judged his powerful deeds to be decisive signs of the dawning eschaton. They ought to have spurred all Galilee to repentance, and for this reason he rejected the demand for a miracle of accreditation, a sign from heaven, which would have matched the sort of signs he was tempted to perform in the desert.[83]

Third, there is his table fellowship with sinners. This was a staggering phenomenon, causing shock and resentment on the part of the religious and sheer delight on that of the irreligious. The religious and moral economy was radically upset, just as it was with Paul's later account of God as one who justifies the ungodly. *For the Baptist, conversion came first and communion second. For Jesus communion came first and conversion second.* "Contact triggered repentance; conversion flowered from communion."[84]

These actions are a perfect translation of his proclamation into action, confirming the motifs he associated with the reign of God, and especially its gratuity and its present realization. What was at stake was the forgiveness and conversion of sinners, as well as their restoration to their rightful family, Israel. His mission was their reconciliation, and this caused for him a great problem in winning over the pious as well, as is reflected in his parables, and especially in that of the prodigal son.[85]

Fourth, we may investigate his public debates and public formulations of his mission. What was at stake in the collision between Jesus and Torah piety? The "system." Jesus' sense of God entailed his own freedom from the religious system. Torah piety was systematic and so liable to entanglement in the system, losing the "craning toward and listening for God which would keep the system open."[86] So much was this the case that his miracles for the well-being of others were interpreted as the infraction of a law.

His public formulations of his mission were in the form of parables. The parable of the mustard seed, for example, means that out of apparently meager and unimpressive beginnings and the unimpressiveness of his following would come the reign of God. His followers are the seed of the vast communion of the saved. He understood himself not only as "the revealer of God's final saving act but as the author of its nascent realization in time."[87] These parables are "filled with warnings and appeals addressed to the unresponsive: the learned, the pious, and the crowds."[88] The eschatological note is disclosed in his initiative toward sinners and in his sabbath conflicts with the representatives of the system.

Even more explicit and more relevant for our present purposes were direct statements about his mission: "I have come ..." These bear on two themes: the salvation of sinners and the revelation of God's will. "I have not come to call the righteous but sinners." His mission was to summon sinners to the banquet of salvation, to search for what was lost and to save it. His mission was also to reveal God's will, to fill to the full what God willed from Israel. Thus he presented his mission as the fulfilment of ancient promises and prophecies.[89]

Finally, there is his entry into Jerusalem and his cleansing of the temple. The entry, the cleansing, and the question about authority "constituted a single narrative unit and reflected a single continuous event."[90] "The cleansing of the temple triggered a sequence of events which brought Jesus to his death."[91] It was

> an explosive act … Everything about the entry into the city and temple and the immediately following expulsion of the temple concessioners was calculated … The temple was the goal of the procession, and the procession was planned … Jesus doubtless intended a real critique and reform of temple practice … [He] brought the capital city and the temple into relation to the reign of God … [T]he temple cleansing signalled the dawn of a new era and a hint of a restoration of a cultic practice appropriate to the new era. The latter was revealed in the final supper he had with his disciples, where the new covenant promised by Jeremiah is explicitly inaugurated.[92]

3.2.3 Convergence of Meanings

On what do the meanings of his public words and actions converge? We begin with his proclamation of the reign of God. The realization of God's intention, pleasure, will was on the point of realization. God had prepared for Israel a climactic and definitive restoration, and for the nations participation in the salvation of Israel. This was being mediated by its proclaimer, and as a pure gift, attesting God's goodness, demanding the renunciation of claims, and offering the joy of repentance. His message was specially directed to the unexpected combination of groups and classes comprising the simple, the afflicted, and the outcasts. These imaged the real situation of Israel vis-à-vis God. They were a type of Israel-to-be-saved. And he gave a completely new valorization of the depressed elements in Israel. Nothing had been so overlooked and unexpected as God's boundless goodness toward the simple, the afflicted, and the outcasts; nothing in his career was so thoroughly misconstrued and resented as his resolute, unabashed, symbol-charged dealings with them. This appeared as a contemptuous trampling on tradition, a dismantling of the Torah. The divisive impact was completely conscious on his part. The meanings converge on a stunningly unexpected restoration of Israel, and his works effected the restoration they signified.

3.3 *Jesus' Teaching to the Disciples*

Distinct from the traditions having to do with Jesus' public words and actions, there are what Meyer calls the esoteric traditions, traditions found in texts depicting Jesus alone with the disciples, uttering teaching reserved for them.

This teaching sublated all else that we have seen, in that it

> promoted Jesus' public performance to the level of explicit thematization, and as solution to riddle, in the sense that it also presented the full scheme of meaning, the interpretative and explanatory perspective, in which he invited his disciples to grasp the whole of his words and acts and, in particular, the significance for Israel and the nations which he attached to his personal destiny.[93]

The core of Jesus' esoteric teaching is reserved for the period following Simon's confession of Jesus as Messiah. The scene at Caesarea Philippi was "the hidden turning point of Jesus' career."[94] After this scene there is played out a twofold set of themes in his teaching to the disciples. First, he interpreted his work of national restoration as the *messianic* task of building on rock, secure against death, *the living temple of the last days*, in other words and in the language of Meyer's early article cited above, *the arrival of the new covenant*. Thus, sayings and teachings surrounding the temple are significant in this period. And second, *the way to building that living temple was to pass through his own rejection, suffering, death, and resurrection*: again, in the terms of the earlier article, *expiatory offering* mediating redemption. There is a thematic progression from Simon's confession of Jesus as Messiah, king, and so temple builder, to the immediate revelation of his coming repudiation, suffering, death, and resurrection. All three synoptic gospels present his word on his coming destiny as the inauguration of a distinct, final phase both in his teaching and in his career, and all three set this final phase under the sign of Simon's recognition and confession of Jesus as the Messiah. This means that the title "Messiah" figures in these traditions as a particular title that Jesus understood to specify thematically the comprehensive aim of his mission. But it was Messiah as suffering Messiah, suffering Son of Man, suffering Servant, all pulled together by him into one complex set of identity markers, where the suffering would be intimately linked to his attitude to the present temple and the living temple that he would build and the expiatory self-offering through which it would be built.

While for Meyer it is the acknowledgment of Jesus as Messiah that is the central presupposition of the data on Jesus' esoteric teaching, with the more recent help of Sigurd Grindheim we should expand on a qualification of this claim, in that, as all acknowledge, Jesus did not embrace any of the commonly held understandings of what precisely "Messiah" meant. He accepted Peter's confession, but also "sternly ordered the disciples not to tell anyone that he was the Messiah" (Matthew 16.2), at least in part because he knew it would be misunderstood, but also because he knew he was far more than the expected Messiah. That "far more" included equality with God, and relativized all else, allowing him to draw together the themes of Messiah, Son of Man, and Servant. Meyer, I will argue against Wright, does not downplay this theme. But the human theme of Messiah is also more important than Grindheim allows it to be.[95] Messiah, Son of Man, and Servant are not divine names but historical realities. Equality with God is something else. But both are important. The New Testament is no more monophysite in practice than is the Council of Chalcedon in a more thematic fashion.

Thus, the messianic thematization of Jesus and his mission is for Meyer the first object of inquiry into his esoteric teaching. He was executed on a charge of political sedition, and the words on the cross establish the charge more exactly: he was executed as one who claimed kingship, which for Jewish ears would mean he was a messianic pretender.[96] But this is not sufficient to indicate anything about *his own* pre-paschal consciousness. It entails only that he was "charged with claiming a status incompatible with Roman policy and punishable by death."[97] It entails nothing either of his self-understanding or of his disciples' understanding of him. But for Meyer we can find in the Markan account of the trial a historically solid point of departure for this inquiry.[98] In an intricate argument that we need not repeat in detail, Meyer finds that Nathan's oracle in 2 Samuel 7, Yahweh's word to David, links the testimony of the false witnesses on Jesus' word about the temple, the question of the high priest, and the response of Jesus. The words "He shall build a house for my name, and I will establish the throne of his reign forever; I will be his father and he shall be my son" (2 Samuel 7.13–14) provide "the clue to the structure of meaning that holds the Markan trial scene together."[99]

The relevant motifs are the destruction and construction of the temple (Mark 14.58, 2 Samuel 7.13), "the Messiah, the Son of the Blessed One" (Mark 14.61, 2 Samuel 7.14), and the theme of definitive enthronement (Mark 14.62, 2 Samuel 7.13). The "hinge word" of the scene is "We heard him say: 'I will destroy this temple that is made with hands and in three days I will build another, not made with hands.'" Some temple saying along these lines was certainly a word of the historical Jesus, and "the building of the temple" carries messianic connotations. But to unriddle the word on the temple calls for "recovery both of its original form and of the full field of meaning in which it has its intelligibility."[100] The form given the first limb of the saying by the witnesses at Jesus' trial did not derive from Jesus, but he did maintain to a chosen inner circle of disciples that the temple would be destroyed, and that this fierce but brief eschatology of trial and tribulation would be followed by the eschatology of grace.

The original or historical form of the first limb of the temple saying may very well be given in John 2.19, "Destroy this temple …," an imperative with the force of a condition. But the second limb, with the time notice "three days," means that the eschatology of tribulation, here the destruction of the temple, is followed swiftly by the eschatology of triumph, here the new temple.[101] "Three days" can mean "in a while, shortly, soon." "The time is determined by God, and the third day signifies the *kairos* of salvation."[102] The accent is on the limitation and shortness of time. "The imminent crisis epitomized in the destruction of the temple would swiftly yield to the salvation epitomized in the new temple to be built by Jesus."[103] This was his word.

"This temple" in the first limb, "Destroy this temple," clearly refers to the temple in Jerusalem. To evoke, even conditionally, its destruction was to touch "not just stone and gold and not only the general well-being but history and hope, national identity, self-understanding, and pride."[104] The new temple to which he refers "no one could build but God himself – or the Messiah transcendently enthroned at God's right hand."[105]

Two other texts that draw on temple motifs may be used to help us understand the eschatological restoration that will come with the new temple, and thus to enter more deeply into what Meyer calls the esoteric teaching of Jesus.

The first is Jesus' response in Matthew 16.17–19 to Simon's declaration of messianic faith. The three verses form a single unit: (17) And Jesus answered him, "Blessed are you, Simon Bar-Jona, for flesh and blood has not revealed [this] to you, but my heavenly Father. (18) And I say to you, You are Peter, and on this rock I will build my church, and the gates of Hades shall not prevail against it. (19) I will give you the keys of the reign of heaven, and whatever you bind on earth heaven shall bind, and whatever you loose on earth heaven shall loose."

Meyer comments: "Verse 18 draws on the master image of the cosmic rock, the divinely appointed site … for the central sanctuary or temple":[106] on this rock I will build my church. The cosmic rock is "the sacred point of contact between heaven and earth."[107] It is for Meyer the key to the content of Jesus' word, and the oracle of Nathan is the key to its context.[108] The central task of the Messiah, Son of the living God, is to build the eschatological temple,[109] and to build it on a rock other than the temple Mount. His work of national restoration was "the messianic task of building on rock, secure against death, the living temple of the last days."[110] The total schematic image (netherworld, rock and temple, gate of heaven) is an equivalent of temple, my church.[111] The result is a new creation. The historical context of the words lies in "Jesus' words and acts bearing on the new temple, the premier symbol of God's eschatological people."[112] The community envisaged in the words "my church" is the eschatological Israel,[113] what Paul will call the Israel of God (Galatians 6.16).

While Jesus addressed this call for faith to all Israel and demanded a positive response, in the esoteric teaching he explained how the call would be divisive of Israel and why he would not retract it on that account. "Israel was destined to find eschatological restoration in those who, like Simon, would come to confess Jesus as 'the Messiah, the Son of [the living] God.' They would be the temple built on rock. The Messiah chose the rock and would build the temple."[114]

The second text has to do with the cleansing of the temple. The cleansing of the temple belonged to the same context as the message "The reign of God is at hand!" and the demand "Repent!" It pointed ahead to imminent judgment and restoration. His act was at once "a demonstration, a prophetic critique, a fulfilment event, and a sign of the future."[115] "The critique pointed straight at temple practice ... It was an act of prophetic indignation ... an attack on 'this generation's' obstinate confidence in [the] status [of the temple]."[116] But it was also restoration, a fulfilment event, comparable in structure and function to the classic biblical "sign," "serving as a present guarantee of the prophecy's future fulfilment." The action "presented itself to the public as a parable demanding to be construed and deciphered and veiling the potent claim to be a hinge moment in the eschatological scenario. It was at once a fulfilment event and a sign of the future, pledging the restoration of temple, Zion, and Jerusalem ... the perfect restoration of Israel."[117] He tried to explain this as best he could to the disciples.

The most distinctive aspect of this act lies in his mode of arrival at the temple. The entry into Jerusalem was "a messianic event, so investing the cleansing of the temple with a messianic dimension ... The entry into Jerusalem and the cleansing of the temple constituted a messianic demonstration, a messianic critique, a messianic fulfilment event, and a sign of the messianic restoration of Israel."[118] The day of the Lord had come because the Messiah was there. "He was the builder of the house of God." He has spoken the word to Simon

> ... in response to a faith that had intuited the secret of his supreme role in the plan of eschatological salvation ... The Messiah was the master builder who would raise on rock the living temple, his *ekklē-sia*. The riddle of the miraculously built temple had its roots here, in Jesus' thematization of his life's work as the bringing of messianic Israel into being.[119]

He "came to the cleansing as messianic judge and restorer."[120] Powering his prophetic indignation was precisely the self-understanding of coming to it as Lord and judge.[121] The cleansing was

> a parable of judgment … and to unbelief Jesus would offer no sign but that of the "other" temple he would build within or after three days of the destruction of "this" one. Like the sign of Jonah, this sign would come too late to serve as a motive for belief, for it would be nothing other than the climactic vindication at which, for good or ill, belief and unbelief would yield to vision.[122]

How did Jesus intend to realize his goal, "the messianic restoration of Israel"?[123] The process would involve both a coming ordeal and its resolution by the triumph or enthronement of the Son of Man.[124]

As for the ordeal, in public preaching Jesus warned the indifferent of the coming crisis. This generation will pay the blood debt for the prophets because it is the last generation, but also because this generation is "engaged in repudiating God's climactic and definitive revealer."[125] For the refusers, "the coming distress … would not be reversed but confirmed by the day of the Son of man."[126] For the disciples, the ordeal would "test and purify, like refining fire."[127] The Abba prayer that he taught them supposed an understanding of the ordeal as test and supposed the ordeal as the setting and context of the prayer. The disciples entered the shelter of his unique relationship to God: our Father.[128] The forgiveness that the prayer stresses would "frustrate evil, break its rhythm, heal its ravages, and convert into redemptive power the energy that evil would otherwise claim for itself."[129] This is the real meaning of the expiation that would mediate the arrival of the reign of God and the new covenant.

As for enthronement, "It is solidly probable that the role played in public proclamation and teaching by the coming of the reign of God was played in esoteric teaching after the confession in the region of Caesarea Philippi by the day of the Son of man."[130] Jesus "supposed for himself a mysterious, unfathomably transcendent condition."[131] The historicity of his words on the main elements of the ordeal is "beyond reasonable doubt," but "the ordeal itself could not possibly be the final state of the future." The final state should rather be "the total reversal of all this … The disciples would be enthroned, the tribes of Israel restored … the temple rebuilt … his vindication would signal [the] reversal [of the ordeal]."[132]

He knew the nation's destiny was at stake in his encounter with his nation. "His mission was to elicit Israel's acceptance of salvation, but not all would accept it," and he knew this. "He would call his countrymen together to a life beyond Torah and [scribal tradition], he would gather them together

in a common renunciation of claims and in mutual forgiveness and reconciliation ... Everything turned on acceptance or refusal."[133] He is speaking
of "an awesome event: the division of Israel and the coming into being of
the messianic 'remnant.'"[134]

"Remnant" does not necessarily mean a separate and organized community. Nor must the remnant be closed. Nor does remnant theology suppose
a lapse of the covenant.[135]

> Jesus' mission was eschatological through and through. He under-
> stood judgment either as an element in the effective imposition of
> God's reign or as the essential prelude to it ... his mission was relative
> to judgment ... he called all Israel but was fully conscious that not all
> Israel accepted or would accept the call ... he made it clear that the of-
> fer and the demand ... were divinely authoritative; the gift was free ...
> but acceptance was requisite ... Jesus pressed a decision on Israel, so
> engendering the crisis that created the remnant of the last days. This
> is the basic context within which the call and sending of the twelve,
> the cures and exorcisms, the dining with publicans and sinners, the
> temple cleansing, all take on their full intelligibility, for all these res-
> toration-intending acts were appeals for faith and acceptance. They
> could all be discounted, misconstrued, rejected. All of them could
> thereby become and did in fact become acts divisive of Israel.[136]

Again:

> Rabbinic Judaism would declare that all Israel had a share in the age
> to come. Jesus declared that the natural heirs or "sons" of the reign
> of God would be cast into the dark and their place taken by the na-
> tions (Matt. 8.11f. par.). The ordeal would continue to divide Israel
> (Matt. 10.34) because restoration would not be a spectacular mira-
> cle nor Israel its passive beneficiary. It would have to be accepted in
> faith as a gift.[137]

The remembrance of what he said about the destiny of the nations (see,
e.g., Matthew 8.11) would later be transformed into the basis of the world
mission of the church.[138]

This is an appeal to "*a transition from the salvation of Israel as ethnic community to the salvation of Israel as religious community,*"[139] where "religious" means
not "national" but "converted." Meyer cites Lonergan to the effect that conversion is intensely personal and utterly intimate, but not so private as to be
solitary. The event on which the *new covenant* was grounded is coterminous
with the whole gospel story, the story of "a trenchant eschatological demand

which effected a division within Israel between those who accepted it and those who rejected it."[140] His aims, and so his self-understanding, explicitly comprehended the ordeal. "He wept over Jerusalem and he recoiled from suffering, but he willed the ordeal and ... instructed his disciples that to launch it was precisely his mission."[141] "[H]e fully intended and willed to press a radically divisive decision on Israel."[142]

The positive aspect was the assembling of the remnant of Israel, who were the heirs of his work of restoration. Matthew 10.12–15 signifies "a broken communion heavy with consequence,"[143] exclusion from the true Israel, the Israel destined for restoration. Those who accepted the invitation were "the seed of the final assembly." The "rock" motif and the Last Supper move in the direction of indicating that he envisaged the emergence of a visible community to embrace his followers.[144]

All of this points to the sense in which the aims of Jesus comprehended a "remnant." This is confirmed by his predilection for the poor and lowly, the simple or childlike, the afflicted, who were "favored beneficiaries of God's reign."[145] He was one of them (Matthew 11.29). The *anawim* are in prophetic tradition the remnant of Israel. But the theme is deepened. Peter's confessing of messiahship is *the condition and signal for the prophecy of suffering.*"[146] More than a simple juxtaposition of themes, the prediction pericope is "an esoteric instruction on messiahship. It does not cancel out this theme but completes and transforms it by integrating the destiny of Jesus into it ... he is Messiah specifically in this context. The way to enthronement will be through repudiation, suffering, and death."[147] There follows what is almost a new call to discipleship: "If anyone would follow me, let him deny himself and take up his cross and *so* follow me."[148] He grasped his imminent death as "a constituent element of the messianic event."[149] This is what was not understood in the common conceptions of "Messiah," but also what is embraced by Jesus' own amalgamation of "Messiah" with the Deutero-Isaian "servant."

From this turning point on, he "repeatedly associated his own death with the coming ordeal."[150] The ordeal was not only "an evil to be reversed" but also "a good somehow *intrinsically designed to generate the reversal*";[151] there is to it "a positive role of somehow *mediating* the dawn of the new age, the consummation and restoration, the reign of God."[152]

His esoteric teaching thus "became a mystagogy centred on suffering and death, the meaning of which somehow depended on the still undefined meaning of his own destiny."[153] The climax and conclusion of the mystagogy is found in Mark's words, which anticipated a motif of Jesus' eucharistic words, "The Son of man has not come to be served but to serve: to give his life as a ransom for many" (Mark 10.45). In the gospels of both Mark and Matthew, these words are spoken right before his entry into Jerusalem. "Man cannot buy life. But he, the Messiah, could ransom the mortal and the dead. He could *give* life to the world."[154]

Here "the Isaian ransom theme (Isa. 43.3f.) is assimilated to the expiatory suffering of the Servant for 'many' (Isa. 52.13–53.12)." And here too we find

> ... the missing link between the salvation of Israel and the salvation of the nations. The expiatory value of the death of Jesus would not be limited to Israel. It would be boundless (Isa. 52.15; 53.4–6, 10–12). With a single stroke this defined Jesus' view of the situation of the nations – their immersion in sin and liability to eschatological death – and supplied its resolution. The paradox that saving one's life was losing it and losing it was saving it (Mark 8.35 parr.) took its sense finally from the destiny of Jesus, which would convert death – in biblical orthodoxy, the punishment for sin – into purification from sin and entry into life.[155]

Vicarious expiation emerges, then, as "the positive sense of Jesus' death" and a theme in Jesus' own self-understanding. It was not an issue he could or did set before Israel, but it

> confirms his understanding of the situation not only of the nations but of Israel as well. Outside the ambit of his own saving mission there was only death and the dead (Matt. 8.22 par.) ... This was not the revelation of some ineluctable necessity structurally intrinsic to salvation ... [but] the revelation of God's pleasure, wisdom, will. The motif of the Servant's universal expiation revealed that it pleased God to restore Israel and save humankind – by Jesus' death.[156]

He "did not aim to be repudiated and killed; he aimed to charge with meaning his being repudiated and killed."[157] Nor was that charging arbitrary. He is revealing the mystery of the redemptive effect for "the many" of the suffering of the one called to mediate the community's restoration. He conceived of life beyond death as on a continuum with his earthly career. Evil would not be crushed by power. "[B]*y subjection to evil Jesus would render it impotent.* Betrayal, desertion, repudiation would only promote and realize his aims. By submitting to evil he would take its measure, establish its futility, shape it to his own purposes."[158] This "followed no pattern of piety attested in contemporary Israel," but it "gave a new and matchless depth to the *anawim* thematic." The "for, on behalf of," *huper*, as in "for many," was "integral to his life, to a convergent mass of acts and words, public and esoteric."[159] Everything is bent in the direction of "the restoration of Israel and ultimately to the benefit of the whole world."[160]

The historicity of both expiation and covenant in this sense is highly probable. He "*interpreted his death as expiatory for the world ... 'forgiveness of sins' ... and as a sacrifice sealing a new covenant ...* This combination of interpretative motifs defined the messianic community to be born of the new covenant as a people whose sins were forgiven."[161] The disciples were "the core of the messianic people to be." They became "bound to one another and to him" in communion, especially by the eucharistic words and their share in the bread and wine. This is not a new direction but "a solemn fulfilment of … table fellowship." The aims of Jesus would be "incarnated in this community, at once the remnant and the first fruits of messianic Israel."[162]

4   Wright's Comments and Contributions

Perhaps the best way to transition to our few comments on the largely complementary work of N.T. Wright is by way of comments Wright makes in his introduction to Meyer's *The Aims of Jesus.* Despite the extraordinary merits Wright finds in the book, Meyer, he says, "never explores the way in which Jesus' [talk about the coming of the Son of Man] must have related to the immediately future public and politically charged events of the destruction of Jerusalem and particularly the Temple."[163] "… if Meyer had worked through the second-Temple material yet once more he might have come to see that Jesus' prophecies of an imminent future had more to do with what we now know as the events of AD 70 and less with the 'parousia' as traditionally conceived."[164] In my view, this connection is one of Wright's most important contributions. Jesus is not talking about the end of the space-time universe but the end of the temple and the destruction of Jerusalem.

Again, for Wright, Meyer never worked out in an integrated way how Jesus' task and vocation would be scheduled for fulfilment precisely as the outcome and reversal of repudiation, suffering, and death.

> He points in emphatically the right direction: the combination of interpretative motifs in Jesus' sayings about his death being "for many," and the cup being "the new covenant in my blood," indicate that he believed that "the messianic community to be born of the new covenant" would be "a people whose sins were forgiven." And he has a deft way of saying both that Jesus knew he would meet a violent end, giving it a scriptural and theological meaning, and that he did not "intend" this death after the manner of a Kamikaze suicide.[165]

Wright quotes Meyer's point that "Jesus did not aim to be repudiated and killed, he aimed to charge with meaning his being repudiated and killed." But, Wright claims, "we can go further, and integrate Jesus' public proclamation still more closely with his death and the meaning he gave to it."[166] Wright also does not think Meyer satisfactorily integrated the way in which Jesus' mission depended for its validation not only on the parousia but also on the resurrection.

I would maintain that Meyer's clear favoring of the Servant motif from Deutero-Isaiah can be raised in evidence in Meyer's favor in this slight dispute. Meyer is not unaware of the importance for Jesus' own self-understanding of the theme of redemptive suffering for the many. The dynamics of this transformation remain to be articulated with systematic precision, but that is a task not for the biblical exegete but for the systematic theologian. I hope the third volume in this set can perform precisely that task.

As for the significance of the resurrection, this is of course where Wright himself makes the essential contribution to this discussion, with his major and all but definitive work, *The Resurrection of the Son of God.*

Again, Wright believes that Meyer misses

> … the origin of the early church's belief that in Jesus the one God of Israel had been personally present in their midst. It is perhaps too much to ask that such a question could even have been raised, head-on, in the 1970s. As it was, Ben was already doing many things that people had said could or should not be done, and this might have been a step too far for even sympathetic readers. Yet the question will not go away, not least in the light of his own insistence that the deepest meanings of a historical character's intentions and achievements are found not simply in his own recorded words and actions but in the traditions they generate. I do not think that Ben himself would have denied that the human being Jesus of Nazareth was mysteriously to be identified with Israel's one true God; but how that identification could be made in terms that a first-century Palestinian Jew could meaningfully think was not a question he even raised, certainly not in this book.[167]

Here again a qualification can be made, I believe, at least in the sense that Meyer's position on pre-existence and incarnation in his reading of Philippians 2.6–11 seems to me to weaken Wright's criticism to some extent.

However, Wright does add to the fruits of exegesis and history that I believe must be carried forward into a contemporary soteriology that would stand in fundamental continuity with the aims and intentions of Jesus. It is now time very briefly to indicate what further materials may be found in Wright's work that could add to our appropriation of the fundamental biblical inspiration of any valid soteriology. Again, I am looking for some exegetical support for at least part of my thesis 90, which I here repeat: "In the process of moving from mission consciousness to self-understanding in the context of mission, Jesus wrought radical changes on, and then integrated, the familiar Jewish conceptions of sin, sacrifice, and expiation, and the familiar Jewish figures of Messiah, Son of Man, and Servant of Yahweh.

The radical changes had to do with the growing realization that redemptive and expiatory suffering in the concrete historical details of his own life, and as mediating a new covenant, would be a principal characteristic of who he was. All of these conceptions were Jewish, human categories, processed and brought together through his developing human self-knowledge. Jesus came to adjudicate them in the light of a further, divine knowledge of his equality with God, which over time became also part of his human self-understanding and was manifest in his doing what his compatriots knew only God could do. All of these developments came to pass as Jesus discovered his mission in the very concrete historical circumstances and details of first-century second-Temple Palestinian Judaism. The basic pattern of what redemption actually means is embodied in his negotiation of those historical details and circumstances."

Why did Jesus act as he did? Obviously, he believed it was his duty, his destiny, his vocation to do so. Why? There are for Wright two major topics and one major theme that must occupy the center of the discussion of this question. The topics are the Jerusalem temple, including the entire sacrificial system, and Torah, and the theme is the return of Yahweh to Zion and the effects this will have on the temple, the sacrificial system, and Torah. For Wright, the crucial narrative within which Jesus understood himself has to do with the return to Zion not only of Israel but also of Israel's God. The return of Israel's God is central to the vocational self-understanding of Jesus. He would embody in his own actions, in his journey to Jerusalem, in his entry into the city, in what he would do there, and supremely in his own death, the long-awaited action of Yahweh. In doing so he would transform the entire religious and political system that had to do with the Jerusalem temple and Torah. Especially in his offering to all and sundry who would believe and follow him the forgiveness of sins and restoration into fellowship with God, he was acting as a one-man temple substitute. And he took on himself the role not merely of a new Moses or of a new Torah, but of a new Torah-*giver*. In short, he believed himself called to be and do things that only Yahweh, Israel's God, could be and do. Moreover, Wright is firm in his position that Jesus did not expect the end of the world but rather the end of the present world order of Gentile domination and the beginning of the time when God would reign in Zion and restore the suffering people's fortunes.[168] Wright understands apocalyptic language and literature as "an elaborate metaphor-system for investing historical events with theological significance."[169] Sociopolitical events were themselves seen as the climactic moment in Israel's history, summoning the nation to repentance precisely as a nation.[170] In so speaking Jesus is not merely a successor to Jeremiah and his like. He is the last in the line. The question about what it means to be the people of God, the people of Yahweh's promise, is at once a theological and a political question. "In such a world, to be non-political is to be irrele-vant."[171] Jesus is concerned with society. "To tell all sides that their vision for the nation is wrong, and to act as if one has glimpsed, and is implementing, a different vision, is to invite" serious political trouble.[172] And it is precisely his suffering that trouble that turns out to be the catalyst of redemption.

Wright highlights four biblical sources as central to Jesus' self-understanding as he went to his death: Daniel 7, Zechariah 14, some Psalms, and Isaiah 40–55. But he also singles out the servant motif as it appears in Isaiah 40–55 as the only one of these four sources that would prompt Jesus' understanding of his suffering precisely as *redemptive*, as catalyzing or mediating redemption. It is in Isaiah 40–55 that we find the claim that the redemption of Israel from exile and the suffering of the messianic figure are linked precisely as effect and cause, or, as Bernard Lonergan would say, as redemption as end (here, redemption from exile) and redemption as mediation (here, the suffering of the servant).[173]

Isaiah 52.7–12 was thematic for the whole work of Jesus.

> How beautiful upon the mountains are the feet of him who brings good tidings, who publishes peace, who brings tidings of good, who publishes salvation, who says to Zion, "Your God reigns." Hark, your watchmen lift up their voice, together they sing for joy; for eye to eye they see the return of the Lord to Zion. Break forth together into singing, you waste places of Jerusalem; for the Lord has comforted his people, he has redeemed Jerusalem. The Lord has bared his holy arm before the eyes of all the nations; and all the ends of the earth shall see the salvation of our God.

Israel's God was becoming king. But how was this to be put into effect? In and through the work of the servant of YHWH, about whom we hear espe-cially in Isaiah 52.13–53.12.

Thus, for Wright:[174]

(1) Jesus announces and enacts the kingdom of YHWH, doing and saying things which dovetail very closely with the message of Isa-iah 40–55 regarding the actions of Israel's God.

(2) The kingdom program of Isaiah 40–55 is put into effect through the work of the servant, specifically his redemptive suffering.

(3) Jesus acts symbolically as though he intends to put his kingdom program into effect through sharing Israel's suffering, and he speaks as if that is indeed what he intends.

(4) One of the relevant sayings of Jesus quotes Isaiah 53 directly, and others can most easily be explained as an allusion to it. The

direct quotation is found in Luke 22.37 ("For I tell you that the scripture that says, 'He shared the fate of criminals,' must come true about me, because what was written about me is coming true"), quoting Isaiah 53.12. The allusions are found in Mark 9.12 ("Why do the scriptures say that the Son of Man will suffer much and be rejected?"), alluding to Isaiah 53.3; Mark 10.45, in a scene that occurs right before the triumphant entry into Jerusalem, for which Zechariah is an important text ("For even the Son of Man did not come to be served; he came to serve and to give his life as a ransom for many"), alluding to Isaiah 53.10 and 53.12; and Mark 14.24 ("Jesus said, 'This is my blood which is poured out for many'"), alluding to Isaiah 53.12.[175]

(5) It is therefore "highly probable"[176] (to put it mildly) that he regarded Isaiah 53 as determinative of his vocation.

(6) Jesus therefore intended not only that he would share Israel's sufferings but also in so doing provide the catalytic action in the divinely appointed plan of redemption for Israel and the world. Eventually a new Israel will emerge from his taking on Israel's sufferings, the Israel whose community celebrations will be patterned not on the temple sacrifices but upon the Last Supper. But the allusions to Isaiah 53 are more than the basis of a theory about his self-understanding; they express what he took to be his vocation. And with this insistence on Wright's part, he links himself in his own way with Meyer's themes of covenant sacrifice and expiatory offering, though without expressing this in so many words.

[Jesus'] work is not to be understood in terms of the teaching of an abstract and timeless system of theology, not even of atonement-theology, but as the historical and concrete acting out of YHWH's promise to defeat evil and rescue his people from exile, that is, to forgive their sins at last. Within this, the allusions to Isaiah 53 should not be regarded as the *basis* of a theory about Jesus' self-understanding in relation to his death; they may be, rather, the tell-tale signs of a vocation which he could hardly put into words,[177] the vocation to be the "herald" of Isaiah 40.9 and 52.7, and thence to be, himself, the servant, representing the Israel that was called to be the light of the world but had so signally failed to live up to her calling. The only way that such a vocation could be articulated without distortion was in story, symbol and praxis: all three came together in the temple, in the upper room, and ultimately on the hill outside the city gate. Jesus' personal reading of Isaiah belongs not so much in the history of ideas, as in the history of vocation, agenda, action, and ultimately passion. And he understood this vocation, agenda, action, and passion as messianic.[178]

For Wright, then, Jesus put together in his own self-understanding the themes and characters of (1) the Danielic Son of Man, (2) the coming king or Messiah, especially as found in Zechariah, and (3) the Servant. To this list we must add with Sigurd Grindheim (4) the one who was equal to God. Wright would not deny this addition, as is manifest in his emphasis on the theme of the return of Yahweh to Zion precisely in the entry of Jesus into Jerusalem.[179]

5   Conclusion

This chapter has been written out of the conviction that the work begun by Ben Meyer, a work that has come to be called the third quest for the historical Jesus, a work furthermore that is rooted in the critical-realist cognitional theory and epistemology of Bernard Lonergan, has the potential to heal the fragmentation of theological endeavors that Lonergan spoke about when he wrote, "Scholarship [built] an impenetrable wall between systematic theology and its historical religious sources."[180] The healing of that fragmentation is required if the method that Lonergan proposes for the overall discipline of theology is really to facilitate a process that proceeds through distinct functional specialties from data to contemporary results. I moved into this preliminary and partial investigation of the aims of Jesus in an effort to help answer the question of his self-understanding, particularly as he embraced his destiny. We have to do something along these lines in order to meet the requirement that, again in Peter Laughlin's words, "a faithful atonement motif will demonstrate a degree of continuity *with the meaning that Jesus of Nazareth constituted for his death.*"[181]

Meyer's work is only a beginning. It has been complemented in more ways than I was able to demonstrate here by the work of Wright. It has not been my intention to write a history of the third quest to date, but rather to demonstrate the kind of exegetical work that will enable the wall to be taken down. Far more elaborate studies of the matters covered in this chapter can be written, but I trust that if they are written in the spirit and with the method exhibited by Meyer's work, they will continue to facilitate the overall theological purpose of moving from the data of historical research to the contemporary results of systematic understanding and the kind of practical pastoral work done in the functional specialty of Communications. That is all I intended in adding this basically nonsystematic chapter to a work in systematic theology. The next volume, *Redeeming History*, will return to the systematic task by proposing the outlines of a contemporary soteriology.

Appendix

Theses Presented in the First Two Volumes of This Work

Thesis 1: A Catholic systematic theology on the level of our time will be

    (a) like all systematic theologies, an attempt to understand the mysteries of Christian faith and the other meanings constitutive of the Christian community;

    (b) grounded in interiorly and religiously differentiated consciousness expressive of four dimensions of conversion: religious, moral, intellectual, and psychic;

    (c) a theological theory of history; and

    (d) expressed in the context of the multi-religious and interreligious world in which we live.

Thesis 2: A contemporary Catholic systematic theology will begin by rearticulating the theology of the divine missions in the contemporary context defined by thesis 1. Thus, renewed Trinitarian, Pneumatological, and Christological articulations will form the dogmatic-theological context for the development of theological doctrines and systematic positions regarding revelation, original sin, redemption, church, sacraments, eternal life, creation, and other emergent elements of Christian constitutive meaning.

Thesis 3: Theological doctrines and systematic positions regarding revelation, original sin, redemption, church, sacraments, eternal life, and creation will catalyze the development of the dogmatic-theological context for yet further understanding. But these doctrinal and systematic positions require a theological theory of history grounded in the Trinitarian, Pneumatological, and Christological context and employing and developing basic categories of history expressed by Lonergan in terms of progress, decline, and redemption, and developed by the present writer in terms of the scale of values and the dialectical structure of personal, cultural, and social values.

Thesis 4: The key to the integrated connection between the mysteries of faith that is the concern of systematics lies in the links that Lonergan has drawn between the four divine relations and four created participations in and imitations of these relations. The starting point in unpacking that four-point hypothesis is the link between sanctifying grace and charity as created participations in, respectively, active spiration and passive spiration. From the standpoint of religiously and interiorly differentiated consciousness, these created participations are (1) the recalled reception (*memoria*) of the gift of God's love (that is, of sanctifying grace as it affects consciousness) grounding a subsequent set of judgments of value (faith), as these together participate in active spiration and so set up a special relation to the indwelling Holy Spirit, and (2) a return of love (charity) participating in the Proceeding Love that is the Holy Spirit, which establishes a special relation to the indwelling Father and Son. Memory and faith combine to imitate and participate in active spiration, and charity imitates and participates in passive spiration.

Thesis 5: Sanctifying grace as participation in active spiration includes also a judgment of value, an ineffable "Yes" that constitutes the universalist faith that is the knowledge born of religious love. As a participation in active spiration, this faith reflects the invisible mission of the Son, the divine Word, the Trinitarian *Verbum spirans Amorem.*

Thesis 6: The Trinitarian structure of created grace provides a psychological analogy for understanding Trinitarian life, an analogy whose structure is isomorphic with the analogies suggested by Augustine, Aquinas, and Lonergan. Thus there is established an analogy for understanding Trinitarian processions that obtains in the supernatural order itself. This analogy joins Augustine in positing *memoria* as the first step, where *memoria* is the retrospective appropriation of the condition in which one finds oneself gifted by unconditional love. *Memoria* and the judgment of value (faith) that follows from it as *verbum spirans amorem* participate in active spiration. The charity that flows from them participates in passive spiration. Together, these form the special basic relations of a systematic theology.

Thesis 7: The divine missions are constituted by God alone as consequent upon the relations of opposition that are the Trinity, but the judgments that affirm the missions require a created term external to God as a consequent condition of the truth of the judgments. In the case of the mission of the Son, that external term is the secondary act of existence that is the base of a real relation of the human nature of Jesus to the eternal Word which, precisely as a divinely constituted relation to the Word, participates in the eternal relation to the Word that is paternity. In the case of the mission of the Holy Spirit, the external term is twofold. "Sanctifying grace" has been the name given the created base of a real relation to the Holy Spirit; that base thus participates in active spiration, the divinely constituted relation to the Holy Spirit, and so in the Father and the Son as together they breathe the Holy Spirit. The disposition of charity flows from that participation in active spiration, and so is the base of a real relation to the Father and the Son that participates in passive spiration, the divinely constituted eternal relation to the Father and the Son, and so in the Holy Spirit. In terms of religiously differentiated consciousness, these may be characterized, respectively, as the reception of the unqualified love of the Father and of the eternal judgment of value that is the Son, both of these in the Holy Spirit, and as the return of love to the Father and the Son, again in the Holy Spirit. These missions are extended in the mission of the church, in part to catalyze non-violent responses to evil. This is part of the grounding statement of a theology of social grace. Finally, the light of glory as the created consequent condition of beatific knowledge is the created supernatural participation in and imitation of filiation, as in the Holy Spirit the Son brings us, his brothers and sisters, children by adoption, perfectly back to the Father. The disposition of hope that flows from the gift of God's love is our present historical participation in this ultimately eschatological relation.

Thesis 8: The notion of sanctifying grace unifies the elements of biblical doctrine by allowing them to be conceived as formal effects.

Thesis 9: The invisible mission of the Holy Spirit is universal. It precedes in time the visible mission of the Son, and is fulfilled by it. Pentecost is the manifestation of that fulfilment.

Thesis 10: The preaching of the reign of God by the incarnate Word can be integrated into a systematic theology by complicating the structure of the scale of values. Thus there emerges the social character of grace.

Thesis 11: As elevation by grace affects every level of consciousness, so it influences also each of the levels of value isomorphic with the levels of consciousness.

Thesis 12: We can identify two meanings of the word "system" as this word is used with reference to theology. There is a methodological meaning that is applied to the "system" of the whole of theology, and there is a strictly theological meaning that refers to the strictly systematic component within that whole.

Thesis 13: The relations among the sets of operations may be schematized as follows.

        5 Horizons

4 Dialectic	Categories 6
3 History	Doctrines 7
2 Interpretation	Systematics 8
1 Research	Communications 9

Thesis 14: The functional specialty that Lonergan calls Foundations should thus be divided into two functional specialties. The specialty called "Horizons" stands outside the other eight and objectifies the concrete universal, the normative subject, that effects the transition from the first phase to the second phase. The first specialty in the second phase is called Categories.

Thesis 15: The first column in the structure of the functional specialties names the operations involved in the mediating phase of theology, the phase that mediates from the past into the present by interpreting, narrating, and evaluating what others have said and done. The second column names the operations entailed in a second phase, when the theologian takes his or her own stand on the issues raised in the mediating phase and in the cultural matrix within which the theologian is operating and states in contemporary terms the positions that have been mediated from the past into the present. Thus this phase may be referred to as the mediated phase. But taking a stance also entails a further mediation from the present into the future, which renders this phase also constitutive, at least in intention. Moreover, each set of operations has its own set of objects.

Thesis 16: In the first phase – research, interpretation, history, dialectic – theology is hermeneutical in the broad sense of understanding what others have said and done; and it is historical in the sense of narrating what was going forward as a result of what others have said and done. The results of this phase, the results of mediating the past into the present, comprise at least the following three aspects: (1) the history of what is regarded in the community as the very action of God in history; thus we speak of "salvation history"; (2) the history of the community's struggles to articulate its salvation history in doctrines and dogma; and finally (3) the history of the discipline of theology itself, which reflects on salvation history and doctrine. All three aspects entail the emergence of meanings and value within specific cultural contexts.

Thesis 17: In the second phase, theologians state not what others have said and done but what they hold to be the case. In Lonergan's words, the second phase is "direct discourse," "oratio recta," while the first is "indirect discourse," "oratio obliqua." If the first phase mediates the tradition into the present, theologians in the second phase state in their own words what they hold to be the mediated tradition. Thus the first phase is "mediating" and the second "mediated." But the second phase also mediates from the present into the future, and in this sense is constitutive, at least in intent.

Thesis 18: Not only does a theology mediate between a cultural matrix and the significance and role of a religion in that matrix, but the mediation in question is a mutual self-mediation. It is for this reason that the second phase in theology not only states the assimilated or mediated tradition but also is at least potentially constitutive of the ongoing tradition.

Thesis 19: The theological and methodological options expressed thus far entail a vast expansion of the range of Catholic theology. The functional specialties of such a theology are now applied to the movement from data to results in the worldwide religious community of humankind.

Thesis 20: The social dimensions of grace are rooted in a level of consciousness that is beyond the four levels of experience, understanding, judgment, and decision and that sublates them. This unitive and inclusive level of consciousness is interpersonal, and when self-transcendent it is marked by love in intimacy, in devotion to the human community, and in the reception of God's love and the return of love for God in charity. The functional specialty Horizons will include this dimension in its mediated object.

Thesis 21: While the four-point hypothesis constitutes the specifically theological dimension of the starting point, it must be joined by a theory of history if our systematics is to integrate the realities named in special categories with those named in general categories. Revelation introduces God's meaning into history. The Incarnation is the personal entrance of God's Meaning into history under intersubjective, aesthetic, symbolic, linguistic, and incarnate carriers. The mission of the Holy Spirit is the inner word of God's meaning in history. Together the four-point hypothesis and the theological theory of history constitute the unified field structure of a contemporary systematics.

Thesis 22: The objects intended in systematic theology must be identified, as far as possible, in categories derived from interiorly and religiously differentiated consciousness.

Thesis 23: While the corresponding element is most often found in intentional consciousness, the experience of the gift of God's love, manifest, for example, in what St Ignatius Loyola calls consolation without a previous cause, introduces complexities regarding the relation of knowledge and love, and so regarding intentional and non-intentional components at the level of theological foundations.

Thesis 24: Lonergan's work on the psychological analogy is required background for the advances being suggested here. It shows how an understanding of human dynamic consciousness in its immanent terms and relations – an understanding of how act proceeds from act in the autonomous spiritual dimension of human consciousness – provides the basic framework for an analogical understanding of Trinitarian processions and relations. In all forms of the analogy, the inner word that provides the analogue for the procession of the divine Word is a judgment of value.

Thesis 25: Religiously differentiated consciousness is to be distinguished into the two moments of being on the receiving end of divine love and loving in return in an unrestricted manner.

Thesis 26: Lonergan's early analogy corresponds to *Insight*'s account of decision and to Ignatius Loyola's third time of election, and his later analogy corresponds to *Method*'s account of judgments of value and decision and to Ignatius's second time of election. Our distinct analogy, a development upon Lonergan's second analogy, reflects participation in divine active and passive spiration.

Thesis 27: The second component of the unified field structure is provided when the general categories of a contemporary systematic theology are focused around the dialectical process of human history.

Thesis 28: The analogy proposed here differs from those of Aquinas and the early Lonergan on two counts: it is explicitly located in the supernatural order, and it initiates a theology of history.

Thesis 29: The proposals being offered here represent an instance of the genetic sequence of systematic theologies. The starting point now becomes a synthetic position that treats together the divine processions and the missions that are identical with the processions joined to a created term as consequent condition of the missions. The missions are the divine processions in history.

Thesis 30: While relations constitute the unifying key to the obscure, analogical understanding of the Trinity considered both immanently and economically, still understanding the divine relations depends on understanding how there can be processions in God.

Thesis 31: The fundamental issue in Trinitarian systematics for Lonergan, namely, how it can be true that (1) the Son is both *a se* and not *a se*, (2) the Holy Spirit is both *a se* and not *a se*, and (3) the way in which the Son is not *a se* is different from the way in which the Holy Spirit is not *a se*, is, with the genetic development being suggested here, swept up into the larger question of a Trinitarian systematics that would be the beginning of a theology of history, namely, how the Trinitarian relations are imitated, and participated in, in history.

Thesis 32: The link between Lonergan's formulation of the fundamental Trinitarian problem and ours is found in identifying the distinct meanings of "emanation" as this term is applied analogically to divine processions, and in identifying the reality of what is so named in terms of relations that are participated in historically through created emanations in human consciousness.

Thesis 33: Lonergan's fundamental Trinitarian problem can be addressed in a manner that links with the present work by understanding his later statement that each of the divine subjects has a unique manner of being subject of the unrestricted act: the Father as originating love, the Son as judgment of value expressing that love, and the Spirit as originated loving.

Thesis 34: What Aquinas refers to as *emanatio intelligibilis* can be formulated in the language of autonomous spiritual procession, where "autonomous" refers to processions of act from act grounded in an intelligible proportion between what proceeds and the principle from which the procession originates.

Thesis 35: The meaning of autonomous spiritual procession is illuminated by contrasting the ordinary and original meaningfulness that Lonergan introduces into his discussion of analytic philosophy, and by identifying autonomy with what occurs in the production of original meaningfulness.

Thesis 36: "Autonomous spiritual procession" means the conscious origination of a real, natural, and conscious act from a real, natural, and conscious act, both within the spiritual dimension of consciousness and also by virtue of the spiritual dimension of consciousness itself as determined by the prior act. Such a procession is exhibited in the procession of concepts from understanding, of judgments from reflective grasp of evidence, and of good decision from an authentic judgment of value. It is only in the procession of act from act that an analogy for the Trinitarian processions can be found.

Thesis 37: The procession of act from act in the spiritual dimension of consciousness is to be sharply distinguished from the procession of act from potency in that same dimension, as well as from all processions in the sensitive-psychic dimension of consciousness.

Thesis 38: The distinction of two ways of being conscious opens us upon the possibility of making a theological contribution to mimetic theory.

Thesis 39: The distinction of the two dimensions of consciousness will enable a clarification of the precise character of the image of God found in the spiritual processions of act from act, whether in the realm of nature or in that of grace.

Thesis 40: Lonergan's first "way of being conscious" is interdividual in many of its manifestations. Psychic development entails the negotiation of this interdividual field in the direction of what Jung calls individuation. But this negotiation calls upon the operations of the second "way of being conscious." Inadequate negotiation of the interdividual field can and will distort this second way, while authentic negotiation of the same field will help the second way flourish in the development of the person. This authentic negotiation is a function of the second way itself, that is, of insight, judgment, and moral responsibility, including the autonomous spiritual processions of act from act at each level.

Thesis 41: If grace in history is a matter of created imitations of the divine relations, sin in history is a matter of quite different kinds of imitations leading to destructive and violent relations. These would be the counterfoil, as it were, to a vision of the social and cultural meaning of grace. The mimetic theory of René Girard helps us identify such infected mimesis.

Thesis 42: Mimetic violence is the story of mutual self-mediation gone wrong. There is another kind of mutual self-mediation established in grace that overcomes conflictual mimesis. The gift of divine love enables consistent fidelity to the transcendental imperatives attached to the notions of the intelligible, the true and the real, and the good, and such fidelity is the key to individuation. But that gift also has a dimension of its own, a dimension that transcends through forgiveness the contamination of human relations brought on by conflictual mimesis. Our love is God's love and so truly without conditions, reservations, or qualifications, when we love our enemies and pray for them, for God's love makes the Father's sun rise on the evil and the good and rain fall for the just and the unjust alike (Matthew 5.44–45).

Thesis 43: Foundationally the image of God lies in the created participation in active and passive spiration that is the share in divine life given us in grace. The historical mission of the Word reveals precisely in what that imitation lies, namely, in the love that returns good for evil. Derivatively, the image of God lies in fidelity to the transcendental imperatives of human consciousness, and particularly in the way these give rise to successive processions of act from act in cognitive and existential subjectivity. The foundational instance, which is first in itself, will be understood by analogy with the derived instance, which is first for us.

Thesis 44: Lonergan's heuristic anticipation in history of (1) a sacralization to be dropped, (2) a sacralization to be fostered, (3) a secularization to be welcomed, and (4) a secularization to be resisted can be specified in terms of his notions of the law of the cross and of the transcendental exigencies of the human spirit, and in terms of Girard's notion of the scapegoat.

Thesis 45: The supreme good into which fidelity to the law of the cross, which enjoins the return of good for evil done, transforms the evils that afflict the human race is the emergence of a new community in history and in the life to come, a community that in theological terms can be understood as the whole Christ, head and members, whether explicitly Christian or not, in all the concrete determinations and relations constitutive of this community.

Thesis 46: The evils transformed by the law of the cross are the distortions of relations that hinder genuine community from ever being realized. These are understood in terms of basic sin and moral evil, both of which are traced ultimately to original sin. With minor qualifications, these realities may be conceptualized more concretely in terms of the failure to reject the mimetic cycle and the consequences of such failure. The new community embodies a new kind of "interdividuation," one that is constituted by the imitation of the four divine relations in grace.

Thesis 47: The law of the cross as embodied in Jesus has a threefold structure: the massive mimesis in which the failure of will that is basic sin is displayed, the transformation of the evil of his suffering and death into a new community, and the resurrection of Jesus as first-born from the dead. This structure, which determines the direction of soteriology, is to be embodied in Christ's members as they lovingly absorb the consequences of basic sin and transform these into new life for the world by returning good for evil.

Thesis 48: The transition from sacral and secular to really sacred and really profane is catalyzed by the emergence of soteriologically differentiated consciousness. This is what provides a key to discriminating which sacralizations are to be dropped and which to be fostered, and which secularizations are to be welcomed and which to be resisted. This statement is compatible with Lonergan's specification of personal, communal, and historical criteria for this transition.

Thesis 49: The same prescription specifies the context of religious development and retardation, both individual and social, within which Lonergan raises these issues.

Thesis 50: Girard establishes a more thorough-going hermeneutic of suspicion regarding the false sacred than does Freud. His understanding of psychic aberration or of what Lonergan calls dramatic bias may be joined with Lonergan's understanding of other biases, and can be put in aid of Lonergan's hermeneutics of the recovery of individual and communal authenticity.

Thesis 51: The legitimate domain of sacralization, the genuine sacred, in history lies in the redemptive religion that overcomes bias and restores progress. The legitimate domain of secularization, the genuine profane, in history lies in the progress that results from human beings being consistently attentive, intelligent, reasonable, and responsible. The appropriate symbolizations will be found primarily in the incarnate meaning of persons and of communities that, gathering in the name of Jesus, radiate peace and joy. But that symbolization is no substitute for the hard work of understanding, judgment, and decision, indeed of collective responsibility, sharing in the invisible mission of the divine Word.

Thesis 52: The word of Hebrew revelation provides progressively clearer indications of precisely what does and does not qualify as the "genuine sacred" in history. The high point of that progressive revelation in the history of Israel is in the Deutero-Isaian vision of the suffering servant. For Christians the clearest revelation of the genuine sacred is in the mind and heart, the human consciousness and knowledge, of Jesus of Nazareth, where revelation itself finds its central locus and primary meaning. And there, in that revelation, we are told that the kingdom of God is a mimesis of the one Jesus called Abba, who "causes his sun to rise on the bad as well as the good, and his rain to fall on the honest and dishonest alike." Imitating Abba means: "love your enemies, and pray for those who persecute you; in this way you will be children of your Father in Heaven." This orientation is central to the very revelation itself that comes through God's word and that is progressively disclosed through the course of the biblical writings. The same orientation is moved into an explicitly systematic-theological framework in the four-point hypothesis regarding the divine missions, where sanctifying grace and charity are created external imitations, mimetic, respectively, of the active spiration of Father and Son breathing the Spirit of Love and of the passive spiration of the Holy Spirit being breathed.

Thesis 53: The psychological analogy that proceeds from nature is helpful if we are to appreciate and understand the psychological analogy in the order of grace that has been proposed here. Firm possession of both analogies also helps to establish the link between religious and personal values in the scale of values. The relevant processions in the order of nature have to do with our existential autonomy, where the procession of a judgment of value from existential-ethical grasp of sufficient evidence for the judgment regarding what it would be good for the existential subject to do and to be provides the analogue for the procession of the Son. From that grasp and that judgment operating together as a single principle there proceeds loving decision to do and to be precisely what has been affirmed, and this is the natural analogue for the procession of the Holy Spirit.

Thesis 54: The movement from the church's confession of faith, "God from God," to the hypothetical understanding of the processions by analogy with human autonomous spiritual procession is mediated by the theological conclusion that divine processions must be according to the mode of *processio operati.* The analogical understanding affirmed in thesis 53 thus provides a hypothetical explanation of how this theological conclusion can be true.

Thesis 55: The structure of the analogy from spiritual autonomy is the only viable structure for a Trinitarian analogy, and the most suitable instance from nature of such spiritual autonomy is the procession of the word of a judgment of value from existentially reflective understanding and the procession of a loving decision from the word of a judgment of value, precisely in the existential issues in which we inquire about ourselves, understand what we ought to be, judge how we can make ourselves be such, and proceed to the existential decisions through which we so constitute ourselves.

Thesis 56: Two and only two divine processions can be conceived by analogy with human autonomous spiritual procession, namely, the procession of the word as a judgment of value from the reflective act of existential self-understanding that utters the word, and the procession of love both from the act of understanding that utters the word of a judgment of value and from the uttered judgment of value itself. It is in this way that we are made in the image and likeness of God. This process from reflective existential understanding to judgment of value and then from the two together to love is a natural imitation of the divine processions.

Thesis 57: Analogies based on the genuine autonomy of the human subject, analogies of act from act in the spiritual dimension of consciousness, are available to us only inasmuch as we have been not only freed from the illusions of false autonomy but also freed into a genuine autonomy through the grace that operates us beyond the deviated transcendence of mimetic rivalry.

Thesis 58: The context is further enriched by the insistence that Lonergan's distinction of insight and word, which occurs in the Scholastic context in which insight grasps intelligibilities resident in corporeal matter, can and must be extended to the fuller hermeneutic epistemology that acknowledges ordinary meaningfulness even at the level of presentations. This distinction in interiorly differentiated consciousness also permits a transposition of the Scholastic notions of active and passive potency into the context of an intentionality analysis heading to self-appropriation.

Thesis 59: The understanding of why we are not able to demonstrate the existence of a divine Word further enriches the natural analogue for the Trinitarian processions. Inner words are required for the integrity, progress, explanatory power, and transcendental reach of human cognitional process. The argument to this effect can be extended to and enriched by the hermeneutical context of the world mediated and constituted by meaning. The enrichment of our understanding regarding the necessity of human inner words contributes to our appropriation of the indemonstrable mystery of the procession of the divine Word, in whose invisible mission our inner words share.

Thesis 60: A still further enrichment occurs when Lonergan's question whether the presence of the beloved within the lover is constituted or produced by love is transformed by the shift of the basic starting point of the analogy from understanding to being in love and from being in love to being on the receiving end of a love that is unqualified and absolute.

Thesis 61: Since the reality of the two divine processions with which the divine missions are identical is the reality to be attributed to relations, the missions themselves will have a thoroughly relational structure. The missions of the Holy Spirit and the Son are themselves missions of relations, sendings of divine relations into the human world mediated and constituted by meaning and motivated by values, and so into the world of human relations. These missions are identical with the divine relations joined to created external terms. The Word and the Holy Spirit are sent or missioned to transform human relations, to lift or elevate them precisely as relations into conformity with the reign of God and so with the entire range of the scale of values.

Thesis 62: The created external terms that are the consequent conditions of the processions and relations also being missions – in Lonergan's hypothesis, the secondary act of existence of the incarnate Word, sanctifying grace, charity, and the light of glory – must (1) be related to one another in a manner that shares in and imitates the order of the divine relations of which they are created external terms, and (2) have implications for an elevation of human relations (not simply of individuals in their authenticity, that is, "personal values") to a participation in divine relations.

Thesis 63: The affirmation that the missions that are identical with the divine processions are real relations and the consequent affirmation that the created terms of these relational missions participate in the relationality that is divine life together constitute the firm theological ground of the theology of social grace already introduced in the first volume. It is in the realm of social grace that there will be found the relations among the created terms of the relational divine missions: the relations to one another of the secondary act of existence, sanctifying grace, charity, and the light of glory.

Thesis 64: The systematic understanding of the doctrine of the universality of salvation lies in a development in the theology of actual grace. At least some instances of actual grace as both operative and cooperative are also sanctifying graces in the strict sense of the term, in that they include the infusion of supernatural charity. This is particularly true of those instances in which insights into the law of the cross and horizon-elevating choices based in such insights offer what Vatican II calls the possibility of sharing in the paschal mystery.

Thesis 65: It is in terms of this theology of actual grace that the universal invisible missions of the Word and of the Holy Spirit are to be understood.

Thesis 66: The scale of values is the key to the notion of social grace. The invisible missions of Word and Holy Spirit are initially, and respectively, the actual grace of divinely given insights into the reign of God in concrete circumstances of human life and divinely prompted elevations of horizon to correspond to the ends dictated by supernatural charity. As the operative grace of these gifts becomes the cooperative grace that enables human assent, the justifying gift of God's love, a created participation in and imitation of divine active spiration, starts into movement the immanent constitution of life in God, the indwelling of the three divine persons. This constitution is the structure of the realm of religious values in the scale of values in the form of elevated *memoria*, faith, charity, and hope. It is the condition of the possibility of sustained personal integrity (personal value). Persons of integrity represent the condition of possibility of genuine meanings and values informing ways of living (cultural values). The pursuit of genuine cultural values is a constitutive dimension in the establishment of social structures and intersubjective habits (social values) that would render more probable something approaching an equitable distribution of vital values to the human community (vital values). The integral functioning of the scale of values represents a set of formal effects of the gift of God's grace at the level of religious values. It constitutes in effect at least a heuristic anticipation of what the reign of God in human affairs would be. And all is marked by participation in the just and mysterious law of the cross.

Thesis 67: Grace, both habitual and actual, effects participation in and graced imitation of the divine relations, and does so in such a way as to transform human relations with God and with one another, introducing human subjects into participation in divine circumincession.

Thesis 68: Quantitative examples of internal and external relations, while easy to point to and understand, are of little existential, historical, or theological significance. The significant issue for our purposes will be to determine what constitutes internal relations between and among human beings. There are ideologies that would treat all relations among human beings as external, as depending only on the existence of the person to whom "this person" is being compared, and not on a primary internal relationality constitutive of what it is to be a human being.

Thesis 69: It will be crucial for the expansion of the theology of divine missions to argue for primary internal relationality as constitutive of the subjects of autonomous spiritual processions. Radical individualism, philosophies of selfishness, and the embodiment of such intellectual inauthenticity in political and economic theories, systems, and budgets display a denial of internal human relationality.

Thesis 70: The social objectification of the terms and relations constituting the normative source of meaning and value in history is provided by the integral scale of values. From the grasp of internal relations in the normative source we may hope to proceed to a grasp of internal relations obtaining in the realm of cultural and social values in which the normative source is objectified.

Thesis 71: Social, political, and economic theories or practices that would in effect deny internal relationality to human subjects would tend to affirm individuals as simply absolute realities. On the other hand, without the breakthrough beyond the primordial mimetic interdividuality analyzed by René Girard to the capacity for autonomous spiritual processions, one is in fact living as if it were the case that one is a simply relative reality, with a center that does not hold. Again, while individualism is in effect a denial of internal relationality in human beings, primal interdividuality prior to any individuation on the part of the subject of autonomous spiritual processions is an existence as if there were a simply relative reality on the part of the subject.

Thesis 72: The four-point hypothesis expresses the created participation of created realities in the four real uncreated relations; the participation is grounded in four created terms that are consequent conditions for these uncreated relations to become "the Trinity in history." These four created terms are also four created bases of created relations to the four uncreated relations in which the four terms participate. As such, their relations to one another participate in the order of the divine relations themselves. As paternity is to filiation, so the secondary act of existence of the incarnation is to the light of glory. As active spiration is to passive spiration, so sanctifying grace is to the circle of operations that constitute the habit or set of schemes of recurrence that constitute charity.

Thesis 73: To say "yes" and to be the "yes" uttered together breathe love. The implication regarding the relation of the terms of the missions to one another, that is, the relation of the secondary act of existence of the Incarnation to sanctifying grace, the gift of God's love, will re-establish in a quite new and thoroughly Trinitarian context that all grace is really the grace of the Son, and is revealed as such in Jesus. To beget the Son and to be begotten of the Father are together also to breathe the Spirit, which would not be breathed without the mutual relations of Father and Son. In this sense, while all mission is in the Spirit, it remains that nothing would be "in the Spirit" were it not the case that the Father eternally begets the Son and the Son is eternally begotten of the Father. For it is only in and through those relations of paternity and filiation, which together are active spiration, that there even is a Holy Spirit. Moreover, just as there is not one procession without the other, so there never is and never can be one mission without the other.

Thesis 74: Despite the real identification of the divine relations, and so of the divine missions, which are the relations joined to created contingent external terms, with the divine processions, persons, personal properties, and notional acts, it remains crucial that the four-point hypothesis speaks of the created contingent external terms as participations in and imitations of the divine relations. This makes "participation" and "imitation" more than purely metaphysical terms. They signify interpersonal relations of knowing and loving between the recipients of divine life and the three divine persons, each of whom is received in a unique manner in accord with the order of the divine relations. Because of the secondary act of existence, the assumed humanity of the historical Jesus of Nazareth is related to the divine Word in a manner analogous to the way in which the Father is eternally related to the same divine Word: as the one who speaks the Word of God the Father. Because of sanctifying grace, the elevated central form or identity of the historical human person is related to the Holy Spirit in a manner analogous to the way in which the Father and Son together are eternally related to the same Holy Spirit: as the Father and Son together are the single principle of the One who does the eternal truth that God is love, so the human being who loves with the love of Father and Son breathes a proceeding love for Father and Son that consciously shares in that same Holy Spirit. Because of charity, which is that created proceeding love, the circle of operations of the historical person who loves with divine love is related to the Father and the Son in a manner analogous to that in which the Holy Spirit is eternally related to the same Father and Son: as the One who receives the eternal love that is then "done." Because of the light of glory the enduring personal identity even of the one who lives after death still awaiting life after life after death, the resurrection of the body, is personally related to the eternal Father in a manner analogous to that in which the Son is eternally related to the same Father: as child of God into whose conscious intelligence and love the divine reality has insinuated itself as primary object or, in metaphysical terms, intelligible species.

Thesis 75: If it is true that for the Father to beget the Son and for the Son to be begotten of the Father is for them together to spirate the Spirit of love, or that for the Father to speak the Word and for the Word to be spoken is for them together actively to breathe Love, then the mutual opposition of Father-Son actively spirates the Spirit, and that active spiration, itself constituted of this mutual opposition, itself stands in mutual opposition to the proceeding Holy Spirit, who is passive spiration.

Thesis 76: An upshot or implication of this for the divine missions is that there is never Spirit without Word or Word without Spirit, whether in the immanent Trinity or in the missions, and whether the mission be "visible" or "invisible." If it is the case that for the Son to be uttered by the Father is also for the Father and the Word actively to spirate the Holy Spirit, then because the missions are the processions and relations joined to created external terms, it follows that for the Son to be sent by the Father is also for the Father and the Word to send the Holy Spirit. This holds for both "visible" and "invisible" missions.

Thesis 77: In contrast with the position of Hans Urs von Balthasar, person is not precisely mission, even in Jesus, whose person is the divine relation of filiation, but in whose human consciousness procession, relation, filiation, person become mission because of the created external term without which they could not be mission. Procession, relation, and person in Jesus are divine and necessary. But mission is contingent, conditioned by the created external term consequent on divine freedom, namely, what Aquinas calls the secondary act of existence. The absolutely supernatural created gift of the secondary act of existence is the condition consequent upon divine decision that makes it possible to say truly, "The second person of the Blessed Trinity is this man Jesus of Nazareth." This contingent "is" is the secondary act of existence.

Thesis 78: The divine consciousness of Jesus is the consciousness precisely of the One who proceeds eternally as Son and Word from the Father, while his human consciousness is the consciousness of the One who has been sent in time as Son and Word made flesh.

Thesis 79: Only spiritual subjects in whom there occur autonomous spiritual processions can possibly be persons on mission.

Thesis 80: Lonergan's discussion of person in his Latin works on the Trinity and Christ must be sublated into a notion that takes more explicitly into account the developments subsequent to Aquinas's definition and to Aquinas's reliance on Boethius's definition as well as the developments in Lonergan's own thinking. As the cognitive levels of consciousness – experience, understanding, and judgment – are sublated by the fourth, existential level, and as these four are sublated by being in love in an unqualified fashion, so the objective of authentic subjectivity sublates being (the objective of the desire to know) into the full range of the scale of values, which is the objective that serves to define what is meant by "person." A person can be defined as a distinct subsistent in a spiritual nature. A human person, then, is a distinct subsistent potentially oriented to commitment to the integral scale of values, and an authentic human person is a distinct subsistent actually oriented to the same commitment. This definition, which is also open to what is meant by "personal value" in the scale of values, really does take into account the developments on the notion of person reached by the turn to the subject in modernity, by the turn to the other in postmodernity, and by the expansions of consciousness beyond cognitional levels in Lonergan's own work.

Thesis 81: The scale of values provides the heuristic structure of the reign of God. A human person can be defined theologically as a distinct subsistent oriented to the reign of God.

Thesis 82: Balthasar's correlation of person and mission needs to be qualified by a distinction that affects its Christological base. With Lonergan we affirm that the divine person of the incarnate Word is a subject of two distinct consciousnesses. His divine consciousness is the consciousness of the one who eternally proceeds as Son from the Father, Word from the Speaker. His human consciousness, ontologically grounded in the secondary act of existence that makes it true to affirm that the second person of the Blessed Trinity is this man Jesus of Nazareth, is the mission consciousness of the Eternal Word become flesh. The two consciousnesses are continuous but also distinct. The first is eternal, uncreated, and necessary. The second is temporal, created, and contingent. They are united in the person of the eternal Word become flesh, who is the subject of both a divine and a human consciousness. This will have implications for the mission of all who, explicitly linked to the visible missions of Son and Spirit or consciously but not knowingly linked to their invisible missions, have a divinely ordained role to play in establishing the reign of God in human affairs. As persons, as personal value, they embrace a mission that, while expressing their place in the whole scheme of things, is not identical with their personhood. Their personhood is located in the autonomous spiritual processions through which, when oriented to the full range of the integral scale of values, they come to grasp, affirm, and choose their divinely ordained missions. And these spiritual processions are primarily identified in the effective history of the Trinitarian theology that begins with Augustine, is transposed by Aquinas, becomes further transposed by Lonergan, and, I hope, rejoins Augustine in my own attempt to create an analogy of memory, word, and love.

Thesis 83: Salvation, the core focus of soteriology, is precisely the reign of God that Jesus announced and inaugurated, the explicit and revealed presence and operation of the God of grace in human history as mediating a participation in and communication of divine life that will extend into a new creation. At its heart is the message of forgiveness, reconciliation, divine compassion and mercy, forgiveness even of those responsible for the crucifixion of the bearer of the good news.

Thesis 84: The community of the church is not the kingdom of God. Its mission is to catalyze the kingdom of God in human affairs, principally by embodying the message of forgiveness in word and deed. *Nulla salus extra regnum Dei*, there is no salvation outside the reign of God, for salvation and the reign of God are coterminous. But the reign of God extends far beyond the church.

Thesis 85: Contemporary soteriologies will inevitably and correctly attempt to seek the redemptive meaning of Jesus' passion, death, and resurrection in categories appropriate to the situations in which these theologies are developed. Our efforts in this direction will be mediated by work on the scale of values. Still, the fundamental criterion for the validity of a soteriology is not its relevance to contemporary issues but its ability to demonstrate a degree of continuity with the meaning that Jesus understood these events to have, that is, with his aims and objectives as his pursuit of them led him to the cross.

Thesis 86: Redemption occurs, in part, in and with respect to concrete historical events, as the inbreaking of the reign of God in history.

Thesis 87: The invisible missions of Word and Holy Spirit are initially, and respectively, the actual grace of divinely given insights into the reign of God in concrete circumstances of human life and divinely prompted elevations of horizon to the ends dictated by supernatural charity. As the operative grace of these gifts becomes the cooperative grace that enables human assent, the justifying gift of God's love, a created participation in and communication and imitation of divine active spiration, starts into movement what in *Missions and Processions* I called the immanent constitution of life in God, the indwelling of the three divine persons, that is, habitual grace.

Thesis 88: This immanent constitution is the structure of the realm of religious values in the scale of values, in the form of elevated *memoria*, from which there proceed faith, charity, and hope.

Thesis 89: Redemption as end in this life and in the life to come is the reign of God, mediated by the suffering, death, and resurrection of the incarnate Word. These events are themselves redemptive mediation. They are also a revelatory event displaying a universal pattern through which the reign of God is advanced, a pattern of returning good for evil and so transforming the evil into a greater good. The greater good is the new community, which continues in this life to mediate the reign of God through the suffering that returns good for evil, and which will enjoy forever in the new creation the most intimate realization possible of God's victory.

Thesis 90: In the process of moving from mission consciousness to self-understanding in the context of mission, Jesus wrought radical changes on, and then integrated, the familiar Jewish conceptions of sin, sacrifice, and expiation, and the familiar Jewish figures of Messiah, Son of Man, and Servant of Yahweh. The radical changes had to do with the growing realization that redemptive and expiatory suffering in the concrete historical details of his own life, and as mediating a new covenant, would be a principal characteristic of who he was. All of these conceptions were Jewish, human categories, processed and brought together through his developing human self-knowledge. Jesus came to adjudicate them in the light of a further, divine knowledge of his equality with God, which over time became also part of his human self-understanding and was manifest in his doing what his compatriots knew only God could do. All of these developments came to pass as Jesus discovered his mission in the concrete historical circumstances and details of first-century second-Temple Palestinian Judaism. The basic pattern of what redemption actually means is embodied in his negotiation of those historical details and circumstances.

Notes

Chapter 1

1 Robert M. Doran, *The Trinity in History: A Theology of the Divine Missions,* vol. 1, *Missions and Processions* (Toronto: University of Toronto Press, 2012). Henceforth this volume will be referred to as *Missions and Processions.*

2 Bernard Lonergan, *The Triune God: Systematics,* vol. 12 in Collected Works of Bernard Lonergan, trans. Michael G. Shields, ed. Robert M. Doran and H. Daniel Monsour (Toronto: University of Toronto Press, 2007) 470–73.

3 For the categories "life after death" and "life after life after death," see N.T. Wright, *Surprised by Hope: Rethinking Heaven, the Resurrection, and the Mission of the Church* (New York: HarperOne, 2008) passim.

4 Bernard Lonergan, "The Supernatural Order," in *Early Latin Theology,* vol. 19 in Collected Works of Bernard Lonergan, trans. Michael G. Shields, ed. Robert M. Doran and H. Daniel Monsour (Toronto: University of Toronto Press, 2011) 65. "The Supernatural Order" is an English translation of Lonergan's "De ente supernaturali," composed in Montreal in 1946.

5 Lonergan, *The Triune God: Systematics* 471, emphasis added. An earlier version of the hypothesis may be found in Lonergan, "Supplementary Notes on Sanctifying Grace," *Early Latin Theology* 630–37.

6 Lonergan, *The Triune God: Systematics* 497, emphasis added.

7 A methodological and foundational background for attempting to understand the mysteries of Christian faith in the context of a philosophical and theological position on *history* may be found in Robert M. Doran, *Theology and the Dialectics of History* (Toronto: University of Toronto Press, 1990) and *What Is Systematic Theology?* (Toronto: University of Toronto Press, 2005).

8 See Doran, *Missions and Processions,* chapter 3.

9 Bernard Lonergan, *Method in Theology*, vol. 14 in Collected Works of Bernard Lonergan, ed. Robert M. Doran and John D. Dadosky (Toronto: University of Toronto Press, 2017) 32–33. See Doran, *Theology and the Dialectics of History* and *What Is Systematic Theology?* for developments of the scale of values.

10 On the dialectic of community, see Doran, *Theology and the Dialectics of History*, chapter 3 and part 3 passim.

11 The distinction "sensitive-psychic and spiritual" as a diagnostic of Girard and Lonergan is my own, but the use in this context of the added traditional theological differential of "elicited and natural" I owe to Neil Ormerod, in a lecture that I heard him deliver in April 2010 at Loyola Marymount University, Los Angeles. See also Neil Ormerod, "Desire and the Origins of Culture: Lonergan and Girard in Conversation," *Heythrop Journal* 54 (2013) 784–95.

12 Lonergan, *The Triune God: Systematics* 139. See the use made of this passage in *Missions and Processions* 103–108, 194–95, and 199–202. For my elaboration of the same point, though without using this passage from Lonergan, see chapter 2 in Doran, *Theology and the Dialectics of History*.

13 The principal works are Bernard Lonergan, *Insight: A Study of Human Understanding*, vol. 3 in Collected Works of Bernard Lonergan, ed. Frederick E. Crowe and Robert M. Doran (Toronto: University of Toronto Press, 1992), and *Method in Theology.* The only step in this process whose dynamics are still subject to some disagreement among students of Lonergan is the move from deliberation to deliberative insights and judgments of value. I have presented my own view on these matters in "Ignatian Themes in the Thought of Bernard Lonergan: Revisiting a Topic That Deserves Further Reflection," *Lonergan Workshop* 19, ed. Fred Lawrence (Boston College, 2006) 83–106. This paper may also be found in the e-book *Essays in Systematic Theology*, essay 19, on the website www.lonerganresource.com. The same material is found more compendiously in *Missions and Processions* 153–62. (Many back issues of *Lonergan Workshop* and of *Method: Journal of Lonergan Studies* have been uploaded to www.lonerganresource.com.)

14 See chapter 2 of Lonergan, *Method in Theology*, on the transcendental notion of value.

15 See, for example, chapter 5 in Bernard Lonergan, *Collection*, vol. 4 in Collected Works of Bernard Lonergan, ed. Frederick E. Crowe and Robert M. Doran (Toronto: University of Toronto Press, 1988). The chapter is entitled "The Natural Desire to See God." An earlier presentation of the natural desire to see God may be found in "The Supernatural Order" 138–79. It should be acknowledged more than is often the case that this latter presentation, probably written without any familiarity on Lonergan's part with Henri de Lubac's *Surnaturel* (also published in 1946), in fact answers the questions that de Lubac raises. Even earlier notes may be found

at 23900DTL040 and 23900DTE040 on the website www.bernardlonergan.
com. These notes were probably written for a course in eschatology that
Lonergan taught in Montreal in 1945. A fine presentation of Lonergan's
position in relation to those of both de Lubac and some contemporary
Thomists is offered by Randall S. Rosenberg, *The Givenness of Desire: Concrete
Subjectivity and the Natural Desire to See God* (Toronto: University of Toronto
Press, 2017). Lonergan's contribution to this discussion is often overlooked.
Rosenberg's book will, I hope, help to change that.

16 See Lonergan, *Insight*, chapters 6 and 7.

17 For the basic statement, see Robert M. Doran, *Subject and Psyche* (Milwaukee:
Marquette University Press, 1994; now available on the website www.
lonerganresource.com, under Scholarly Works/Books). For the theological
implications, see Doran, *Theology and the Dialectics of History* passim.

18 See Doran, *Missions and Processions* 203–204, and Index, "Autonomy."

19 Mutual self-mediation is instanced wherever the self-understanding of one
person or group is a function of communication with another person or
group and the self-understanding of the other person or group is a function
of the same communication. The category is explained in detail by Lonergan
in "The Mediation of Christ in Prayer," in *Philosophical and Theological Papers
1958–1964*, vol. 6 in Collected Works of Bernard Lonergan, ed. Robert C.
Croken, Frederick E. Crowe, and Robert M. Doran (Toronto: University of
Toronto Press, 1996) 160–82. Unfortunately, Lonergan limits his exposition
of mutual self-mediation to the relations between and among individuals.
What is required is an elucidation of the mutual self-mediation of groups,
communities, cultures, even religions. But for the moment, my point is that
such attempts as the present chapter to bring Lonergan and Girard into
communication with each other can be enriching to both.

20 See Lonergan, *Insight*, chapter 11, and *Method in Theology*, chapter 1.

21 See Robert M. Doran, "Invisible Missions: The Grace That Heals Disjunctions,"
in *Seekers and Dwellers: Plurality and Wholeness in a Time of Secularity*, ed. Philip
J. Rossi (Washington, DC: The Council for Research in Values and Philosophy,
2016) 247–67. Some of the themes in this essay will be taken up in chapter 3,
"Actual Grace and the Elevation of the Secular."

22 See Robert M. Doran, "Trinitarian Elements in a Theology of Religion:
A Tribute to Frederick E. Crowe," in *The Promise of Renewal: Dominicans
and Vatican* II, ed. Michael Attridge, Darren Dias, OP, Matthew Eaton, and
Nicholas Olkovich (Hindmarsh, SA, Australia: ATF Theology, 2017) 207–24.
See also Robert M. Doran, "Functional Specialties for a World Theology,"
Lonergan Workshop 24 (2013) 99–111. These essays may also be found in
Essays in Systematic Theology on www.lonerganresource.com, essays 42 and 36
respectively.

23 Lonergan, *The Triune God: Systematics* 471.

24 See Lonergan, "The Supernatural Order" 69 and 71, where it is stated that only Jesus, as divine and human, claims by right operations through which God is attained in Godself. The remote proportionate principle of such operations, the communication of the divine nature, finds its primary instantiation in the hypostatic union and its secondary instantiation in the habitual grace whereby we become children of God and sharers in the divine nature.

25 See Karl Rahner, "Some Implications of the Scholastic Concept of Uncreated Grace," in *Theological Investigations*, vol. 1, trans. Cornelius Ernst (London: Darton, Longman & Todd, 1961) 319–46. Lonergan does not refer to Rahner's position on the issue. Rahner's essay appeared in 1946. They both acknowledge that the usual Scholastic manner of conceiving the relation of created and uncreated grace mistakenly has the divine gift constituted by something created. While teaching a course on grace in 1947–48, Lonergan realized that he had fallen into the mistake that de facto Rahner had flagged, though Lonergan does not refer to Rahner; and he corrected himself in mid-course. But he arrived at a different, and in my opinion better, solution than did Rahner. I am currently editing student notes on Lonergan's 1947–48 course. Whether or not Lonergan had read Rahner's essay by the time he realized his own mistake while teaching (see Doran, *Missions and Processions* 25–26) will probably remain unknown. No evidence one way or the other has emerged thus far – which may itself be sufficient evidence for a negative answer.

26 See Bernard Lonergan, "Fragments toward a Seventh Chapter of *De Deo trino: Pars systematica*," METHOD: *Journal of Lonergan Studies* ns 5:2 (2014, published 2016) 1–21.

27 On the notion of a circle of operations, see Bernard Lonergan, "System and History," in *Early Works on Theological Method 2*, trans. Michael G. Shields, ed. Robert M. Doran and H. Daniel Monsour, vol. 23 in Collected Works of Bernard Lonergan (Toronto: University of Toronto Press, 2013) 298–312.

28 In chapter 3 of the present volume, an attempt will be made to incorporate into these dynamics what has traditionally been called actual grace.

29 See Charles Hefling, "Revelation and/as Insight," in *The Importance of Insight: Essays in Honour of Michael Vertin*, ed. John J. Liptay and David S. Liptay (Toronto: University of Toronto Press, 2007) 97–115.

30 On the qualifications to be made on the invisible and visible missions of the Son and the Holy Spirit, see Robert M. Doran, "Social Grace and the Mission of the Church," in *A Realist's Church: Essays in Honor of Joseph A. Komonchak* (Maryknoll, NY: Orbis Books, 2015) 169–84. These are advances beyond the position expressed in vol. 1 regarding the relation of the mission of the Son to that of the Holy Spirit. They are incorporated again here in chapter 3. See especially pp. 52–54.

31 See Lonergan, *Method in Theology* 112–14. See also Doran, *Theology and the Dialectics of History*, chapter 8.

32 See Doran, "Trinitarian Elements in a Theology of Religion."

33 See, for example, the opening pages of René Girard, *Deceit, Desire, and the Novel: Self and Other in Literary Structure*, trans. Yvonne Freccero (Baltimore: Johns Hopkins University Press, 1966).

34 See the following remark by Jean-Michel Oughourlian in René Girard, *Things Hidden since the Foundation of the World* (Stanford, CA: Stanford University Press, 1987) 199, emphasis in the text: "… the real human *subject* can only come out of the rule of the Kingdom; apart from this rule, there is never anything but mimetism and the "interdividual." Until this happens, the only subject is the mimetic structure." Girard's response (ibid.): "That is quite right." "Interdividual" refers to the same dimension that Lonergan calls "primordial intersubjectivity," where dramatic and group bias function. Girard adds the insistence on the mimetic character of this dimension. On intersubjectivity, see Lonergan, *Insight* 237–42.

35 The confusions in Jungian theory are a function of not distinguishing two kinds of opposites: contraries, which can be reconciled with one another, and contradictories, which cannot. Consciousness and the unconscious are contraries, as are the masculine and feminine dimensions of the psyche. Good and evil are contradictories. See chapter 10 in Doran, *Theology and the Dialectics of History* for details.

36 Augustine, *Confessions*, book 1, chapter 1. See *The Confessions of St. Augustine*, trans. John K. Ryan (New York: Doubleday Image, 1960) 44.

37 Lonergan, *Insight* 215. Girard enables us to link the "blind spot" with the intersubjectivity that Lonergan discusses later in his treatment of bias. That link is not explicit in Lonergan's account.

38 See Girard, *Things Hidden since the Foundation of the World* 7.

39 Bernard Lonergan, "Christology Today: Methodological Reflections," in *A Third Collection*, vol. 16 in Collected Works of Bernard Lonergan, ed. Robert M. Doran and John D. Dadosky (Toronto: University of Toronto Press, 2017) 91.

Chapter 2

1 On the notion of a unified field structure, see Doran, *Missions and Processions* xii–xiii. References are provided there for further documentation. But see especially Doran, *What Is Systematic Theology?* index: Unified field structure.

2 Bernard Lonergan, "The Dehellenization of Dogma," in *A Second Collection*, vol. 13 in Collected Works of Bernard Lonergan, ed. Robert M. Doran and John D. Dadosky (Toronto: University of Toronto Press, 2016) 24. See Lonergan, *The Triune God: Systematics* 376–91.

3   Lonergan, *The Triune God: Systematics* 231, emphasis added.

4   Ibid. 236–37.

5   See Lonergan, *Method in Theology* 47–50.

6   For a general statement, see Lonergan's references in thesis 12 of *The Incarnate Word* to the continuity in John's gospel between God the Father and the words that Jesus the man speaks. Bernard Lonergan, *The Incarnate Word*, vol. 8 in Collected Works of Bernard Lonergan, trans. Charles C. Hefling, Jr, ed. Robert M. Doran and Jeremy D. Wilkins (Toronto: University of Toronto Press, 2016) 664–69.

7   See Wright, *Surprised by Hope.*

8   "… general basic terms name conscious and intentional operations. General basic relations name elements in the dynamic structure linking operations and generating states. Special basic terms name God's gift of his love and Christian witness." Lonergan, *Method in Theology* 317. To this list I add, "The special basic relations are the created participations in the divine relations of active and passive spiration, through being on the receiving end of God's love in *gratia gratum faciens* and loving God in return in charity." Doran, *Missions and Processions* 39.

9   Bernard Lonergan, "*Existenz* and *Aggiornamento,*" in *Collection* 230–31.

10 I owe this affirmation to Eric Mabry. Chapter 5 below represents my own development of it.

11 On the scale of values, see Lonergan, *Method in Theology* 32–33, and Doran, *Theology and the Dialectics of History*, chapter 4 and passim. The other principal set of categories in the theory of history proposed in the latter book is found in the analogy of the dialectics of the subject, culture, and community, that is, in analogous structures at the levels of personal, cultural, and social values. Together the scale of values and the analogy of dialectic provide that portion of the unified field structure of a contemporary systematics that is provided by the general categories, the categories shared by theology with other disciplines. The portion of the unified field structure that has to do with theology's special categories is provided by the structure of "religious values" presented in its basic form in chapter 2 of *Missions and Processions,* "The Immanent Constitution of Life in God." That chapter offers a hypothesis regarding the basic structure of universal divine mission in the world.

12 Lonergan, *Method in Theology* 33.

13 On formal effects, see Lonergan, "Supplementary Notes on Sanctifying Grace," in *Early Latin Theology* 622–24.

14 That John 1.9 does not refer simply to the light of reason but to the divine Word who enlightens believers and nonbelievers alike is stressed by Lonergan in "Fragments toward a Seventh Chapter of *De Deo trino: Pars systematica.*"

Chapter 3

1　See Bernard Lonergan, "Sacralization and Secularization," in *Philosophical and Theological Papers 1965–1980*, vol. 17 in Collected Works of Bernard Lonergan, ed. Robert C. Croken and Robert M. Doran (Toronto: University of Toronto Press, 2005) 259–81.

2　Lonergan's position on actual grace is found in thesis 5 of "The Supernatural Order": "Interior actual grace essentially consists in vital, principal, and supernatural second acts of the intellect and the will." Our transposition to "divinely communicated insights and divinely effected transformations in the willing of the end or the establishment of one's fundamental option" honors Lonergan's own movement from faculty psychology to intentionality analysis.

3　"… the fundamental theorem, as it were, is transforming evil into good, absorbing the evil of the world by putting up with it, not perpetuating it as rigid justice would demand. And that putting up with it acts as a blotter, transforms the situation, and creates the situation in which good flourishes." Bernard Lonergan, "The Mediation of Christ in Prayer" 182.

4　For Lonergan's comments on Max Scheler's adaptation of Nietzsche on *ressentiment*, see Lonergan, *Method in Theology* 34 and note 7.

5　See, for example, Acts 8.26–40, the story of Philip and the Ethiopian eunuch.

6　Bernard Lonergan, "The Future of Christianity," *A Second Collection* 133. At this point Lonergan quotes approvingly C.F.D. Moule, *The Phenomenon of the New Testament* (London: SCM Press, 1967) 14: "At no point within the New Testament is there any evidence that the Christians stood for an original philosophy of life or an original ethic. Their sole function is to bear witness to what they claim as an event – the raising of Jesus from the dead." With N.T. Wright I would want strenuously to press Moule to go further, and I hope Lonergan would as well. The revelation in Christ Jesus *is* "a new way of construing what it meant to be human." That this is connected to the claim regarding Jesus' resurrection is clear. But Moule's language of "sole function" is misleading, suggesting as it does that the resurrection does not really make that much of a difference. See N.T. Wright, *The New Testament and the People of God* (Minneapolis: Fortress Press, 1992) 365 and note 28.

7　See Bernard Lonergan, *The Redemption*, vol. 9 in Collected Works of Bernard Lonergan, trans. Michael G. Shields, ed. Robert M. Doran, H. Daniel Monsour, and Jeremy D. Wilkins (Toronto: University of Toronto Press, 2018) 199.

8　Ibid. 218–21.

9　Lonergan, *Insight* 720.

10　See Lonergan, *The Triune God: Systematics* 512–21.

11 In the next volume I will indicate something of the origin of Lonergan's dynamics of basic sin and moral evil, as a transposition of the medieval notions of *malum culpae* and *malum poenae.* I will stress that the transposition, while important, introduces complications that need to be delineated with more precision than appears in Lonergan's work.

12 See Lonergan, *Method in Theology* 34.

13 For these questions see Doran, *Missions and Processions* 235.

14 Ibid.

15 Ibid. 236.

16 See ibid. 237.

17 See above, p. 216, note 24. The connection between habitual or sanctifying grace and actual grace in these instantiations has yet to be drawn. See pp. 47–50.

18 On the notion of a soteriological differentiation of consciousness, see Doran, *Theology and the Dialectics of History*, index, at Soteriological differentiation.

19 See *Missions and Processions* 242–43.

20 Ibid. 243.

21 "Gratia vero gratum faciens … dupliciter accipitur: uno modo pro ipsa divina acceptatione, quae est gratuita Dei voluntas; alio modo pro dono quodam creato, quod formaliter perficit hominem, et facit eum dignum vita aeterna." Thomas Aquinas, *De veritate*, q. 27, a. 5.

22 "… omnem effectum quem Deus facit in nobis ex gratuita sua voluntate, qua nos in suum regnum acceptat, pertinere ad gratiam gratum facientem …" Ibid.

23 See Bernard Lonergan, *Grace and Freedom: Operative Grace in the Thought of St Thomas Aquinas*, vol. 1 in Collected Works of Bernard Lonergan, ed. Frederick E. Crowe and Robert M. Doran (Toronto: University of Toronto Press, 2000) 35.

24 The text and Thomist references are found in Jacques Maritain, *The Range of Reason* (New York: Scribner, 1952). See Thomas Aquinas, *Summa theologiae*, 1-2, q. 89, a. 6.

25 The dates of the *De veritate* are 1256–59 and of the *Prima secundae* 1271–72. The *Quodlibetum primum* was written slightly before the *Prima secundae.*

26 See, for instance, René Girard, *I See Satan Fall like Lightning*, trans. James G. Williams (Maryknoll, NY: Orbis, 2002) 161–69.

27 Lonergan, "The Supernatural Order," in *Early Latin Theology* 229.

28 See Lonergan, *Method in Theology* 41, 118, 223, 252.

29 Lonergan, "The Supernatural Order" 229. Translation modified.

30 See Lonergan, *Grace and Freedom* 161.

31 Lonergan, "The Supernatural Order" 229. Lonergan rejects the notion that vital acts must be produced by the faculty in which they are received. See, for example, Lonergan, *The Triune God: Systematics* 546–53.

32 Lonergan, "The Supernatural Order" 229.

33 Ibid.

34 Ibid. 231.

35 Ibid.

36 Material in this and the following two sections is based on what I wrote in my paper "Invisible Missions: The Grace That Heals Disjunctions."

37 Thomas Aquinas, *Summa theologiae*, 1, q. 38, aa. 1 and 2.

38 For my initial statement of this position, see Robert M. Doran, "Consciousness and Grace," *Method: Journal of Lonergan Studies* 11:1 (1993) 51–75.

39 See Hefling, "Revelation and/as Insight."

40 See Bernard Lonergan, "Prolegomena to the Study of the Emerging Religious Consciousness of Our Time," *A Third Collection* 52–69, at 68–69.

41 Bernard Lonergan, "The Method of Theology Spring 1963," *Early Works on Theological Method 3*, vol. 24 in Collected Works of Bernard Lonergan, trans. Michael G. Shields, ed. Robert M. Doran, and H. Daniel Monsour (Toronto: University of Toronto Press, 2013). See especially pp. 11–18. In the human sciences, philosophy, and theology, there is (1) the common-sense understanding that characterizes the object of the science, (2) the understanding of that object that the human scientist is searching for, which is not coincident with (1), (3) the mutual influence between (1) and (2) so that (1) itself undergoes a *Wendung zur Idee* under the influence of the human science that studies it, (4) the experimental correction of (2) as history goes forward, (5) the histories that are written about (1), (2), (3), and (4), and finally (6) crises that affect (1), (2), (3), (4), and (5). See my paper "'No Other Gospel': Ecclesial Integrity in the Appropriation of the Second Vatican Council," presented at the West Coast Methods Institute, April 2013, Loyola Marymount University, now uploaded to www.lonerganresource.com as essay 48 in *Essays in Systematic Theology: An E-book*. The paper applies this schema to the *Wirkungsgeschichte* down to 2013 of Vatican II. (Significant positive developments have happened since 2013, of course, due to the pontificate of Pope Francis.)

42 For details on the triad, see chapter 2 of my *Missions and Processions*, "The Immanent Constitution of Life in God." What is added to that discussion here is the role of actual grace.

43 See chapter 4 of *Theology and the Dialectics of History* for an overview. The elaboration of the scale of values constitutes the principal point of the book. Part 2 is devoted to personal values, part 3 to social values or the good of order, and part 4 to cultural values. The entire scale is isomorphic with the levels of consciousness as worked out by Lonergan. This is the source of its exceptional validity and normative capacity.

44 On revelation and the Incarnation, see again Hefling, "Revelation and/as Insight."

45 Frederick E. Crowe, "Son of God, Holy Spirit, and World Religions," in *Appropriating the Lonergan Idea,* ed. Michael Vertin (Toronto: University of Toronto Press, 2006) 324–43.

46 See the concluding comments in Frederick E. Crowe, *Christ and History* (Toronto: University of Toronto Press, 2015).

47 See Doran, "Functional Specialties for a World Theology."

48 See Robert M. Doran, "The Ninth Functional Specialty," *METHOD: Journal of Lonergan Studies* ns 2:1 (2011) 12–16. This paper can also be found in *Essays in Systematic Theology,* as essay 38.

49 For the sake of convenience, I take my references here from George F. McLean, "Introduction: Disjunctions in the 21st Century," in *Church and People: Disjunctions in a Secular Age,* ed. Charles Taylor, José Casanova, and George F. McLean (Washington, DC: The Council for Research in Values and Philosophy, 2012) 1–14. The quotations that specify each disjunction are taken from p. 1 in McLean's Introduction.

50 See Bernard Lonergan, "Dialectic of Authority," in *A Third Collection* 3–9.

51 See Charles Taylor, "The Church Speaks – To Whom?" in *Church and People* 21. Compare Lonergan: "By a model is not meant something to be copied or imitated. By a model is not meant a description of reality or a hypothesis about reality. It is simply an intelligible, interlocking set of terms and relations that it may be well to have about when it comes to describing reality or to forming hypotheses. As the proverb, so the model is something worth keeping in mind when one confronts a situation or tackles a job." Bernard Lonergan, *Method in Theology* 4.

52 Lonergan, *Method in Theology* 271, with reference to Olivier Rabut, *L'expérience religieuse fondamentale* (Tournai: Castermann, 1969) 168.

53 See Bernard Lonergan, *Early Works on Theological Method 2* 339–40. Among the examples of premature systematization that Lonergan lists is clericalism, which, it may be argued, remains today the single greatest obstacle to the implementation of Vatican II reforms.

54 See Bernard Lonergan, "Dimensions of Meaning," in *Collection* 245.

Chapter 4

1 Bernard Lonergan, *The Triune God: Doctrines,* vol. 11 in Collected Works of Bernard Lonergan, trans. Michael G. Shields, ed. Robert M. Doran and H. Daniel Monsour (Toronto: University of Toronto Press, 2009) 409.

2 Lonergan, *The Triune God: Systematics* 234–35.

3 Ibid. 238–39.

4 Ibid. 246–47.

5 Ibid. 256–57.

6 For a basic component of the transformation of relations among human beings, see Matthew 18.15: "If another member of the church sins against you, go and point out the fault when the two of you are alone. If the member listens to you, you have regained that one. But if you are not listened to, take one or two others along with you, so that every word may be confirmed by the evidence of two or three witnesses. If the member refuses to listen to them, tell it to the church, and if the offender refuses to listen even to the church, let such a one be to you as a Gentile and a tax collector." How often the first step in this word of wisdom is neglected even among Christians!

7 The teaching of Gilbert involved the implication of accidental perfections in the divine essence, by which this essence is what it is. DB 389.

8 Joachim posited a quaternity in God: the three persons and a really distinct divine substance. DB 431–32, DS 803–804.

9 On the Scotist formal distinction, see Lonergan, *The Triune God: Systematics* 298–305.

10 Lonergan refers to DB 54 and 691. DB 54 (DS 125) is the *Symbolum Nicaenum* and so treats the procession of the Son. DB 691 (DS 1300) is from the *Decretum pro Graecis* of the Council of Florence concerning the procession of the Holy Spirit.

11 Lonergan refers to the sophisticated formula of the *Symbolum Fidei* of the Council of Toledo (AD 675): "… though we have said that these three persons are one God, we are not allowed to say that the same one is the Father who is the Son, or that He is the Son who is the Father, or that He who is the Holy Spirit is either the Father or the Son. For He is not the Father who is the Son, nor is the Son He who is the Father, nor is the Holy Spirit He who is the Father or the Son, even though the Father is that which the Son is, the Son that which the Father is, the Father and the Son that which the Holy Spirit is, that is, one God by nature. For, when we say, He who is the Father is not the Son, we refer to the distinction of persons; but when we say, The Father is that which the Son is, the Son that which the Father is, and the Holy Spirit that which the Father is and the Son is, this clearly refers to the nature or substance, whereby God exists, since in substance they are one; for we distinguish the persons, but we do not divide the Godhead." DB 280, DS 530, translation based on Neuner-Dupuis, *The Christian Faith in the Doctrinal Documents of the Catholic Church* (New York: Alba, 1982) §§ 313–14.

12 It must be added that a critical realism that regards the "real world" as not only mediated but also constituted by meaning and motivated by value must also account for *the relations that obtain among meanings and values*. Thus, the subject and term of a relation may be meanings and values as well as things and their characteristics. For an initial foray into these matters regarding meaning, from a Lonergan-based perspective and relying on the often overlooked chapter 17

of *Insight*, see the even more overlooked chapter 19 in Doran, *Theology and the Dialectics of History*, "The Ontology of Meaning." Obviously as well, everything I have said in many places regarding the scale of values is a theoretical position on the relations that obtains among different "levels" of value.

13   Ibid. 703.

14   For the background to this discussion, see *Missions and Processions*, chapters 8 and 9.

15   Lonergan, *The Triune God: Systematics* 733.

16   Ibid. 735 and 737.

17   See Doran, *Missions and Processions* 358 note 17, where the instance highlighted in that volume is summarized: "The immanent constitution of life in God has two orderings: from sanctifying grace to the Holy Spirit, and from charity to the Father and the Son. There are three terms, but two relations."

18   I presume here the three assertions contained in Lonergan's chapter on the processions, which immediately precedes the chapter on the relations. Those assertions, treated extensively in *Missions and Processions* chapters 8 and 11, read as follows.

Assertion 1: "The divine processions, which are processions according to the mode of a *processio operati*, are understood in some measure on the basis of a likeness to intellectual emanation; and there does not seem to be another analogy for forming a systematic conception of a divine procession." Ibid. 145.

Assertion 2: "Two and only two divine processions can be conceived through the likeness of intellectual emanation, namely, the procession of the Word from the Speaker, and the procession of Love from both the Speaker and the Word." Ibid. 181.

Assertion 3: "Generation in the strict sense of the term is implied by the divine emanation of the Word, but not by the divine emanation of Love." Ibid. 189.

19   *Lonergan, The Triune God: Systematics* 234–35.

20   For the *via analytica* in Trinitarian theology, see Lonergan, *The Triune God: Doctrines*. For what is perhaps Lonergan's most extensive treatment of the analytic and synthetic ways in general, see Lonergan, *The Triune God: Systematics* 58–77.

21   Ibid. 235.

22   Ibid. That this procession is not generation is explained in Lonergan's treatment of the third assertion on the processions.

23   Ibid.

24   See ibid. 181 and 355.

25   Ibid. 237.

26   Ibid.

27   We have already seen this relation of sanctifying grace, and so of paternity and filiation, to charity, as well as the relation of charity to paternity and

filiation. See Doran, *Missions and Processions,* chapter 2. It remains that we fill out the relation of the secondary act of existence to the light of glory and proceed from there to the relations of these two terms to sanctifying grace and charity.

28 "Processiones ratione distinguuntur a relationibus et realiter cum relationibus identificantur." Ibid.

29 Lonergan refers here to Thomas Aquinas, *Summa theologiae,* 1, q. 45, a. 2, ad 3m, and ibid. a. 3.

30 See Lonergan, *The Triune God: Systematics* 239 and note 3.

31 "Quae quattuor relationes sunt subsistentes." Lonergan, *The Triune God: Systematics* 238–39.

32 "Sicut ergo deitas est Deus, ita paternitas divina est Deus Pater." Thomas Aquinas, *Summa theologiae,* 1, q. 29, a. 4.

33 *Lonergan, The Triune God: Systematics* 240–41.

34 Ibid. 242–43.

35 Ibid. 244–45.

36 "Non enim proprietates personales sic intelliguntur advenire hypostasibus divinis, sicut forma subiecto praeexsistenti: sed ferunt secum sua supposita, inquantum sunt ipsae personae subsistentes, sicut paternitas est ipse Pater."

37 Lonergan, *The Triune God: Systematics* 231. See ibid. 237: "The processions are conceptually distinct from, but really identical with, the relations."

38 Ibid. 323. See ibid. 325: "The real, subsistent divine relations, really distinct from one another, are properly called and are persons."

39 Ibid. 451.

40 ibid. 453.

41 Ibid. 247 note 9, with reference to Thomas Aquinas, *Summa theologiae,* 1, q. 40, introduction.

42 Ibid. 369.

43 See Lonergan, *The Incarnate Word* 540, thesis 11: "The human nature of Christ is adorned by habitual grace, together with the virtues and gifts in singular fullness."

44 "Tres relationes reales in Deo secundum mutuam oppositionem realiter inter se distinguuntur." *The Triune God: Systematics* 246–47. "… tres: nempe, paternitas, filiatio, spiratio passiva." Ibid.

45 See *Missions and Processions,* chapter 2.

46 Lonergan, *The Triune God: Systematics* 252–53.

47 I have slightly changed Lonergan's order of exposition here. He relates paternity and filiation, then active and passive spiration, then paternity and active spiration, then filiation and active spiration, then passive spiration and both paternity and filiation. See ibid. 252–55. However, my order of exposition follows the order of Lonergan's original list of comparisons (see the reference in the previous note).

48 Ibid. 254–55, emphasis added.

49 "Relationes divinae reales ratione a divina essentia distinguuntur et realiter cum ea identificantur." Ibid. 256.

50 DB 432 (DS 804 – the Fourth Lateran Council): "… una quaedam summa res est, incomprehensibilis quidem et ineffabilis, quae veraciter est Pater, et Filius, et Spiritus sanctus; tres simul personae, ac singillatim quaelibet earundem" ("… one supreme reality, incomprehensible and ineffable, which is truly the Father and the Son and the Holy Spirit: three persons taken together, and each of them taken individually").

51 Lonergan, *The Triune God: Systematics* 259.

52 I did go into these parts of the chapter in the paper "Bernard Lonergan's Treatment of the Divine Relations: A Commentary." See above, p. 65.

Chapter 5

1 Robert M. Doran, "The First Chapter of *De Deo Trino: Pars Systematica*: The Issues," *METHOD: Journal of Lonergan Studies* 18:1 (2000) 27–48; "*Intelligentia Fidei* in *De Deo Trino, Pars Systematica*: A Commentary on the First Three Sections of Chapter One," *METHOD: Journal of Lonergan Studies* 19:1 (2001) 35–83; "The Truth of Theological Understanding in *Divinarum Personarum* and *De Deo Trino, Pars Systematica*," *METHOD: Journal of Lonergan Studies* 20:1 (2002) 33–75. These three also constitute essays 7, 8, and 9, respectively, in Robert M. Doran, *Essays in Systematic Theology: An E-book*, on www.lonerganresource.com.

2 For further treatment see Robert M. Doran, "System and History: The Challenge to Catholic Systematic Theology," *Theological Studies* 60:4 (1999) 652–78, and "System Seeking Method: Reconciling System and History," *Il Teologo e la Storia: Lonergan's Centenary (1904–2004)*, ed. Paul Gilbert and Natalino Spaccapelo (Rome: Gregorian University Press, 2006). These constitute essays 6 and 16, respectively, in Doran, *Essays in Systematic Theology* on the website www.lonerganresource.com. My most complete treatment of the issues is in chapter 10 of *What Is Systematic Theology?*

In 1956–57, and so before the publication of *Divinarum personarum*, Lonergan stated in lectures on the positive or dogmatic part of Trinitarian theology, "The time will come when theology will be more comprehensive and synthetic and at the same time more concrete, resulting from … historical syntheses … But let us not call for that synthesis before it is possible; there is not yet any method sufficiently developed that is capable of that sort of research. What our times need most of all is patience; otherwise we shall easily err – like St Anselm who, endowed as he was with great intelligence and being engrossed in all the most difficult questions, wanted to solve them at a time that still lacked the conceptual foundations necessary for doing that. Merely seventy-five years later, Peter Lombard arrived on the scene, collecting the documents needed for the new requirements of systematics. And the same can be said of Abelard's premature doctrines. The positions of contemporary authors are being abandoned because they have been developed too prematurely. Their importance, however, lies in their influence on contemporary authors in developing methods better adapted to the newer demands of human thinking and by which the same truth can be understood in an ever more comprehensive way." Bernard Lonergan, "The Triune God," lectures at the Gregorian University, Rome, 1956–57, reconstituted from notes taken by students, trans. Michael G. Shields, translation edited by Robert M. Doran. These notes are posted to the Lonergan Archive website www.bernardlonergan. com at 14500DTL060 (Latin notes) and 14600DTE060 (English translation).

3 The definitive work to date on the fifth level is Jeremy W. Blackwood's doctoral dissertation, "Love and Lonergan's Cognitional-Intentional Anthropology," available on www.lonerganresource.com under Scholarly Works/Dissertations. It has been published in revised form by Marquette University Press, *"And Hope Does Not Disappoint": Love, Grace, and Subjectivity in the Work of Bernard JF Lonergan, SJ* (Milwaukee: Marquette University Press, 2017). The significance of Blackwood's work is that it is now clear that anyone who wishes to deny a fifth level of consciousness is disputing not just with Blackwood nor just with me, but with Lonergan.

4 Bernard Lonergan, "Natural Right and Historical Mindedness," *A Third Collection* 163–76.

5 On social grace, see Doran, *Missions and Processions*, index at "Social grace."

6 Hans Urs von Balthasar, *Theo-Drama: Theological Dramatic Theory*, vol. 3, *Dramatis Personae: Persons in Christ*, trans. Graham Harrison (San Francisco: Ignatius Press, 1992) 227.

7 Ibid. 228 note 68.

8 Ibid. 229 note 68.

9 Ibid.

10 Ibid. Balthasar is not of course denying the real distinction, which is central to his thought. What he seems to be questioning is the significance of the real distinction for understanding the ontological constitution of Christ.

11 This course, Lonergan writes, "convinced me that there could not be a hypostatic union without a real distinction between essence and existence" (Bernard Lonergan, "*Insight* Revisited," *A Second Collection* 223). Lonergan's own appreciation of Aquinas seems to have taken a positive turn at this point.

12 Lonergan, *The Triune God: Systematics* 377.

13 Ibid. 386–89, with emphases added, and with one slight change in translation (from "as to existence" to "as existing").

14 "Between the divine and the created natures [of Christ] there is an essential abyss." Balthasar, *Dramatis Personae* 220.

15 As I have already indicated, in using the expression "autonomous spiritual processions" I am drawing on Lonergan's explanation of "emanatio intelligibilis" in the second chapter of *The Triune God: Systematics.* But he does not himself use this expression. See Doran, *Missions and Processions* 176–95.

16 See Lonergan, *The Incarnate Word,* thesis 10.

17 Ibid. 465.

18 Lonergan made a comment in a question-and-answer session at the 1974 Lonergan Workshop at Boston College that supports this interpretation. The comment may be found on the website www.bernardlonergan. com at 810AODTE070, at page 5. The comment was to the effect that the Jungian position on the development of the ego "is something that is quite interesting from the viewpoint of the consciousness of Christ, for example, for theologians." Obviously he is speaking of the human consciousness of Christ, since the divine consciousness did not develop. From this remark I began to wonder whether the *systematic understanding* of the psychological unity of the one subject of two consciousnesses in Christ *might* be formulated on an *analogy* with something like Jung's notion of the relation between the self and the ego. This is a systematic question. I am still not prepared to answer it. What Lonergan's remark revealed is that he recognized the validity of the question that I had been asking, namely, the systematic question, How are we to understand what we have already affirmed as a theological doctrine, that is, that there are two consciousnesses in Christ and that there is a psychological unity to the one subject of these two consciousnesses? To draw one's systematic analogy from Jung is fraught with difficulties, most of which have to do with the imprecision of Jung's own language. But the potential fruitfulness of such a procedure should be acknowledged.

19 Lonergan, *Insight* 619.

20 Bernard Lonergan, "*Insight* Revisited," *A Second Collection* 277.

21 Bernard Lonergan, *De constitutione Christi ontologica et psychologica* (Rome: Gregorian University Press, 1956). Now available in Latin and English facing pages as *The Ontological and Psychological Constitution of Christ,* vol. 7 in Collected Works of Bernard Lonergan, trans. Michael G. Shields, ed. Frederick E. Crowe and Robert M. Doran (Toronto: University of Toronto Press, 2000).

22 This is not to negate the importance and validity of the ethics of *Insight.* Elsewhere I have likened this presentation to St Ignatius of Loyola's third time of election, as presented in the *Spiritual Exercises.* If I am correct, then the ethics of *Insight* presents one valid procedure of moving to decision. But Ignatius proposes two other procedures as well, and Lonergan's later thoughts on the matter are much more illuminative of these other methods, and much more expansive in their delineation of a fourth level

of consciousness. For details, see Robert M. Doran, "Ignatian Themes in the Thought of Bernard Lonergan: Revisiting a Theme That Deserves Further Reflection," *Lonergan Workshop* 19, ed. Fred Lawrence (Boston: Boston College, 2006) 83–106. This appears as essay 19 in Doran, *Essays in Systematic Theology.*

23　"… when we ask 'Three what?' or 'Three who?' we are led to find some specific or generic word under which we may include all three, and none has occurred to us." Augustine, *De trinitate,* VII, iv, 7. "[Human limitation] asked what it should call the Three. And it replied 'substances' or 'persons.' By these names it did not wish to convey any idea of diversity, but it wished to avoid any idea of singleness, so that not only would unity be understood by speaking of one essence, but also trinity would be understood by speaking of three substances or persons." Ibid. 9. These two quotations are cited by Lonergan, *The Triune God: Systematics* 308–309. I have changed the translation provided in *The Triune God: Systematics,* so that "general" becomes "generic" and "special" becomes "specific." Later in the same section, Augustine concedes that "person" is a generic term, but that no specific term can be found. "Substance" here translates the Greek "hypostasis," and is obviously not used in the same sense as Aquinas and Lonergan use "substantia" to speak of one divine substance, but rather in the sense meant by Greek theologians in speaking of "hypostasis," as in "hypostatic union," union in and on the basis of the person. Augustine is clear on this at the very beginning of the sections here cited. But see the discussion below of Boethius's definition of person.

24　Lonergan, *The Triune God: Systematics* 323.

25　Hans Urs von Balthasar, "On the Concept of Person," *Communio* 13 (Spring 1986) 18.

26　Balthasar, *Dramatis Personae* 211. Andresen's study is "Zur Entstehung und Geschichte des trinitarischen Personbegriffs," *Zeitschrift für die neutestamentliche Wissenschaft* 52 (1961) 1–39.

27　Balthasar, "On the Concept of Person" 18, emphasis in text.

28　Balthasar, *Dramatis Personae* 204.

29　Ibid. 207. Jungian "individuation," it may be argued, refers precisely to the qualitative distinction that Balthasar correlates with personhood. Whether it can be achieved without an explicit relation with God is debated among those who study Jung.

30　Balthasar, "On the Concept of Person" 19.

31　The distinction of cosmological, anthropological, and soteriological is made not by Jaspers but by Eric Voegelin, *Order and History,* vol. 1: *Israel and Revelation* (Baton Rouge: Louisiana State University Press, 1956) 56. I have developed the distinction for my own purposes in Doran, *Theology and the Dialectics of History*, passim, but especially in the sections that treat the dialectic of culture. See the index for references.

32 For an indication of the complexity of this question, see Barnabas Lindars, "Ezekiel and Individual Responsibility," *Vetus Testamentum* 15 (1965) 452–67.

33 Balthasar, "On the Concept of Person" 18.

34 Ibid.

35 Ibid.

36 Ibid. 20. We may think here of what Lonergan writes on the dramatic pattern of experience as well as, of course, Balthasar's own *Theo-Drama*.

37 Tertullian, *Adversus Praxean*, 27.11, quoted by Balthasar in "On the Concept of Person" 21. Translation: "We see plainly the twofold state, which is not confounded, but conjoined in One Person – Jesus, God and Man" (www. newadvent.org/fathers/0317.htm). For another but distinct reference to Tertullian see Balthasar, *Dramatis Personae* 211.

38 Balthasar, "On the Concept of Person" 20–21.

39 Ibid. 21–22, emphasis added.

40 Ibid. 22, emphasis added.

41 Ibid. 21.

42 Ibid. 22.

43 Lonergan, "Christology Today" 93.

44 The text of Aquinas in question reads, in translation: "Although we cannot use 'person' of God in its original sense we can extend this perfectly well for our present purpose. Since in comedies and tragedies famous men were represented, the word 'person' came to be used in reference to men of high rank. It then became customary in the ecclesiastical world to refer to personages of rank. This is why some theologians define person by saying that a person is 'a hypostasis distinguished by dignity.' To subsist in rational nature is a characteristic implying dignity and hence, as already mentioned, every individual with rational nature is called 'person.' Of course the dignity of divine nature surpasses all other, and so it is completely fitting to use 'person' of God."

45 Balthasar, "On the Concept of Person" 23.

46 Balthasar quotes this from Richard's *De Trinitate*, 4.28, and refers to the edition by Jean Ribailler (Paris: J. Vrin, 1958) 181.

47 See Balthasar, "On the Concept of Person" 22 and note 12.

48 Richard of St Victor, *De Trinitate* 5.25.

49 I rely here on Paul Burgess, "Three Are the Perfection of Charity: The *De Trinitate* of Richard of St. Victor," www.paulburgess.org/richard.

50 See Lonergan, "Fragments toward a Seventh Chapter of *De Deo trino: Pars systematica*" (see above, p. 218, note 12).

51 Balthasar, "On the Concept of Person" 23–24.

52 Ibid. 24, emphasis added.

53 Ibid. 24–25.

54 Ibid. 25. He refers here to the volume of his *Theo-Drama* that we also are relying on.

55 Ibid.

56 Balthasar, *Dramatis Personae* 201.

57 See Lonergan, *The Triune God: Systematics* 313.

58 Ibid.

59 Ibid. 323.

60 Recall the statement that we cited above, "… we cannot ascribe a twofold consciousness to the Logos-made-man." Balthasar, *Dramatis Personae* 227.

61 See Lonergan, *Early Works on Theological Method 1*, vol. 22 in Collected Works of Bernard Lonergan, ed. Robert M. Doran and Robert C. Croken (Toronto: University of Toronto Press, 2010) 571: "… what is conscious is not yet an object."

62 See Lonergan, *The Ontological and Psychological Constitution of Christ*, parts 5 and 6 passim.

63 "… we should not overlook what apparently misleads many in this matter, namely, that as there are two realisms, naive and critical, so also 'real,' 'object,' 'evident,' 'to know,' and similar notions have two different meanings. The first is a meaning of reality, objectivity, evidence, and knowledge according to which a kind of animal faith is carried toward a world of objects that are each already, out, there, now, and in this sense, 'real.' The other, quite different meaning of these very same notions is that according to which the mind, led by questions, conceives the natures of things from an understanding of what it has experienced, affirms the true from grasping an unconditioned, and apprehends being in the true as in a medium." Lonergan, *The Triune God: Systematics* 321.

64 Ibid.319, emphasis added.

65 Lonergan, *Method in Theology* 273.

66 John D. Dadosky, "Is There a Fourth Stage of Meaning?" *Heythrop Journal* 51 (2010) 768–780.

67 Lonergan, *The Triune God: Systematics* 323, 325.

68 Lonergan, "The Subject," in *A Second Collection* 74.

69 See, for example, Lonergan, *Early Works on Theological Method 1* 97.

70 See Lonergan, *Insight* 402–407.

71 See Lonergan, *The Triune God: Systematics* 324–25.

72 See Robert M. Doran, "Aesthetics and the Opposites," originally published in *Thought* in 1977 and reproduced in *Theological Foundations*, vol. 1: *Intentionality and Psyche* (Milwaukee: Marquette University Press, 1995) at 118; this volume is now available on www.loneranresource.com, under Scholarly Works/Books; John D. Dadosky, "Desire, Bias, and Love: Revisiting Lonergan's Philosophical Anthropology," *Irish Theological Quarterly* 77

(2012) 247–52. Dadosky also indicates a contribution by Mark Morelli to this discussion. See ibid. 251.

73 Bernard Lonergan, "*Existenz* and *Aggiornamento*," in *Collection* 222–31.

74 Bernard Lonergan, *Topics in Education*, vol. 10 in Collected Works of Bernard Lonergan, ed. Robert M. Doran and Frederick E. Crowe (Toronto: University of Toronto Press, 1993) 92, emphasis added.

75 Lonergan, *Method in Theology* 33.

76 Ibid. 14: "There is a still further dimension to being human, and there we emerge as persons, meet one another in a common concern for values, seek to abolish the organization of human living on the basis of competing egoisms and to replace it by an organization on the basis of man's perceptiveness and intelligence, his reasonableness, and his responsible exercise of freedom."

77 See Lonergan, *The Triune God: Systematics* 399–413.

78 See above, p. 227, note 6.

79 Balthasar, *Dramatis Personae* 51. In terms of the definition of theological person presented in our thesis 81, we might say that Balthasar's insistence on the role of mission in the person understood theologically intends a specification of how each individual is concretely "oriented to the reign of God."

80 Ibid. 52.

81 Ibid. 53.

82 Ibid. 54.

83 Ibid. 92–93. This will be emphasized again in our treatment of Ben F. Meyer in chapter 7.

84 Ibid. 149.

85 See Frederick E. Crowe, *Christ and History: The Christology of Bernard Lonergan from 1936 to 1982* (Toronto: University of Toronto Press, 2015).

86 See above, pp. 99–101.

87 Balthasar, *Dramatis Personae* 226.

88 Ibid. 150.

89 Ibid. 224.

90 Ibid. 227.

91 Ibid. 150.

92 Ibid. 220. Compare Lonergan's insistence that "there is no discontinuity between God the Father and the words that Jesus the man speaks." See Lonergan, *The Incarnate Word* 665.

93 Lonergan, "Christology Today" 91.

94 Ibid. 94.

95 Ibid., emphasis added.

96 Ibid.

97 See Doran, *Missions and Processions*, chapter 2.

Chapter 6

1 For Schwager, see especially his *Jesus in the Drama of Salvation: Toward a Biblical Doctrine of Redemption*, trans. James G. Williams and Paul Haddon (New York: Crossroad, 1999).

2 See Doran, *Missions and Processions*, chapter 3, relying on Lonergan, *The Triune God: Systematics* 442–99.

3 See Jonathan Bernier, *The Quest for the Historical Jesus after the Demise of Authenticity: Toward a Critical Realist Philosophy of History in Jesus Studies* (London, New York: Bloomsbury T&T Clark, 2016) 3.

4 An entire section of the newly formed International Institute for Method in Theology is devoted to the development of critical-realist hermeneutics. I must count on that group, under the leadership of Joseph Gordon, to develop further the materials I have had to limit myself to in these chapters. I am convinced there is no better place to start than with the work of Meyer and Wright, but nonetheless that work remains but a beginning.

5 See Peter Laughlin, *Jesus and the Cross: Necessity, Meaning, and Atonement* (Eugene, OR: Pickwick Publications, 2014).

6 N.T. Wright, *The New Testament and the People of God* (Minneapolis: Fortress Press, 1992) 476. These are the final words in this text. Wright prefers to use the lower-case "god" up to a point in his recovery of New Testament theology.

7 Ben F. Meyer, *The Aims of Jesus*, with a new introduction by N.T. Wright (Eugene, OR: Pickwick Publications, 2002; henceforth *Aims*) 251. Quotations from *The Aims of Jesus* are used by permission of Wipf and Stock Publishers, www.wipfandstock.com.

8 See Lonergan, *The Triune God: Systematics* 386–89 and above, p. 101.

9 The "place" of the Holy Spirit in Jesus' relational human consciousness will be addressed in the soteriology that we will attempt to develop in the next volume.

10 Again, let me suggest that Lonergan's off-hand comment about the possible relevance of an analogy with Jung's notion of the relation between self and ego might contribute to the illumination of the formal structures of this movement. See above, p. 228, note 18.

11 N.T. Wright, *Jesus and the Victory of God* (Minneapolis: Fortress Press, 1996) 14. Henceforth this book will be referred to as *JVG*.

12 See Laughlin, *Jesus and the Cross* 6.

13 Lonergan, *The Incarnate Word* 572, thesis 12: "Living on this earth, Christ had human knowledge both effable and ineffable, besides his divine knowledge. As a beholder, he immediately knew God by that ineffable knowledge which is also called beatific, and in the same act, though mediately, he also knew everything else that pertained to his work. As a pilgrim, however, he elicited by effable knowledge those natural and

supernatural cognitional acts which constituted his human and historical life." Much work remains to be done on this position, both to understand it and to draw out its implications, before it can join the fruits of critical-realist exegesis and history, but I believe the position itself will survive that work.

14 See Bernard Lonergan, "Natural Right and Historical Mindedness," *A Third Collection* 163–76. Lonergan takes the expression "historical mindedness" from Alan Richardson. See ibid. 165. I suspect this was a quite deliberately chosen alternative to "historical consciousness," since what he is talking about is more than "consciousness" in Lonergan's technical understanding of the latter term.

15 Lonergan, *Method in Theology* 258.

16 Laughlin, *Jesus and the Cross* xiii.

17 See Doran, "The Ninth Functional Specialty."

18 "… if modern theologians were to transpose medieval theory into the categories derived from contemporary interiority and its real correlatives, they would be doing for our age what the greater Scholastics did for theirs."Lonergan, *Method in Theology* 327–28.

19 For my suggestions on transposition, see Robert M. Doran, "Generalized Isomorphism: The Key to Transposition," *Divyadaan* 28:1 (2017) 43–64. This will soon appear also in *Essays in Systematic Theology* on the website www. lonerganresource.com.

20 Wright, *JVG* 122.

21 See N.T. Wright, *The Contemporary Quest for Jesus* (Minneapolis: Fortress Press, 2002) 88–91.

22 I would maintain that Wright's work in this area is very much in harmony with what I had in mind when writing about the effect of psychic conversion on hermeneutics. See Doran, *Theology and the Dialectics of History*, chapter 20. To present a detailed argument for this claim is beyond what is possible in the present book.

23 See Meyer, *Aims* 245–49.

24 See ibid.

25 I base this notion of revelation as occurring not only through but also *in and for* the historical Jesus of Nazareth in my reading of Hefling, "Revelation and/as Insight." That the insights of which Hefling speaks in this extremely illuminating paper are actual graces would seem to follow from Lonergan's thesis on actual grace in "The Supernatural Order." See Lonergan, *Early Latin Theology* 228–55. I have interpreted and developed that notion in chapter 3 of the present volume. That these insights can be understood in terms of communication between Jesus' divine and his human consciousness and his divine and human knowing seems clear, though we have yet to work out the categories in which to express that communication. Again, I believe an analogy with Jung's notion of the relation of self and ego may prove helpful.

26 See Wright, *JVG* 8.

27 For a similar judgment see Bernier, *The Quest for the Historical Jesus after the Demise of Authenticity* 2.

28 Neil Ormerod, "Foreword" to Laughlin, *Jesus and the Cross* ix.

29 Ibid. ix–x.

30 Ibid. x.

31 Ibid.

32 Laughlin, *Jesus and the Cross* xiii.

33 Wright, *JVG* 541, emphasis added.

34 Laughlin, *Jesus and the Cross* 1.

35 Wright, *The Contemporary Quest for Jesus* 1.

36 Ibid. 1–2.

37 Ibid. 2.

38 Ibid. 4–5.

39 Ibid. 5.

40 A succinct treatment is found in ibid., to p. 28, and a much more thorough one in *JVG* 1–82.

41 It should be added that 1 Peter 2.21 is the beginning of a passage in which the obvious reference is to the Deutero-Isaian servant.

42 Laughlin, *Jesus and the Cross* 2.

43 Ibid. 4.

44 See ibid.

45 Ibid.

46 Ibid. 6, emphasis Laughlin's.

47 Ibid. 7.

48 David Brondos, "Why Was Jesus Crucified? Theology, History and the Story of Redemption," *Scottish Journal of Theology* 54 (2001) 485, quoted by Laughlin, *Jesus and the Cross* 7.

49 Laughlin, *Jesus and the Cross* 9.

50 Ibid. 10.

51 Ibid.

52 Ibid. 24.

53 In the first chapter of *Jesus and the Cross*, Laughlin studies the soteriological views of Alan Mann, Mark Heim, and John Milbank, and finds them all lacking the concern for the actual intentions of Jesus that he insists must ground our systematic soteriology.

54 Lonergan, *Method in Theology* 54, emphasis added.

55 Ibid. 272, emphasis added.

56 Ibid. 335, emphasis added.

57 Lonergan, "The Mediation of Christ in Prayer," in *Philosophical and Theological Papers 1958–1964* 182, emphasis added.

58 For a strictly exegetical statement supporting this position, see Stanislas Lyonnet and Léopold Sabourin, *Sin, Redemption, and Sacrifice: A Biblical and*

Patristic Study (Rome: Biblical Institute Press, 1970) 69–78. Thus, "… the salvation wrought by God through Christ brings forth, here on earth, at least some of its fruits." Ibid. 75.

59   See Doran, *Missions and Processions* 83: "The preaching of the reign of God by the incarnate Word can be integrated into a systematic theology by complicating the structure of the scale of values. Thus there emerges the social character of grace."

Chapter 7

1   See Meyer, *Aims* 60–69.

2   Ibid. 60.

3   See N.T. Wright, *The Resurrection of the Son of God* (Minneapolis: Fortress Press, 2003) 3–10.

4   See Meyer, *Aims* 61.

5   I will cite the translations Meyer employs, which are his own. See ibid. 9.

6   Ibid. 62.

7   Ibid. 62–63.

8   Ben F. Meyer, "The Expiation Motif in the Eucharistic Words: A Key to the History of Jesus?" *Gregorianum* 69 (1988) 487, emphasis added.

9   Ibid. Emphasis added.

10   Ibid.

11   Ibid.

12   Michael J. Gorman, *The Death of the Messiah and the Birth of the New Covenant: A (Not So) New Model of the Atonement* (Eugene, OR: Cascade, 2014).

13   See Meyer, *Aims* 62.

14   Lonergan, "The Mediation of Christ in Prayer" 182.

15   See Meyer, *Aims* 63.

16   Ibid. 64.

17   Ibid. 63.

18   See ibid. 65.

19   Ibid.

20   Ibid.

21   See ibid.

22   Ibid. 66, emphasis added.

23   See ibid.

24   Ibid.

25   Ibid. 69.

26   Ibid.

27   Ibid. 70–75.

28   Ibid. 74.

29   See ibid. 72–73.

30 Ibid. 220, emphasis added.

31 Ibid. 115.

32 Ibid. But Wright regards the thesis of the cessation of prophecy to be overblown. See Wright, *JVG* 151.

33 Meyer, *Aims* 115–16.

34 Ibid. 116.

35 Ibid. 117.

36 Ibid.

37 Ibid. 123.

38 Ibid.

39 Ibid.

40 Ibid. 128.

41 Ibid. 129.

42 While Wright rearranges things under different categories, he maintains the distinction of proclamation and public actions and lists under the latter the same events as those specified by Meyer.

43 Meyer, *Aims* 129.

44 Ibid. 220–21.

45 Ibid.

46 Ibid.

47 Ibid. 130.

48 Ibid.

49 Ibid.

50 Ibid.

51 Ibid.

52 Ibid. 130–31.

53 Ibid. 131.

54 Ibid.

55 Ibid.

56 Ibid. 132.

57 Ibid. 132.

58 Ibid.

59 Ibid. 132–33.

60 Ibid. 133.

61 Ibid. 133–34.

62 Wright will emphasize more strongly the identification of "the forgiveness of sins" with "the definitive end of exile."

63 Meyer, *Aims* 136.

64 Ibid.

65 Ibid. 137, emphasis added.

66 Ibid. 136.

67 Ibid.

68 Ibid.

69 Ibid. 137.

70 See ibid. 137–42.

71 Ibid. 142.

72 Ibid.

73 Ibid. 143.

74 See ibid. 142–47.

75 See ibid. 151.

76 Ibid.

77 Ibid.

78 See ibid. 152–53.

79 Ibid. 153.

80 See ibid.

81 See ibid. 154.

82 Ibid.

83 For the material summarized in this paragraph, see ibid. 154–58.

84 Ibid. 161. For the materials summarized in this paragraph, see ibid. 158–61.

85 See ibid. 161–62. For Wright's unique perspective on this parable, see *JVG* 126–31.

86 Meyer, *Aims* 163.

87 Ibid. 164.

88 Ibid. 165.

89 See ibid. 167.

90 Ibid. 168.

91 Ibid. 170.

92 Ibid. 170.

93 Ibid. 174.

94 Ibid. 188.

95 See Sigurd Grindheim, *God's Equal: What Can We Know about Jesus' Self-Understanding?* (London, New York: T.&T. Clark, 2011) chapter 1.

96 See Meyer, *Aims* 178.

97 Ibid.

98 Ibid. 179.

99 Ibid. 180.

100 Ibid. 181.

101 See ibid. 181–82.

102 Ibid. 182.

103 Ibid.

104 Ibid. 183.

105 Ibid. 184.

106 Ibid. 185.

107 Ibid.
108 Ibid. 186.
109 Ibid.
110 Ibid. 188.
111 See ibid. 194.
112 Ibid. 195.
113 See ibid. 196.
114 Ibid. 197.
115 Ibid.
116 Ibid. 198.
117 Ibid.
118 Ibid. 199.
119 Ibid. 201.
120 Ibid.
121 Ibid. Meyer uses the word "consciousness" for what I am here calling "self-understanding."
122 Ibid. 201–202.
123 Ibid. 202.
124 See ibid. 206, following on a review of exegetical literature.
125 Ibid. 207.
126 Ibid.
127 Ibid. 208.
128 See ibid.
129 Ibid.
130 Ibid. 209.
131 Ibid.
132 Ibid.
133 Ibid. 210.
134 Ibid.
135 See ibid.
136 Ibid. 211.
137 Ibid.
138 See ibid. 247.
139 Ibid. 212.
140 Ibid. 213.
141 Ibid.
142 Ibid.
143 Ibid. 214.
144 Ibid. 215.
145 Ibid.
146 Ibid.
147 Ibid.

148 See ibid. 216, emphasis in text.

149 Ibid. 217.

150 Ibid. 216.

151 Ibid., emphasis added.

152 Ibid., emphasis added.

153 Ibid. 217.

154 Ibid.

155 Ibid. 217–18.

156 Ibid. 218.

157 Ibid.

158 Ibid.

159 Ibid.

160 Ibid. 219.

161 Ibid., emphasis added.

162 Ibid.

163 N.T. Wright, "Introduction," in Meyer, *Aims* 9i.

164 Ibid. 9k.

165 Ibid. 9i.

166 Ibid.

167 Ibid. 9j.

168 See Wright, *JVG* 95.

169 Ibid. 96.

170 See ibid. 97.

171 Ibid. 98.

172 Ibid.

173 See Lonergan, *The Redemption* 30–39. We will take up this distinction in the third volume of this work. Obviously of course, for Lonergan redemption as end has little to do with the redemption of Israel from exile. In his presentation of the law of the cross, Lonergan is emphasizing that the suffering of the messianic figure has catalyzed or mediated a far more extensive redemption as end. But how is such an expanded notion of redemption as end linked with the redemption of Israel from exile that was uppermost in the Jewish context informing Jesus' mentality and aims? Wright and Meyer raise and help to answer this question.

174 See Wright, *JVG* 601–602.

175 To this must be added, I believe, Luke's account (22.20), "This cup which is poured out for you is the new covenant in my blood"; see also 1 Corinthians 11.25, "This cup is the new covenant in my blood," which Paul "received from the Lord." See the account above of Meyer's treatment of the Pauline passage, p. 169. This addition also probably moves Jeremiah 31.31–34 onto the list of biblical sources central to Jesus' self-understanding. See also Gorman, *The Death of the Messiah and the Birth of the New Covenant.*

176 Wright, *JVG* 603.
177 Compare Lonergan on the effable and ineffable human knowledge of Jesus, in *The Incarnate Word* thesis 12.
178 Wright, *JVG* 603–604, emphasis in text.
179 I also want to add Jeremiah 31.31–34 as a central biblical contribution to Jesus' self-understanding, supporting the emphases of Gorman in *The Death of the Messiah and the Birth of the New Covenant.*
180 Lonergan, *Method in Theology* 258.
181 Laughlin, *Jesus and the Cross* 6, emphasis Laughlin's. But see above, p. 160, for my reservations with the word "constituted" in this context.

Index

Note: The index does not include the appendix, a great deal of which is taken from volume 1, *Missions and Processions,* and the rest of which repeats verbatim material treated earlier in this volume.

Abelard, Peter, 160, 227

Absolute: individuals as simply a. in neo-liberal thought, 73; and "is," 72; a. objectivity, 131; and real relations, 73–74, 85; simply a., simply relative, and a. and relative in qualified way, 71–73

Act: first a. and second a., 51, 52; notional a., 11; notional and essential a., 101; potency, form, and a., 126; principal a., *see* Principal act(s); pure a., 19, 26, 30, 66, 67, 87, 92–93; secondary a. of existence, *see* Secondary act of existence; supernatural a., 51, 52; vital a., 51

Act from act, 16, 21, 26, 147; and act from potency, 16–17, 19. *See also* Autonomy; Autonomous spiritual processions; Spontaneity

Active spiration: analogue for, 26, 88, 89, 99; defined, 75; and divine essence, 94; a.s. as Father and Son together, 10, 12, 68, 84, 85; a.s. of Father and Son is one, 92; and filiation, 78, 85, 86, 91–92; and four divine relations, 10, 30, 66, 75,

76; and four-point hypothesis, 3; identity of a.s. with paternity-filiation, 78, 84–87, 90, 92; and mutual acknowledgment of lovableness by Father and Son, 92; as mutual opposition of Father and Son, 90, 94; in mutual opposition to proceeding Holy Spirit, 85; one a.s. in God and two in us, 93; and passive spiration, 85, 91, 92; and paternity, 78, 85, 86, 91, 92; and sanctifying grace, 3, 14, 20, 26, 30, 31, 33, 50, 55, 77; as subsistent (Spirator), 78, 80, 81; term of, 86; and Trinitarian structure of habitual grace, 14, 15, 164, 165

Acts of the Apostles, 167, 168, 170, 219 n. 5

Actual grace, 27–28, 34, 37; and apprehension of and consent to solution, 41; and Christian theology of religions, 62; and circumincession, 65; and conversion, 48; and discerning grace/genuine sacred everywhere, 37, 38, 42, 59, 60; and elevation, 41; and fundamental option, 38, 45; and insights, 38, 45, 50, 51, 52, 58, 61,